The White Savior Film

MATTHEW W. HUGHEY

The White Savior Film

Content, Critics, and Consumption

TEMPLE UNIVERSITY PRESS
PHILADELPHIA

TEMPLE UNIVERSITY PRESS
Philadelphia, Pennsylvania 19122
www.temple.edu/tempress

Library of Congress Cataloging-in-Publication Data

Hughey, Matthew W. (Matthew Windust)
  The white savior film : content, critics, and consumption /
Matthew W. Hughey.
      pages cm
  Includes bibliographical references and index.
  ISBN 978-1-4399-1000-9 (cloth : alk. paper) —
ISBN 978-1-4399-1001-6 (paperback : alk. paper) —
ISBN 978-1-4399-1002-3 (e-book)   1. Whites in motion pictures.
2. Race in motion pictures.   3. Motion pictures—Social aspects—
United States.   I. Title.
  PN1995.9.W45H85 2014
  791.43'652909—dc23

                                        2013043278

♾ The paper used in this publication meets the requirements of the
American National Standard for Information Sciences—Permanence
of Paper for Printed Library Materials, ANSI Z39.48-1992

Printed in the United States of America

2 4 6 8 9 7 5 3 1

For Desie, who saves herself

Naming "whiteness" displaces it from the unmarked, unnamed status that is itself an effect of dominance. . . . To look at the social construction of whiteness, then, is to look head-on at a site of dominance. . . . To speak of whiteness is, I think, to assign everyone a place in the relations of racism. It is to emphasize that dealing with racism is not merely an option for white people— that, rather, racism shapes white people's lives and identities in a way that is inseparable from other facets of daily life.

—Ruth Frankenberg,
White Women, Race Matters

Contents

Acknowledgments   ix

1 The Savior Trope and the Modern Meanings of Whiteness   1

2 White Savior Films: *The Content of Their Character*   18

3 Reviewing Whiteness: *Critics and Their Commentary*   72

4 Watching Whiteness: *Audience Consumption and Community*   125

5 The Significance of White Saviors in a "Postracial" World   160

Appendix A: Data and Methodology for Content Analysis of Film   175

Appendix B: Data and Methodology for Film Reviews   184

Appendix C: Data and Methodology for Film Audiences   189

References   193

Index   211

Acknowledgments

I am grateful to the friends and colleagues who informally helped with my research and to those who officially served as my research assistants: Cherish Forsman, Menaka Kannan, Rodderick Benton, Sheena Gardner, and Bianca Gonzales-Sobrino. I thank them for their assistance with data collection and editing. Their time, energy, and dedication helped extend my reach and sight.

Additionally, I remain incredibly thankful to those who agreed to be interviewed, to serve as focus group members, and to read my preliminary notes and analyses. The words of these participants became the bedrock of data in Chapter 4. I appreciate their giving so freely of their time and opinions on what some consider indelicate issues that engender passion and discord. Without their honesty and forthrightness, this book would be lacking.

I owe an epistemological debt to the authors of notable articles and books that helped me wrestle down myriad ideas and debates over race and media: David L. Altheide, Shyonn Baumann, Howard Becker, Joyce Bell, Eduardo Bonilla-Silva, Ronald E. Chennault, Troy Duster, David G. Embrick, Tyrone Forman, Henry Giroux, Andrew M. Gordon, Doug Hartmann, Michèle Lamont, Amanda Lewis, George Lipsitz, Alan A. Marcus, Wendy Leo Moore, Gregory S. Parks, Jennifer Pierce, Vincent F. Rocchio, Clara E. Rodríguez, Jeremy D. Stoddard, Hernán Vera, and Howard Winant. My words remain indebted to theirs.

I am obliged to thank many other individuals who assisted my analysis and afforded me valuable resources that aided different stages of this book's development. Special thanks go to Sarah Brauner-Otto, David Brunsma, Woody Doane, Yasmiyn Irizarry, and Wendy Leo Moore. In particular, I thank Donald Shaffer for the many humanities-and-social-science-synthesized conversations about the trope of the savior, its manifestation in social life, and the correct methods for its evaluation. Our conversations helped unsettle many a text. I hope the social scientist in him enjoys the tables and figures herein.

This book is better off because of the suggestions about and criticism of various ideas presented in preliminary form at the 2010 Media, Democracy, and Diversity Conference at the University of Virginia (Charlottesville); the 2010 annual meeting of the American Sociological Association (Atlanta, Georgia); and the 2011 annual meeting of the Southern Sociological Society (Jacksonville, Florida). This book also draws from ideas published in Matthew W. Hughey, "Racializing Redemption, Reproducing Racism: The Odyssey of Magical Negroes and White Saviors," *Sociology Compass* 6, no. 9 (2012): 751–767, and Matthew W. Hughey and Sheena Gardner, "Film Reviewers and Framing Race: Recuperating a Post-racial Whiteness," *Darkmatter* 9, no. 2 (2012), available at http:// www.darkmatter101.org/site/2012/11/29/film-reviewers-and-framing-race -recuperating-a-post-racial-whiteness/. I extend my gratitude to the anonymous reviewers and editors of these publications who provided early feedback on the sociological study of the white savior film.

Thanks go to the librarians at Mississippi State University, the University of Virginia, and the University of Connecticut. Their knowledge and acumen were welcome aids in my research. I offer thanks also to the Media Studies faculty at the University of Virginia—namely, Hector Amaya, Aniko Bodroghkozy, Siva Vaidhyanathan, and especially David Golumbia (now at Virginia Commonwealth University). I thank them for setting me out on a path of media investigation, scrutiny, and analysis.

I am extremely grateful to the Department of Sociology and the Institute for African American Studies at the University of Connecticut for providing an institutional space for bringing this project home. In particular, I am appreciative of the confidence that Bandana Purkayastha and Jelani Cobb have in my work and me.

This book came to Temple University Press through the insight of Mick Gusinde-Duffy, then senior acquisitions editor at Temple (now editor in chief of the University of Georgia Press). He convinced me that Temple was the right place for the text. Editor in chief Janet Francendese then provided a windfall of support in terms of hands-on editing and numerous phone and e-mail conversations that guided the book's formal development. I extend thanks to Janet for all her work and her unwavering belief in the book. To the remainder of people at Temple—its editorial board, its support staff, and the anonymous reviewers of the text—I offer thanks for their assistance and professionalism.

Thanks go to Sherrill and Michael Hughey for instilling in me a critical eye for injustice and inequality, regardless of its overt or subtle manifestation. I am pleased to have a partner, Desie, who is supportive of my work. I thank her for putting up with my countless hours of research, the playing and replaying of miles of film footage, the dissecting of pages upon pages of film reviews, and the earbud-implanted evenings of transcribing interviews and focus group discussion. I am grateful for her patience and understanding.

1

The Savior Trope and the Modern Meanings of Whiteness

The media and the cinematic racial order are basic to the understanding of race relations in any society.

—Norman Denzin, "Symbolic Interactionism, Poststructuralism, and the Racial Subject"

Color-Blind Sided: The Curious Case of Sandra Bullock

As she accepted the 2010 Oscar for Best Actress for her role as Leigh Anne Tuohy in the 2009 film *The Blind Side*, Sandra Bullock gushed, "There's no race, no religion, no class system, no color, nothing, no sexual orientation that makes us better than anyone else. We are all deserving of love" ("Oscars 2010" 2010). The film, based on a true story, centers on the Tuohys, a white, Republican family in the Deep South who adopt a homeless African American teenager named Michael Oher. The Tuohys, and especially the formidable Leigh Anne, teach Michael valuable life lessons and the sport of football. Because of their help, Oher excels on the field to such a degree that he earns a scholarship at the University of Mississippi and a career in the NFL. *The Blind Side* garnered wide attention from reviewers and prize committees, including a nomination for the Eighty-Third Annual Academy Award for Best Picture. Commentators hailed Bullock's performance (which also received the Golden Globe Award for Best Actress and the Screen Actors Guild Award for Outstanding Performance by a Female Actor in a Leading Role) as her best work to date. The *Chicago Tribune*'s Michael Phillips wrote, "The star is Sandra Bullock, whose character, Leigh Anne Tuohy, is conceived as a steel magnolia with a will of iron and . . . righteous gumption" (Phillips 2009).

But some commentators did not join the applause. They saw the movie as another instance of a "white savior film"—the genre in which a white messianic character saves a lower- or working-class, usually urban or isolated, nonwhite character from a sad fate. In one example of this perspective, the day after Bullock received her first Oscar, movie star Vanessa Williams appeared on ABC's

The View and broke from the daytime television script of apolitical pleasantries to state, "It brings up a theme for black folks, that, okay, here's another white family that saves the day. In terms of another black story that needs a white person to come in and lift them up." Interrupting Williams with a color-blind retort, Barbara Walters stated, "I have to disagree with you. . . . It was a wonderful story, and it was a story of closeness between two races, so I don't agree with you" (Deane 2010). The mildly cross interaction between Williams and Walters demonstrates how the prism of race and cinema refracts our worldviews. Despite dissent from some, many on both sides of the color line seemed to largely adore—to the tune of $255 million—*The Blind Side*.

But mere days after Bullock embarked, Oscar in hand, on a journey toward increased stardom and accolades, news broke that Bullock's husband, Jesse James, had had an extramarital affair with neo-Nazi pinup girl Michelle McGee (a woman with white-power and swastika tattoos adorning her body) and that Bullock and James had adopted (in January 2010) a young African American boy from New Orleans. Bullock's interracial adoption and husband's flirtation with white supremacy prompted a storm of public debate. Some saw Bullock's move as kind-hearted benevolence, whereas others were a bit more skeptical, such as the author of the following editorial in the *Chicago Defender*:

> Now Bullock can be both the female victim icon and the liberal white heroine at the same time. . . . Essentially we have a woman being praised in the national media for adopting a Black child and attempting to raise him for a time with her neo-Nazi husband. . . . Just because someone is white and rich doesn't mean they know what's best for an African American child, especially when they clearly aren't too concerned with sharing a bed with white power fanatics. (Johnson 2010)

The dustup over, and slippage between, Bullock's reel- and real-life interracial drama reflects the uneasy place of the white savior motif in our contemporary world. It captures public attention and drives contentious debate in venues far beyond movie theaters.

Given the diverse locations in which the white savior resonates, the anxious allure of saviorism has saturated our contemporary logic. This trope is so widespread that varied intercultural and interracial relations are often guided by a logic that racializes and separates people into those who are redeemers (whites) and those who are redeemed or in need of redemption (nonwhites). Such imposing patronage enables an interpretation of nonwhite characters and culture as essentially broken, marginalized, and pathological, while whites can emerge as messianic characters that easily fix the nonwhite pariah with their superior moral and mental abilities.

While some might argue that such racially charged saviorism is an essentially conservative, postcolonial device that rationalizes right-wing paternalism, I argue that it knows no political boundaries and is pliable to contradictory and seemingly antagonistic agendas. For example, the left-leaning and Pulitzer Prize–

winning journalist Nicholas Kristof admits to the intentional use of the savior motif in his journalism. In the *New York Times*, Kristof penned the following:

> Very often I do go to developing countries where local people are doing extraordinary work, and instead I tend to focus on some foreigner, often some American, who's doing something there. And let me tell you why I do that. The problem that I face—my challenge as a writer—in trying to get readers to care about something like Eastern Congo, is that frankly, the moment a reader sees that I'm writing about Central Africa, for an awful lot of them, that's the moment to turn the page. It's very hard to get people to care about distant crises like that. One way of getting people to read at least a few [paragraphs] in is to have some kind of a foreign protagonist, some American who they can identify with as a bridge character. And so if this is a way I can get people to care about foreign countries, to read about them, ideally, to get a little bit more involved, then I plead guilty. (Kristof 2010)

And ironically, the conservative journalist David Brooks decries the white savior motif as an overdrawn plot device. In reviewing the 2009 film *Avatar* in the *New York Times*, he writes:

> It rests on the stereotype that white people are rationalist and technocratic while colonial victims are spiritual and athletic. It rests on the assumption that nonwhites need the White Messiah to lead their crusades. It rests on the assumption that illiteracy is the path to grace. It also creates a sort of two-edged cultural imperialism. Natives can either have their history shaped by cruel imperialists or benevolent ones, but either way, they are going to be supporting actors in our journey to self-admiration. It's just escapism, obviously, but benevolent romanticism can be just as condescending as the malevolent kind—even when you surround it with pop-up ferns and floating mountains. (Brooks 2010)

The trope of the white savior has saturated popular imagination and casual conversation on blogs (Gates 2012), on Twitter (Cole 2012), in newspaper op-eds (Lange 2013), and on television. The sketch comedy television show *MADtv* (Leddy 2007) even parodied the genre in the skit "Nice White Lady":

> White School Administrator: Forget it. These are minorities. They can't learn and they can't be educated.
>
> White Schoolteacher: With all due respect, sir, I'm a white lady. I can do anything.

Feeding off both use and ridicule, the trope survives and sets off controversy with each new manifestation, especially in cinema. Whether arguing over the content of the films themselves, the evaluations of film critics, the meaning-making of these films by a heterogeneous consumer public, people wrangle over the site and suitability of the white savior and stake out a position along the spectrum of evaluations: good to bad, progressive to racist, and stereotype to true story. The repetition of heated debate over every film that showcases a white protagonist attempting to save a person of color might lead one to think that a major step either forward or backward in race relations is at stake when the curtain goes up.

Using this background as a touchstone for analysis, I set out in this book to investigate the full circle of white savior films: from their cinematic content to their reception by professional film critics, to their consumer base and interpretation. But first, before we investigate the synthesis of race and saviorism, what is this thing we commonly call "white"?

Race and the Modern Meanings of Whiteness

"Race," wrote the famous anthropologist Ashley Montagu, is "man's most dangerous myth" (1942). Contemporary scholars now assert that race is a "social construction"—a set of ideological beliefs, interactive practices, and institutional locations, used to justify the division of people by arbitrary phenotypical features and the unequal allocation of resources and privileges. Viewing race as a social construction means that it is not a naturally occurring or essential human characteristic. Rather, race is an invented category that, over time, people have come to treat as verifiable, real, and the cause of serious consequences, what sociologists call a "social fact."[1]

A long literature on the evolution of the concept of race and the division of humanity into racialized categories need not be summarized here. For my purposes in this book, the key concept is that whiteness perches atop the racial hierarchy in the United States (and arguably, almost everywhere else), reserving a host of material and symbolic privileges.[2] Given this position, whiteness

---

1. The origins of the concept of race grew out of the synthesis of colonialism, globalization, and early philosophical and scientific thought about human variation (Smedley 1993). For example, the belief in divinely decreed or biologically derived racial differences rationalized the transatlantic slave trade, the extermination and removal of Native Americans, the barring of Asian immigrants from the United States, and the belief in the innate superiority of whiteness from Hitler's Germany and Pinochet's Chile to South African apartheid and the Jim Crow United States. But these racialized interactions have not always been around, and they are not preordained. Ancient societies failed to divide people according to physical differences (they generally established in- and out-groups by way of citizenship, religion, status, and language usage) (Snowden 1983: 63). Moreover, race holds no genetic reality (Graves 2005). Recent advances in molecular biology and genetic mapping have enabled the expedient study of population differences (Bliss 2012). Still, race is imbued with a special potency we might call "common sense." Most people believe that race holds a biological reality. And when people define a situation as real, the situation will be real in its consequences (Thomas and Thomas 1928: 572). We live in a racialized society in which racial meanings, expectations, and institutions differently constrain and enable peoples' lives.

2. Examples of material privilege include better access to higher education or safe neighborhoods in which to live, and symbolic privilege includes conceptions of beauty or intelligence that are conflated with whiteness but that implicitly exclude the intellectual

is associated with either normativity or idealism—linked sets of behaviors, achievements, and statuses to which all who desire social and economic mobility should aspire (Hughey 2012).

This white normativity is often hidden in plain sight. As scholars Nelson Rodriguez and Leila Villaverde write, "Whiteness has historically been appropriated in unmarked ways by strategically maintaining as colorless *its* color (and hence its values, belief systems, privileges, histories, experiences, and modes of operation) behind its constant constructions of otherness" (2000: 1). Because whiteness can be akin to an invisible "knapsack" of privileges (McIntosh 1988), contemporary white dominance and privilege often go unquestioned (at least by most whites) or are justified in reference to whites' supposed possession of "good values," such as a strong work ethic and commitment to sovereign individualism. Rather than recognize such values as the result of half a millennium of a social order heavily slanted in one group's favor, this view assumes the inherent superiority of whiteness. The sociologist Ruth Frankenberg maintains, "Whiteness, as a set of normative cultural practices, is visible most clearly to those it definitively excludes and those to whom it does violence. Those who are securely housed within its borders usually do not examine it" (1993: 228–229).

Because race, and thus whiteness, is a socially derived category, the meanings and privileges we assign to it and different racial groups are not static. Economic, legal, social, demographic, and cultural tremors sometimes shake the foundations on which these categories are built and create confusion within or between groups. As a result, the dominant racial group might seek to shore up those foundations (Doane 1997a). For example, recent years have seen a string of social shifts that many whites interpret with apprehension and anxiety. Media outlets increasingly report census projections that whites will lose their majority status in the United States by 2050 ("Minorities Expected" 2008). In concert with these findings, a June 2011 report blazed across national headlines to inform audiences that "more than half of the children under age 2

---

contributions or aestheticism of people of color. That even economically vulnerable white working class can reap the benefits of whiteness was a point recognized early in the twentieth century by the pioneering sociologist W.E.B. Du Bois: "The white group of laborers, while they received a low wage, were compensated in part by a sort of public and psychological wage. They were given public deference and titles of courtesy because they were white. They were admitted freely with all classes of white people to public functions, public parks, and the best schools. The police were drawn from their ranks, and the courts, dependent on their votes, treated them with such leniency as to encourage lawlessness. Their vote selected public officials, and while this had small effect upon the economic situation, it had great effect upon their personal treatment and the deference shown them" ([1935] 1999: 701). Today, whites are often assumed to be the standard, or normative, group and the identity all should assimilate into and aspire to resemble and to which society's central institutions cater: from examples as mundane as "flesh"-colored Band-Aids (when is the last time you saw a dark brown Band-Aid?) to the wide representation on television, in radio, in newsprint, and on the Internet of white people as positive leaders of, and central contributors toward, civilization (even now, in the age of Obama, when is the last time you saw more than a handful of black political or social leaders portrayed in mainstream media?) (McIntosh 1988).

in the U.S. are minorities, part of a sweeping race change and a growing age divide between mostly white, older Americans and fast-growing younger ethnic populations that could reshape government policies" (Yen 2011). These demographic changes come at a time of increased worry over the perceived normalization of economic instability in the housing, stock, and loan markets and increased overall unemployment levels amid the white working and middle classes. Moreover, recent years have been marked by concern over illegal immigration manifest in nativist laws and policies in states such as Arizona, Georgia, and Alabama; a rising discourse opposing affirmative action; and a largely white Tea Party that exhorts us to "take our country back!" This angst was highlighted in a March 2010 *Time* article titled "The White Anxiety Crisis" by Gregory Rodriguez:

> Despite the extraordinary progress of the past 50 years, the sense of white proprietorship—"this is our country and our culture"—still has not been completely eradicated. . . . This [white backlash] won't take the form of a chest-thumping brand of white supremacy. Instead, we are likely to see the rise of a more defensive, aggrieved sense of white victimhood that strains the social contract and undermines collectively shared notions of the common good.

A year later, CNN ran the story "Are Whites Racially Oppressed?," documenting that 44 percent of Americans believe discrimination against whites is equal to bigotry aimed at blacks and other racial minorities. The article began:

> They marched on Washington to reclaim civil rights. They complained of voter intimidation at the polls. They called for ethnic studies programs to promote racial pride. They are, some say, the new face of racial oppression in this nation—and their faces are white. . . . A growing number of white Americans are acting like a racially oppressed majority. They are adopting the language and protest tactics of an embattled minority group. (Blake 2011)

By 2012 the first black presidency, in Barack Obama; the first female Speaker of the House, in Nancy Pelosi; the first Latina member of the Supreme Court, in Sonia Sotomayor; and the news that nonwhite births accounted for more than half of all U.S. births led many to an interpretation of these circumstances that was shaded with a fear of disenfranchisement. "Take our country back!" could be a poignant yet ultimately futile battle cry among a new white minority. Simply put, more and more whites regard themselves as oppressed and are creating a varied social backlash against the racial "others" who they believe are the new oppressors. Many whites interpret the changes in the racial landscape as threats to white normality, privilege, and culture—a culture that some understand as inherently superior and moral. Yet, despite the ominous tone that threads together this worldview, the white backlash is far from new. Such discourse was present when whites discussed slave revolts during the eighteenth century, when whites resisted the handful of newly elected black congressmen during Reconstruction, and when whites disapproved of the civil rights movement (Doane 1997b; Gallagher 2003; Wise 2009).

But the notion of a white backlash may somewhat oversimplify, and even obscure, a fundamental characteristic of white racial identity. While some whites rebel against recent civil rights gains, some fight to protect them. In fact, some whites, regardless of their political or ideological stances, are trying to settle what it means to be white in a time of rapidly changing racial demographics, virulent racial discourse, and apocalyptic and nihilistic messages about the future of the nation and white people. Many whites are in the midst of a crisis of meaning inherent to the very character of whiteness. That is, whiteness is not so much *in* crisis as it is an identity constructed *as* crisis. Whiteness is perpetually a crisis of legitimation given that it must constantly engage in the Herculean feat of claiming a superior and righteous subject position regardless of the external changes around it. In so doing, the foundational sense of white superiority actually sows the seeds of its own frailty. As Alastair Bonnett writes, "Whiteness has often been experienced as something very vulnerable, as an identity under threat. . . . [T]he fragility of whiteness is a direct product of the extraordinary claims of superiority made on its behalf" (2000: 39).

These social, political, economic, and demographic changes to the U.S. racial landscape certainly roughen and fracture what was once smooth terrain for the unfettered travel of white racial superiority. These social undulations, while hardly mountainous changes to the racial order, threaten uncontested white dominance. And while these cracks may result in only slight tremors that barely shake our racialized social order, many whites experience these vibrations as a cataclysmic earthquake that threatens to collapse the house in which they lived as blatant lord and master.

During a time when some perceive an assault on white racial superiority, mainstream media narratives of triumphant white do-gooders should not surprise anyone. As the *Atlantic*'s Teju Cole (2012) writes, "From [Jeffrey] Sachs to Kristof to Invisible Children to TED, the fastest growth industry in the US is the White Savior Industrial Complex." Such stories—especially mass-produced, reviewed, and consumed cinema—appear to support our collective reinterpretation of whites as sentimental interracial benefactors. No longer, so we are told, are whites the racists of Jim Crow. Now they stand on the side of racial righteousness. White actors such as Tom Cruise as advisor to post-Meiji Japanese samurai in *The Last Samurai* (2003), Matthew McConaughey as civil rights lawyer in *A Time to Kill* (1996) and *Amistad* (1997), Emma Stone as Southern girl writing a munificent exposé in *The Help* (2011), and Sandra Bullock as steel magnolia mentoring a homeless black child in *The Blind Side* (2009) all represent characters whose innate sense of justice drives these tales of racial cooperation, nonwhite uplift, and white redemption. These narratives help repair what is truly the most dangerous myth of race—a tale of normal and natural white paternalism (Hughey 2010).

Whether helping people of color who cannot or will not help themselves, teaching nonwhites right from wrong, or framing the white savior as the only character able to recognize these moral distinctions, these films show whites going the extra mile across the color line. In a climate in which many whites believe they are victimized, feel fatigued by complaints of racial inequality, and hold a latent desire to see evidence of a postracial era of reconciliation, films that demonstrate a messianic white character certainly resonate. These interracial depictions of friendly and cooperative race relations thus eschew any blatant dispatch of white supremacy. Rather, they rely on an implicit message of white paternalism and antiblack stereotypes of contented servitude, obedience, and acquiescence. Whiteness emerges as an iron fist in a velvet glove, the knightly savior of the dysfunctional "others" who are redeemable as long as they consent to assimilation and obedience to their white benefactors of class, capital, and compassion. But from where did this modern cinematic trope emerge?

A Genealogy of the White Savior

Terms such as "noble savage," "manifest destiny," "white man's burden," and "great white hope" refer to previous iterations of the complex relationship between the tropes of the white savior and the dysfunctional and dark "other" in need of saving. A "trope" is a recurring cinematic motif that conveys a specific and poignant symbolic meaning (Manchel 1990: 134). Films are often driven by tropes that then come to define particular genres, whether stories about an outsider teacher in an urban school or a lone cowboy in an exotic land. Hernán Vera and Andrew Gordon explain in *Screen Saviors: Hollywood Fictions of Whiteness* that the white savior genre is recognizable through the presence of a white person as "the great leader who saves blacks from slavery or oppression, rescues people of color from poverty and disease, or leads Indians in battle for their dignity and survival" (2003: 33). Examples include *Conrack* (1974), *Glory* (1989), *Dances with Wolves* (1990), *Dangerous Minds* (1996), *Sunset Park* (1996), *Amistad* (1997), *Music of the Heart* (1999), *Finding Forrester* (2000), *Hardball* (2001), *The Last Samurai* (2003), *Half Nelson* (2006), *Gran Torino* (2008), *Avatar* (2009), *The Blind Side* (2009), and *The Help* (2011), to name just a few.

Producers, critics, and audiences often present these films as straightforward and impartial narratives about heroic characters, intercultural friendships, and the humanistic struggle to overcome daunting odds (usually "based on a true story," to boot). Yet they are sites of both purposeful ideological labor and implicit explanations about race so normalized as common sense that many may fail to recognize them as ideological. To unpack the nuance of the present-day white savior trope, one must dig into its earlier manifestations. Hence, it is necessary to identify its origins to gain purchase on the assumptions and cultural logic that drive its modern incarnation.

Race is a relational concept. It holds meaning through the identification and division of people from one another. Especially in the North American context, the meanings of race remain structured by a white-nonwhite binary. The logic of hypodescent (the one-drop rule) and the conflation of whiteness with both superiority and normality helped create a racial order in which nonwhiteness (particularly blackness) was understood as impure and inferior.

Against this backdrop, the predecessor to the modern white savior trope emerges in tandem with the character of the "noble savage." The term first appeared in John Dryden's *The Conquest of Granada* (1672) as an idealized picture of "nature's gentleman." This character was thought worthy because it was unspoiled by material developments and the trappings of modernity. It was often billed as a nonwhite, indigenous, and exotic savage that the white explorer would discover on his colonizing mission. "In the Eurocentric imagination of the eighteenth century, Africans and indigenous 'new world' peoples were said to have noble qualities: harmony with nature, generosity, child-like simplicity, a disdain of materialistic luxury, moral courage, natural happiness even under duress, and a natural or innate morality" (Hughey 2009: 564). This racialized idea fit well with the romanticized and uneasy belief that a burgeoning industrial society was moving away from its time-honored roots, thus losing touch with humanity's true moral instincts. With growing colonial contact and an increasingly media-saturated world, the notion of a white messianic penetrant of a naturally pure and unspoiled culture of noble savages slowly trickled into the popular imagination. Soon the characters of the noble savage and the white colonizer became staples of popular culture and an all-too-seductive device by which racial difference and interaction were interpreted.

In the United States, the term "manifest destiny" came to symbolize a synthesis between racial and religious paternalism. Coined in 1845 in the *United States Magazine and Democratic Review* (J. Pratt 1927), the notion of manifest destiny carried with it the implicit assumption that white Americanness was exceptionally virtuous and was divinely inspired to spread that virtue to others, even if against their will. This ideology was practiced, most notably, in white attitudes toward black slaves and in the westward expansion that would "save" Native Americans from themselves. Hence, the policy of "Kill the Indian, and Save the Man" (R. Pratt [1892] 1973) was instituted as indigenous land was stolen and Native Americans were forced to attend schools designed to strip away their cultural practices in order to "civilize the savages." Such white saviorism was protected and propagated in the legal and policy positions of the time as well as within the dominant and de facto assumptions regarding interracial interactions. White domination vis-à-vis white racial paternalism—a move from the iron fist to the velvet glove of white supremacy—was rationalized through "racial stereotypes (the cognitive aspect), metaphors and concepts (the deeper cognitive aspect), images (the visual aspect), emotions (feelings such as fear), and inclinations (to take discriminatory action)" (Feagin 2006: 27). Whites were socially constructed as heroic and virtuous saviors, a framing that Ronald Takaki (1979) calls "virtuous republicanism"—concentrated repositories of an 1800s Protestant ethic that carried purchase relative to nonwhite pathologies and problems in need of white control.

As the nineteenth century closed, Rudyard Kipling's 1899 poem "The White Man's Burden" (first published in *McClure's Magazine*) further refined the notion of a white savior. Written for Queen Victoria's Diamond Jubilee and altered to address the U.S. acquisition of the Philippines from Spain in the Spanish-American War, the poem received mixed reaction. Some thought it direct praise of white colonization over darker-skinned nations. In this rendering, the "burden" is the moral responsibility of white men to rule over darker and dysfunctional people for their own good. As a result, many came to see the poem as emblematic of racism, colonization, and white superiority complexes that continue to frame the world in terms of a stark civilized-savage dichotomy. Others saw the poem as a satirical critique and tongue-in-cheek parody of the prevailing racial and cultural imperialist attitudes of the day. Regardless of the debate, the phrase came to symbolize an increasingly taken-for-granted weltanschauung: a world populated by dysfunctional people of color thought unredeemable without righteous white paternalism.

As a vociferous movement for human rights and decolonization by people of color in the United States and in nations under the yoke of American and European control gained momentum, the white savior took on a more sinister shade. As the first black heavyweight-boxing champion, Jack Johnson (1908–1915), gained fame and the ire of white America, some demanded a white boxer reclaim the title. As a series of white boxers tried and failed to beat Johnson, they were each labeled the "great white hope." These challengers were, in many ways, propitious white saviors. The black possession of the heavyweight belt was thought an unnatural and dangerous situation that would encourage social equity, threaten to debunk the myth of white superiority, and even cause race riots. In fact, the 1912 U.S. Congress was so convinced that images of Johnson pummeling his white opponents would cause race riots that they passed legislation making it illegal to transport a fight film across state lines (with the penalty of a $1,000 fine, a year in prison, or both) ("Cinema" 1940).

Since the days of Johnson, the term "great white hope" has been repeatedly used in relation to white challengers to heavyweight champs, such as Joe "the Brown Bomber" Louis in the 1930s. In particular, Nazi boxer Max Schmeling's twelfth-round defeat of Louis prompted Adolph Hitler to claim the victory as proof of Aryan supremacy. The trope continued into the 1980s as Larry "the Hitman" Homes fought Gerry Cooney in a fight so racially charged that both white supremacist groups and black activist organizations claimed they would attend the match. While these white challengers were not white saviors in the conventional sense—in that they directly sought to beat, rather than help, people of color—they labored to reproduce a social situation in which whites would occupy positions of paternalistic authority over people of color. In this sense, the "great white hope" became a personified trope for white racial anxiety. A moribund white supremacist order required a racial savior whose very social presence promised to cement white racial clout and control, which would in turn reestablish an order premised on the expertise of white benefactors and the gratitude of nonwhite recipients.

The Widespread White Savior

Scholarship interrogating the diffuse iterations and evolution of the white savior has flourished since the middle of the twentieth century. Historians have demonstrated how the white savior was a very real character during the formation of the United States. The historian James Axtell finds that Native people saw soldiers, missionaries, and teachers as a troubling presence. Upon capturing some of these white interlopers, they would often return them to their American and European kindred because they "in general regarded their white saviors as barbarians and their deliverance as captivity" (Axtell 1975: 62). Similarly, myriad studies in fields as diverse as religion, environmental conservation, education, and politics have pointed to the troubling nature of the concept of the white savior and the damage done by those who have seen themselves suited to such a label. Given its religious foundation, saviorism is often discussed favorably. But now it is commonly understood as a seductive and likely harmful and dangerous orientation toward ministry. Tim Sisk, the director of the Office of Christian Outreach at Wheaton College, states, "We try to do cross-cultural training. We want [graduates] to go out there not with a white savior mentality, but as a learner, sometime who can learn from other cultures and be a better person" (quoted in Riley 2005: 159).

Environmental conservation and protection advocates also now recognize prior missteps in use of the white savior device:

> Diverse iconic figures in conservation such as Theodore Roosevelt, Jacques Cousteau and Jane Goodall have played starring roles in wildlife films in order to communicate their respective views on conservation. The common narrative of these films represents a reoccurring motif, or trope, in wildlife film that has evolved over time and prominently persists today—the trope of the Environmental Savior. This trope is justifiably condemned in its predominant form in mainstream wildlife film for casting a white westerner as environmental savior in a foreign ecosystem. (Winston 2010: v)

Others have found the white savior trope to invade educational pedagogy. Connie Titone discovered that some white teachers did "not see any difference between rightness and whiteness" and adopted the identity of a "white savior" in which they teach "African American, Cajun, and Vietnamese adolescents to succeed academically . . . [,] assimilate into mainstream ways of speaking and acting, learn the given Eurocentric curriculum, gain access to the social and economic system as it was, and thus be successful" (1998: 161–162). Moreover, programs such as Teach for America have increasingly come under fire for reproducing a neocolonial practice in which first-time white teachers hone their skills on dark-skinned at-risk students, all under the logic of a controlling form of charity (Seward 2010).

In the realm of politics, the white savior proves so flexible a device that it is used across the political spectrum of red and blue. For example, Reynolds

Scott-Childress finds that artistic depictions of Abraham Lincoln relied on the trope of the "white savior above. Lincoln's acts of abolition and the slave's initial awakening are really two separate narratives . . . between great man and lowly slave" (1999: 33–34). In stark contrast, the founder of the American Nazi Party, George Lincoln Rockwell, writes, "Future generations will look upon Adolf Hitler as the White Savior of the twentieth century, and the Fuehrerbunker in Berlin as the Alamo of the White race" (quoted in Thayer 1968: 27). The white savior is a device so malleable that it can frame the nearly ultimate benefactor of people of color in the personage of Lincoln or as the definitive white supremacist of Hitler. The trope has also been used by nonwhite cultures when discussing their light-skinned political leaders, such as the Mexican leader Álvaro Obregón, who has been "described as the 'white savior' and compared to Hernán Cortés" (Appelbaum, Macpherson, and Rosemblatt 2003: 218).

Expanding to the larger geopolitical realm, understandings of Hawaii and its incorporation into the United States have been fraught with the "narrative that portrays [Father] Damien as the white savior of powerless Hawaiians who improved conditions of unfortunate 'lepers' and tragically died from the disease himself in the process" (Moran 2007: 226). Such a story justified white efforts to dominate Hawaiian political systems and created a hallowed image of the sacrificing messianic white father-savior who gave his life so that Hawaiians would be better off. In contemporary political discourse regarding U.S. political intervention in foreign lands, scholars have recently demonstrated how "policymakers and corporate media have consistently named their aggressive, illegal military interventions into Haiti (among many other countries) as 'saintly' and 'noble.' . . . This propaganda perpetuates the paternalism of white supremacy that depicts the United States as the white savior of a childlike Haiti" (Malott 2011: 131).

Over time, the white savior metaphor has stabilized and reduced the complexity of an array of interracial and intercultural interactions into a digestible narrative of redemption, individuality, and sacrifice. As witnessed above, increasing numbers of scholars and stakeholders now recognize and critique the prior and continued usages of the savior motif as a mechanism to legitimate and rationalize asymmetrical social relations. But when it comes to film, many still maintain that such evaluations are unfounded and that criticisms of white characters as white saviors fail to see film as harmless entertainment (Shaw 2008). Hollywood film, as a relatively recent and extremely popular media form, offers a prescient opportunity to examine how the savior metaphor works in relation to contemporary understandings of race, particularly that of interracial interactions.

White Saviors on Silver Screens

What role does film play in white racial meaning-making and in repairing the myth of inherent white racial superiority? Given the trepidation, disquiet, and anomie experienced by whites' place and purpose in the age of Obama, some might find it strange to turn to cinema. However, the social practice of consuming film has proved an efficacious strategy for promoting economic stability, stabilizing national identity, and endorsing both implicit and explicit racial messages since the first films appeared. Indeed, entertainment and consumption have often been officially hailed as a solution—or at least a distraction—from the problems of the real world. Terry Cooney thus writes in *Balancing Acts: American Thought and Culture in the 1930s*, "Whether films offered visions of order restored, affirmations of work-centered values, or celebrations of a culture rooted in the mythic American village, they also held out images of competing worlds that might be entered through mimicry or consumption" (1995: 39).

During the Great Depression, when nearly 25 percent of the country was unemployed near its peak in 1933, approximately 60–70 million Americans still packed theaters each week. In 1935 President Franklin Roosevelt stated, "During this Depression, when the spirit of the people is lower than at any other time, it is a splendid thing that for just 15 cents an American can go to a movie and look at the smiling face of a baby and forget his troubles" (quoted in Welling and Valenti 2007: 101).

As film stepped into the 1940s, and the United States moved into World War II, the Hollywood film industry sputtered because of the loss of foreign markets but then quickly rebounded domestically with film advances in sound recording, special effects, cinematography, and use of color. After the war, Hollywood had its most profitable year with then all-time highs in theater attendance (Dirks, n.d.a). Yet in 1944 Dr. Lawrence Reddick, the curator of the Schomburg Collection of Negro Literature of the New York City Public Library, surveyed one hundred films from the beginning of silent films to the 1940s, finding over 75 percent of them to be "anti-Negro" (Reddick quoted in Leab 1975: 3).

The 1950s era of McCarthyism and the birth of the Cold War generated fear that Communists lurked behind every corner. The House Un-American Activities Commission targeted many in Hollywood, which prompted the creation of anti-Communist films such as *Invasion, U.S.A.* (1952), *Red Planet Mars* (1952), and *Walk East on Beacon!* (1952). These films coalesced a sense of U.S. identity qua hyperpatriotism, while fears were temporarily alleviated through the entertainment afforded by the 10.5 million television sets that graced U.S. homes by 1950 and the new trend of drive-in theaters (of which there were approximately four thousand by 1959) (Dirks, n.d.b).

Films from the 1960s reflected the signs of tremendous social changes and contested cultural practices. The one-screen "picture palaces" adorned in art deco gave way to the birth of the multiplex theater (the first built in 1963) that seated hundreds with multiple showings of different films (Dirks, n.d.c). These theaters broadcast films taken from race-based literature, such as Lorraine Hansberry's *A Raisin in the Sun* (1961) and Harper Lee's *To Kill a Mockingbird* (1962), one of the first white savior films. These films gave 1960s audiences an overt cinematic take on race relations not seen since D. W. Griffith's film

Birth of a Nation (1915), based on the novel *The Clansman* (1905) by Thomas Dixon Jr.

As the 1970s took hold, the blaxploitation genre emerged as a reflection of social discontent over racial inequality or a new marketing strategy for bringing blacks to theaters. Melvin Van Peebles's X-rated, confrontational cult film *Sweet Sweetback's Baadasssss Song* (1971) caused controversy for its militancy, explicit sex, antiwhite sentiment, and violence. The same year, a more palatable black hero emerged in the Gordon Parks–directed *Shaft* (which many called the black version of Clint Eastwood's *Dirty Harry*), which was a counterbalance to the trope of the white savior. Approximately two hundred blaxploitation films made it to theaters throughout the decade (Dirks, n.d.d), and the genre catapulted many black careers and forced audiences into watching a take-no-nonsense black character who refused to kowtow to whites (Entman and Rojecki 2001).

In possible reaction to the explosion of on-screen diversity from the previous decades, the 1980s bore witness to the first group of white savior films, such as *Cry Freedom* (1987), *Mississippi Burning* (1988), *A Dry White Season* (1989), *Glory* (1989), and the Indiana Jones trilogy (1981, 1984, 1989). Moreover, the rise of HBO and Showtime via cable television, the creation of the VHS tape, and the proliferation of movie theaters with multiple screens across the United States placed cinematic narratives about race and whiteness in the mainstream (Gray 1995). This trend continued in the 1990s, a decade marked by a proliferation of "race films," leading some scholars to view televisual media as a dynamic medium receptive to public demands for diversity and empowerment (Gray 1995; Nama 2003: 24). Despite this increased diversity, other scholars note that black characters were still locked in stock caricatures of black stereotypes, leading the media scholar Robin Means Coleman (2000) to call the 1990s the "Neo-Minstrel Era." Along with the release of black stereotypical films, the pace quickened on the production of rather overt white savior films such as *Dances with Wolves* (1990), *Dangerous Minds* (1995), *Ghosts of Mississippi* (1996), *Amistad* (1997), and *Music of the Heart* (1999). The frequency and popularity of white savior films only increased in the 2000s as several films and their lead actors were nominated for Academy Awards: for Best Actress, Halle Berry in *Monster's Ball* (2001), Rachel Weisz in *The Constant Gardener* (2005), and Sandra Bullock in *The Blind Side* (2009) and for Best Picture, *Crash* (2005). *Avatar* (2009) garnered nine Oscar nominations on its own and was domestically the highest grossing film of the year.

How and why did these movies resonate in recent years? Consider that since the 1980s there has been a kind of racial schizophrenia in the United States. On the one hand, various institutions began a process of resegregation. The continued effects of racial segregation, years after *Brown v. Board of Education* (1954), contributes to negative outcomes for nonwhites (Massey and Denton 1993). Such enduring inequality manifests in racialized effects in gentrification and home mortgage lending, health disparities, unemployment, and the wealth gap, to name just a few. On the other hand, many now remark or believe that the United States has reached a postracial state in which racism is either dead or the providence of only a few bad apples (Hughey 2011). Especially after President Obama's election, many claim that race plays little to no role in people's everyday lives (except when "politically correct" policies discriminate against whites). Especially among whites, many seem weary of even discussing the continued legacy of racial inequality and seem to suffer from a kind of racial fatigue.

Given the cultural abyss between our dominant postracial discourse and the very real material results of racial inequality, cinema is an important site for publicly accessible and entertaining narratives that reconcile these competing stories. In fact, because of the hypersegregated character of the United States, few within its borders spend substantive time interacting with people of different racial or ethnic groups (Massey and Denton 1993). This point is particularly true for whites. Eighty-six percent of suburban whites live in communities where the black population is less than 1 percent (Oliver and Shapiro 1997), and "according to the 2000 Census, whites are more likely to be segregated than any other group" ("Race Literacy," n.d.). As a result, popular films that highlight interracial interactions offer the public, especially whites, a view of experiences they will rarely have in real life. In the absence of lived experience, films are often understood as accurate reflections of reality, especially when the film begins with the caveat "based on a true story." The historian George Lipsitz notes that films about past race relations "probably frame memory for the greatest number of people" (1998: 219), and Vincent Rocchio, a communications scholar, writes, "The contemporary status of race in mainstream American culture is intimately bound to the process of representations within and through the mass media" (2000: 4).

During unsettled times of conflict, cultural producers "face the challenge of presenting 'collective' sentiments among the tensions, struggles, and crises of contested norms" (Pescosolido, Grauerholz, and Milkie 1997: 444). Hollywood has responded with a cadre of racial redemption stories in which blacks and whites reach across the color line to supposedly help one another. In this light, white savior films emerge as powerful cultural devices that attract, seduce, and command the U.S. public in a time of unsettled understandings of race, racism, and racial identity. In a climate in which many whites believe they are unfairly victimized and losing dominance, many people are exhausted with talking about race, and there is a latent desire to see evidence of interracial reconciliation and amity, films that showcase strong, kind, and messianic white characters assisting nonwhite, down-on-their-luck characters deliver just the right touch.

The white savior film is an important cultural device and artifact because it helps repair the myth of white supremacy and paternalism in an unsettled and racially charged time. The white savior film perpetuates, in subtle and friendly terms, the archaic paradigm of manifest destiny, the white man's burden, and the great white hope. As the film scholar Daniel Bernardi writes, "Cinema is everywhere a fact of our lives, saturating our leisure time, our conversation, and our perceptions of each other and of self. Because of this, race in cinema is neither fictional nor illusion. It is real because it is meaningful and conse-quential; because it impacts real people's lives" (2007: xvi). Whether in *Dances with Wolves, Finding Forrester, Dangerous Minds, Gran Torino, Freedom Writers, The Last Samurai,* or *The Blind Side,* the based-on-a-true-story message is strikingly similar and provides a roadmap for the navigation of race relations.

The Circuit of Meaning: Content, Critics, and Consumption

In three chapters that follow, I investigate the production, distribution, and consumption of the white savior film. These three aspects of film are a part of a feedback loop, or what the cultural theorist Stuart Hall calls a "circuit of culture" (1997: 1).

Chapter 2, "White Savior Films: The Content of Their Character," relies on a content analysis of fifty white savior films produced in a recent quarter century (1987–2011). The chapter highlights the central pillars that uphold the white savior motif. The question that guides my content analysis of these films is how do the dominant messages of these films manifest and what are their visual and discursive structures?

In Chapter 3, "Reviewing Whiteness: Critics and their Commentary," I ex-amine how the dominant racial meanings of North America become manifest in the cultural form of film reviews about the fifty films covered in Chapter 2. In specific, I examine a large number (2,799) of film reviews culled from not only mainstream print-based sources such as the *Atlanta Journal-Constitution* and the *Washington Post* but also web-based sources such as *Reeling Reviews* and *Rotten Tomatoes* and the race- or gender-specific sites *Black Flix* and *The Movie Chicks.* I then observe the dominant racial patterns manifest in these reviews in relation to changes in U.S. race relations measured by descriptions of events involving African Americans, Asian Americans, Latino/Hispanic Americans, racial relations, and hot-button racial topics such as affirmative ac-tion, civil rights, and hate groups as listed in the *New York Times Index* (1987–2004). By exploring the relationship between the interpretive community of film reviewers and perceptions of U.S. race relations, I come to ask: How do variations in race relations relate to the interpretive strategies used to under-stand racialized films?

Chapter 4, "Watching Whiteness: Audience Consumption and Commu-nity," affords a view of how audiences make meaning of white savior films. Relying on interviews with eighty-three people and eight focus groups who watched three white savior films, the chapter examines how interpretations of this genre vary or align in patterned repetition and how different demographic positions influence audience meaning-making; how audiences accept, reject, or modify the dominant meanings of these films; and how their interpersonal interactions affect their interpretations of this cinematic genre. Accordingly,

I ask: How do demographic, contextual, and social variables relate to various audience interpretations of white savior films?

Having investigated the production, distribution, and consumption of white savior films, I turn in Chapter 5, "The Significance of White Saviors in a 'Postracial' World," to driving home the global and domestic significance of white savior films in a growing neoliberal context that is punctuated by discursive claims of being either postracial or color-blind. I highlight how—woven throughout the content, critics, and consumption of white savior films—the import and centrality of race (particularly meanings of white paternalism and contented black servitude) are often downplayed, made invisible, and even contested. Of consequence, given the globalization of Hollywood film, their images labor to disavow the existence and effects of modern racism, which in turn allows the perpetuation of racial hierarchies and reconsolidation of white racial interests across the world.

2

White Savior Films

The Content of Their Character

The messianic white self is the redeemer of the weak, the
great leader who saves blacks from slavery or oppression,
rescues people of color from poverty and disease, or leads
Indians in battle for their dignity and survival. This is a
narcissistic fantasy found in many Hollywood movies.

—Hernán Vera and Andrew Gordon, *Screen Saviors: Hollywood
Fictions of Whiteness*

For centuries, magicians, messiahs, and martyrs have played the role of
helpful guides and aides to embattled protagonists in an array of mythological tales. Athena's assistance to Odysseus, Merlin's shepherding of
King Arthur, Mephistopheles's supervision of Faust, and Dante's use of Virgil
and Beatrice all share a common denominator. Through their enchanted calcu-
lus, they help the disheveled and struggling hero solve problems that, over time,
represent formulaic redemption stories and morality tales.

That such stories and characters are widely shared across time and space is
no coincidence. These narratives carry resonance because they provide scripts
that instruct audiences on the means of receiving redemption, either in a secular or theological sense, during times of social upheaval and change. In modern
times, these characters are a staple of the culture industry. They litter the media
landscape. Especially in film, a border-crossing, white, messianic figure is an
oft-used device. These characters provide both uncertainty and dénouement
for narrative structure. In the former, they represent unknown forces; their origins, intentions, and powers afford a sense of austerity and allure. In the latter,
they bring their charmed or uncanny vision to bear on the central problem of
the film: saving people of color who lack the fortitude, wisdom, resources, or
plain old willpower to rescue themselves.

To many, the white savior film does not seem to address issues of race at
all. I argue the opposite. These films commit a great deal of labor in constructing and fortifying both the category of white racial identity and a normative
(and even moral or progressive) pattern of interracial interaction. That is, in
a quarter century (1987–2011) of marked racial tension, unease, progress, and

conflict, these films work to repair the myth of a great white father figure whose benevolent paternalism over people of color is the way things not only have been but should be.

To unpack this story, I analyze fifty films (produced between 1987 and 2011) deemed white savior films by independent sociologists and media studies scholars (see Bernardi 2007; Chennault 1996; Giroux 1997; Moore and Pierce 2007; Rodríguez 1997; Stoddard and Marcus 2006; Vera and Gordon 2003). I move systematically through these films to consider their content and development (see Table 2.1 for a listing of these films and Appendix A for an account of the methodology employed). By providing an overview of fifty white savior films produced over the past twenty-five years, this chapter stands as the first systematic and critical examination (via a blend of sociological and media studies perspectives) of the genre.

The Production of White Savior Films: A Primer

Table 2.1 shows that many different companies between 1987 and 2011 produced these films. Yet a trend of vast media conglomeration also marks this period. When *Cry Freedom* was released in 1987, approximately fifty corporations controlled most of American media, including magazines, books, music, newspapers, radio and television, and certainly movies. By 1992 that number had dropped to twenty-five. By 2000 (remaining the same in 2012) five corporations controlled most U.S. media: Time Warner, Disney, News Corporation, Bertelsmann, and Viacom. Media scholar Ben Bagdikian (2004) calls such consolidation a "cartel." And with the cartel's expansion into global markets (Bertelsmann is a German company), these companies are increasingly responsible for the content and character of information the world over ("Who Owns the Media?" 2006).

In specific terms of film production, only six parent units controlled the market share by 2012. Those six are Comcast (owner of Universal Pictures and Focus Features), News Corporation (owner of Fox Searchlight and Twentieth Century Fox), Disney (owner of Pixar, Miramax, and Marvel Studios), Viacom (owner of Paramount Pictures), Time Warner (owner of Warner Bros), and Sony (owner of Columbia Pictures). In terms of U.S. and Canadian market share of film in 2011, Viacom took in 19 percent, Time Warner 18 percent, Sony 13 percent, Disney 12 percent, Comcast 11 percent, and News Corporation 11 percent ("Market Share," n.d.). The Big Six thus controlled 85 percent of the cinematic market share in 2011 (together grossing over $8 billion), which was twice as much as the next 140 studios combined ("Studio Market Share," n.d.; Subers 2012). This control stretches beyond the theater releases of films. The communications professor Thomas Schatz writes:

> At present, these "Big Six" media conglomerates own not only the Hollywood film studios, but also all four of the US broadcast television networks

TABLE 2.1. WHITE SAVIOR FILMS (1987–2011)

Title and Year	Production Company/Director	Gross U.S./Gross Worldwide (including U.S.)
Cry Freedom (1987)	Universal/Richard Attenborough	$5,899,797/Unknown (U)
The Principal (1987)	Dorica Film/Christopher Cain	$19,734,940/U
Mississippi Burning (1988)	Orion Pictures/Alan Parker	$34,603,943/U
Rambo III (1988)	Carolco Pictures/Peter MacDonald	$16,745,418/$189,015,611
A Dry White Season (1989)	Davros Films/Euzhan Palcy	$3,766,879/U
Glory (1989)	TriStar Pictures/Edward Zwick	$26,830,000/U
Indiana Jones and the Last Crusade (1989)	Paramount Pictures/Steven Spielberg	$197,171,806/$494,800,000
Dances with Wolves (1990)	Tig Pictures/Kevin Costner	$184,208,848/$424,200,000
The Long Walk Home (1990)	Dave Bell Associates/Richard Pearce	$4,803,039/U
Black Robe (1991)	Allied/Roland Joffé	$8,211,952/U
City of Joy (1992)	Allied/Roland Joffé	$14,683,921/U
Medicine Man (1992)	Cinergi/John McTiernan	$45,500,797/U
Thunderheart (1992)	TriStar Pictures/Michael Apted	$22,660,758/U
Schindler's List (1993)	Universal/Steven Spielberg	$96,045,248/$317,100,000
On Deadly Ground (1994)	Seagal/Nasso Productions/Steven Seagal	$38,590,500/U
Stargate (1994)	Canal+/Roland Emmerich	$71,565,669/$196,600,000
Dangerous Minds (1995)	Hollywood Pictures/John N. Smith	$84,919,401/$177,900,000
Losing Isaiah (1995)	Paramount Pictures/Stephen Gyllenhaal	$7,603,766/$8,500,000
A Time to Kill (1996)	Regency/Joel Schumacher	$108,706,165/$145,600,000
Ghosts of Mississippi (1996)	Castle Rock/Rob Reiner	$13,052,741/U
The Substitute (1996)	Dinamo Entertainment/Robert Mandel	$14,752,141/U
Sunset Park (1996)	Sony Pictures/Steve Gomer	$10,000,000/U
Amistad (1997)	Dreamworks SKG/Steven Spielberg	$44,175,394/U
Bulworth (1998)	20th Century Fox/Warren Beatty	$26,525,834/U

Music of the Heart (1999)	Craven-Maddalena/Wes Craven	$14,859,394/U
The Matrix (1999)	Warner Bros./Andy and Lana Wachowski	$171,479,930/$402,079,930
Snow Falling on Cedars (1999)	Universal/Scott Hicks	$14,378,353/U
Finding Forrester (2000)	Columbia Pictures/Gus Van Sant	$51,768,623/U
Monster's Ball (2001)	Lee Daniels Entertainment/Marc Forster	$31,252,964/U
Hard Ball (2001)	Paramount Pictures/Brian Robbins	$40,219,708/U
K-Pax (2001)	IMF/Iain Softley	$50,315,140/U
Pavilion of Women (2001)	Beijing Film Studio/Ho Yim	$35,938/U
Tears of the Sun (2003)	Cheyenne Enterprises/Antoine Fuqua	$43,426,961/$86,468,162
The Last Samurai (2003)	Warner Bros./John Woo	$111,110,575/$456,758,981
The Matrix Reloaded (2003)	Warner Bros./Andy and Lana Wachowski	$281,492,479/$742,128,461
The Matrix Revolutions (2003)	Warner Bros./Andy and Lana Wachowski	$139,259,759/$412,000,000
Crash (2004)	Bob Yari Productions/Paul Haggis	$54,580,300/$98,410,061
The Constant Gardener (2005)	Focus Features/Fernando Meirelles	$33,579,797/$81,079,798
Amazing Grace (2006)	Four Boys Films/Michael Apted	$21,208,358/$27,213,386
Blood Diamond (2006)	Warner Bros./Edward Zwick	$57,312,489/U
Children of Men (2006)	Universal/Alfonso Cuarón	$35,286,428/$68,327,768
Half Nelson (2006)	Hunting Lane Films/Ryan Fleck	$2,694,973/U
The Last King of Scotland (2006)	Fox Searchlight/Kevin Macdonald	$17,605,861/U
Freedom Writers (2007)	Paramount Pictures/Richard LaGravenese	$36,605,602/$43,090,741
Pathfinder (2007)	20th Century Fox/Marcus Nispel	$10,232,081/U
Gran Torino (2008)	Matten Productions/Clint Eastwood	$148,055,047/U
Avatar (2009)	20th Century Fox/James Cameron	$760,507,625/$2,782,275,172
The Blind Side (2009)	Alcon Entertainment/John Lee Hancock	$255,950,375/U
The Soloist (2009)	Dreamworks SKG/Joe Wright	$31,670,931/U
The Help (2011)	Dreamworks SKG/Tate Taylor	$169,705,587/U

and the vast majority of the major cable networks. Their holdings in other media-related industries are extensive but varied, including music and print publishing, video games, consumer electronics, theme parks, toy manufacturing, cable and satellite systems and online media. (2009: 45)

Media conglomerates are in the midst of a dominant horizontal integration. That is, they are gaining a foothold on the ability to sell one product across varied and numerous markets.

Over one-third (eighteen of the fifty analyzed, or 36 percent) of the white savior films listed in Table 2.1 were produced by these six media conglomerates: two films by Sony, three films by Universal, four films by Paramount, four by either Twentieth Century Fox or Fox Searchlight, and five by Warner Bros. Those companies not media conglomerates, such as Dreamworks SKG (three films) or TriStar (two films), still hold some influence over the market and have done well in recent box office sales ("Studio Market Share," n.d.). In particular, these films were well cited and rewarded. Table 2.2 presents an overview of how many were nominated for or won one or more of the five major film-industry awards: (1) the Academy Award (the Oscar), (2) the American Film Institute award, (3) the Golden Globe award, (4) the Screen Actors Guild Award, and (5) the Writers Guild of America award.

The media conglomeration that began in the 1980s coincides with three related trends. First, as conglomeration quickened, the making of independent ("indie") films also quickened pace.[1] This dichotomization between mainstream and indie films resulted in fewer mainstream films being produced, with a greater focus on big-budget and hopeful blockbusters. Second, with more now riding on less, major film studios began relying heavily on testing and screening their film in progress and story lines to reduce financial and critical risk. Whereas studios used the sneak preview in the 1960s and 1970s to generate buzz about a film, the Big Six began to employ surveys, focus groups, and interviewing to predict what types of stories appealed to the greatest number of viewers. Third, the success of Steven Spielberg's *Jaws* (1975) and *Raiders of the Lost Ark* (1981) and George Lucas's *Star Wars* (1977) captured Hollywood's attention. Major studios began investing in sequels and the development of genres based on hot-button social issues. To many people's surprise, and with the civil rights movement in the not-so-distant past, audiences paid to see movies about social controversy, inclusive of race and racism.

With the arrival of big-budget, socially researched, and culturally relevant mainstream film, the white savior genus sprang on the scene. It encompassed action films, movies about historical events, tales of political tribulations overseas, and narratives of educational inequalities. Accordingly, by the 1980s the white savior strode into films about South African apartheid (*Cry Freedom*, 1987; *A Dry White Season*, 1989), Afghanistan and communism (*Rambo III*,

---

1. "Indies" are films produced mostly or completely outside the major film studio system, often have lower budgets, and generally witness limited distribution and release.

TABLE 2.2. MAINSTREAM AWARDS

Title and Year	Award (no. won, no. nominated)
Cry Freedom (1987)	AA (3N); GG (4N)
The Principal (1987)	
Mississippi Burning (1988)	AA (1W, 6N); GG (4N)
Rambo III (1988)	
A Dry White Season (1989)	AA (1N); GG (1N)
Glory (1989)	AA (3W, 2N); GG (1W, 4N); WGA (1N)
Indiana Jones and the Last Crusade (1989)	AA (1W, 2N); GG (1N)
Dances with Wolves (1990)	AA (7W, 5N); GG (3W, 3N); WGA (1W)
The Long Walk Home (1990)	
Black Robe (1991)	
City of Joy (1992)	
Medicine Man (1992)	
Thunderheart (1992)	
Schindler's List (1993)	AA (7W, 5N); GG (3W, 3N); WGA (1W)
On Deadly Ground (1994)	
Stargate (1994)	
Dangerous Minds (1995)	
Losing Isaiah (1995)	
A Time to Kill (1996)	GG (1N)
Ghosts of Mississippi (1996)	AA (2N); GG (1N)
The Substitute (1996)	
Sunset Park (1996)	
Amistad (1997)	AA (4N); GG (4N); SAGA (1N)
Bulworth (1998)	AA (1N); GG (3N); WGA (1N)
Music of the Heart (1999)	AA (2N); GG (1N); SAGA (1N)
The Matrix (1999)	AA (4W)
Snow Falling on Cedars (1999)	AA (1N)
Finding Forrester (2000)	
Monster's Ball (2001)	AA (1W, 1N); AFI (2N); GG (1N); SAGA (1W); WGA (1N)
Hard Ball (2001)	
K-Pax (2001)	
Pavilion of Women (2001)	
Tears of the Sun (2003)	
The Last Samurai (2003)	AA (4N); AFI (1W); GG (3N); SAGA (1N)
The Matrix Reloaded (2003)	
The Matrix Revolutions (2003)	
Crash (2004)	AA (3W, 3N); AFI (1W); SAGA (1W; 2N); WGA (1W)
The Constant Gardener (2005)	AA (1W, 3N); GG (1W, 2N); SAGA (1W); WGA (1N)

(continued)

TABLE 2.2. (*continued*)

Title and Year	Award (no. won, no. nominated)
Amazing Grace (2006)	
Blood Diamond (2006)	AA (5N); GG (1N); SAGA (2N)
Children of Men (2006)	AA (3N)
Half Nelson (2006)	AA (1N); AFI (1W); SAGA (1N)
The Last King of Scotland (2006)	AA (1W); GG (1W); SAGA (1W); WGA (1N)
Freedom Writers (2007)	
Pathfinder (2007)	
Gran Torino (2008)	AFI (1W); GG (1N)
Avatar (2009)	AA (3W, 6N); GG (1W, 2N); WGA (1N)
The Blind Side (2009)	AA (1W, 1N); GG (1W); SAGA (1W)
The Soloist (2009)	
The Help (2011)	AA (1W, 3N); AFI (1W, 3N); GG (1W); SAGA (3W, 1N)

Note: AA = Academy Award; AFI = American Film Institute; GG = Golden Globe; SAGA = Screen Actors Guild Award; WGA = Writers Guild of America

1988), race and the Civil War (*Glory*, 1989), race and the civil rights movement (*Mississippi Burning*, 1988), treasure-seeking anthropologists who fight Nazis (*Indiana Jones and the Last Crusade*, 1989), and white teachers in majority black and dysfunctional schools (*The Principal*, 1987). At their core, these films hold close to a kindly white figure who possesses the moral fiber, cognitive acumen, and/or physical strength to teach darker-skinned subordinates right from wrong and in so doing redeems or sacrifices him- or herself for the greater good.

The Common Denominators of the White Savior

In what follows, I examine seven key dimensions of the white savior character and genre over the 1980s, 1990s, and 2000s. I do not approach these films as if their meanings live in a vacuum. Rather, I examine the films' content in the context of race relations and political climate—a strategy that situates the cinematic narrative in three key moments of those decades (see Table 2.3). First, the interplay of a growing 1980s neoliberalism that was characterized by a culture war over the place of race and institutional authority; second, the 1990s period of race relations characterized by the 1992 Los Angeles riot, black church burnings, the O. J. Simpson trial, assaults on social welfare, news discourse that imagined a racial Armageddon, and a white racial backlash against civil rights gains; and third, the 2000s large-scale embrace of postracialism, particularly with the ascent of Barack Obama to the White House. Simply put, I systematically cover each film within the context of these distinct, but related, periods to highlight their structure and shared features.

TABLE 2.3 THE COMMON DENOMINATORS OF THE WHITE SAVIOR (NUMBER OF FRAMES)

Title (Year)	Crossing the Color and Culture Line	His Saving Grace	White Suffering	The Savior, the Bad White, and the Natives	The Color of Meritocracy	White Civility, Black Savagery	"Based on a True Story": Racialized Historiography	Total Ratio and Percentage
Cry Freedom (1987)	16	8	11	6	8	7	2	58/314 (18.47%)
The Principal (1987)	11	24	6	8	16	9	0	74/218 (33.94%)
Mississippi Burning (1988)	20	21	8	6	14	7	3	79/256 (30.86%)
Rambo III (1988)	22	26	5	17	4	8	1	83/204 (40.69%)
A Dry White Season (1989)	14	17	8	15	16	15	3	88/194 (45.36%)
Glory (1989)	18	13	6	10	9	8	2	66/244 (27.05%)
Indiana Jones and the Last Crusade (1989)	15	18	3	9	0	9	0	54/246 (21.95%)
Dances with Wolves (1990)	23	11	17	14	2	4	0	71/362 (19.61%)
The Long Walk Home (1990)	5	8	17	5	0	2	2	39/194 (20.10%)
Black Robe (1991)	22	18	13	4	3	2	0	62/202 (30.69%)
City of Joy (1992)	5	11	6	3	2	4	0	31/264 (11.74%)
Medicine Man (1992)	7	4	3	2	0	7	0	23/212 (10.85%)
Thunderheart (1992)	13	2	4	11	4	4	2	40/238 (16.81%)
Schindler's List (1993)	3	15	13	2	3	1	4	41/390 (10.51%)
On Deadly Ground (1994)	7	10	8	0	2	3	0	30/202 (14.85%)

(continued)

TABLE 2.3. (*continued*)

Title (**Year**)	Crossing the Color and Culture Line	His Saving Grace	White Suffering	The Savior, the Bad White, and the Natives	The Color of Meritocracy	White Civility, Black Savagery	"Based on a True Story": Racialized Historiography	**Total Ratio and Percentage**
Stargate (1994)	14	18	3	16	7	16	0	74/242 (30.58%)
Dangerous Minds (1995)	17	13	18	15	17	5	0	85/198 (42.93%)
Losing Isaiah (1995)	5	8	2	8	6	11	0	40/222 (18.02%)
A Time to Kill (1996)	18	13	17	18	5	7	0	78/298 (26.17%)
Ghosts of Mississippi (1996)	11	12	6	13	4	3	2	51/260 (19.62%)
The Substitute (1996)	4	7	3	12	3	6	0	35/228 (15.35%)
Sunset Park (1996)	9	9	6	7	5	9	0	45/198 (22.73%)
Amistad (1997)	10	14	5	3	7	13	3	55/310 (17.74%)
Bulworth (1998)	3	2	0	3	6	2	0	16/216 (7.40%)
Music of the Heart (1999)	5	11	7	6	13	3	2	47/248 (18.95%)
The Matrix (1999)	10	9	5	6	7	3	0	40/272 (14.71%)
Snow Falling on Cedars (1999)	11	6	8	2	5	6	0	38/254 (14.96%)
Finding Forrester (2000)	6	6	8	8	5	4	0	37/272 (13.60%)
Monster's Ball (2001)	8	6	5	1	0	1	0	21/222 (9.46%)
Hard Ball (2001)	12	5	7	5	2	3	0	34/212 (16.37%)
K-Pax (2001)	3	2	1	4	1	0	0	11/240 (4.58%)
Pavilion of Women (2001)	3	1	3	5	0	2	0	14/232 (6.03%)
Tears of the Sun (2003)	11	4	1	5	2	1	2	26/242 (10.74%)

								Total Ratio and Percent
The Last Samurai (2003)	18	11	6	1	6	0	3	45/308 (14.61%)
The Matrix Reloaded (2003)	3	6	2	0	1	3	0	15/276 (5.43%)
The Matrix Revolutions (2003)	4	8	2	0	2	4	0	20/258 (7.75%)
Crash (2004)	10	6	8	1	5	2	0	32/224 (14.29%)
The Constant Gardener (2005)	5	5	3	2	1	3	2	21/258 (8.14%)
Amazing Grace (2006)	8	7	2	12	3	2	3	37/234 (15.81%)
Blood Diamond (2006)	8	5	6	8	6	1	3	37/286 (12.94%)
Children of Men (2006)	6	4	4	7	4	4	0	29/218 (13.30%)
Half Nelson (2006)	11	8	5	5	8	2	0	39/212 (18.39%)
The Last King of Scotland (2006)	9	4	4	13	0	4	3	37/242 (15.29%)
Freedom Writers (2007)	13	6	4	12	13	6	0	54/246 (21.95%)
Pathfinder (2007)	4	3	5	10	2	8	0	32/198 (16.16%)
Gran Torino (2008)	16	8	7	0	15	9	0	55/232 (23.71%)
Avatar (2009)	18	3	4	16	10	15	0	66/324 (20.37%)
The Blind Side (2009)	8	3	4	7	11	12	2	47/258 (18.22%)
The Soloist (2009)	5	4	0	5	5	4	0	23/234 (9.40%)
The Help (2011)	10	4	5	8	7	5	1	40/292 (13.69%)
Total Ratio and Percent	517/12,414 (4.16%)	447/12,414 (3.60%)	304/12,414 (2.45%)	356/12,414 (2.87%)	277/12,414 (2.23%)	269/12,414 (2.17%)	45/12,414 (0.36%)	**2,215/12,414 (17.84%)**

Crossing the Color and Culture Line

A defining characteristic of the white savior film is the white interloper's intrusion on a nonwhite culture that is, or soon will be, under assault. Akin to Virgil's *Aeneid* or Chaucer's *Canterbury Tales*, the point of the journey is not its completion but what the central characters discover about themselves and their culture along the way. Accordingly, in thirty-one of the fifty (62 percent) films in this sample, the white savior entered a setting entirely unfamiliar or even hostile.

The white savior could be part of an invading or colonizing military force, a teacher assigned to a failing urban school, or a capitalist seeking riches and resources. Not long after the protagonist enters the foreign land, he or she learns that the original reason for the journey was wrong and slowly becomes uncomfortable with his or her role. The savior then comes to admire the noble savagery and lack of pretense among the native, indigenous, or local culture. And slowly the savior comes to learn about the native techniques for defending themselves from the few bad white people of whom the savior was formerly a part. In the end, the savior might even identify more with the natives to the point of turning his or her back on the colonizing force, the school administration, or the white legal structure. Films such as *Dances with Wolves* (1990), *The Last Samurai* (2003), *The Constant Gardener* (2005), and even the quasi-computer-generated film *Avatar* (2009), in which a paraplegic marine becomes the savor of the Na'vi, readily evidence this characteristic.

These films rely on both racial and xenophobic narratives to propel the exoticism of the foreign and dark "others" for U.S. audiences. However, white saviors also intrude on domestic areas as long as those settings are a priori understood as dangerous and backward—for example, northern urban ghettos full of black criminals or the rural settings of the Deep South choked with white racists. The films *To Kill a Mockingbird* (1962), *Mississippi Burning* (1988), *Glory* (1989), *Ghosts of Mississippi* (1996), *Sunset Park* (1996), *Hardball* (2001), *Gran Torino* (2008), and the like serve as potent stomping grounds on which the white savior may enact his or her mission.

All that is required is a racialized culture change. In some cases, the boundary, not the savior, may move, bringing the white protagonist into contact with the "others" without having to leave his yard. For example, in *Gran Torino*, Walt Kowalski (Clint Eastwood) is a white Korean War veteran living alone in his once-gentrified neighborhood in Detroit, Michigan. The neighborhood experiences white flight; several Asian families move in, and a Hmong family moves in next door. Without making a move, Kowalski finds himself in a foreign land, a predicament that draws out the racism he implicitly carries. Yet with time, he comes to understand some of the Hmong culture and traditions, even respecting the values they are shown to place on cooperation, hard work, and family. After one encounter with the Hmong family, Walt excuses himself to the bathroom, where he looks in the mirror and states, "God, I've got more in common with these gooks than I do with my own rotten, spoiled family."

The "stranger in a strange land" motif propels much of the rising action in white savior films. The narrative arc begins with a racist, greedy, close-minded, or otherwise dysfunctional white character. The protagonist then learns the ways of the "natives" and comes to respect them. And finally, the protagonist transforms into their savior; he rescues them from the problems thought endemic to the culture of their own racial group or rises in power to lead them against some native enemy.

For example, in *The Last Samurai*, protagonist Nathan Algren (Tom Cruise), a former Army captain under the infamous General George Custer, is approached by an old Army buddy, Zebulon Gant (Billy Connolly). Gant takes Algren to meet his former commanding officer Colonel Bagley (Tony Goldwyn), whom Algren despises for Indian massacres in which he was ordered to participate. Bagley offers Algren a job training conscripts of the new Meiji government of Japan to suppress a samurai rebellion. But Algren is now a bitter alcoholic, haunted by the memories of previous killings. He is skeptical of his mission as simply an instructor of warfare but accepts it as his fate:

> Algren: You want me to kill Jappos, I'll kill Jappos—
> Bagley: We're not killing anybody—
> Algren: You want me to kill the enemies of Jappos, I'll kill the enemies of Jappos. Or Rebs or Sioux or Cheyenne, for 500 bucks a month, I'll kill whoever you want. [*Leans close*] But keep one thing in mind. I'd happily kill you for free.

Algren arrives in Japan and is soon captured by the samurai. After being kept in the samurai village for just a few months, he mysteriously masters the language, Japanese swordplay, domestic customs, gender relations, and philosophy and becomes enamored with the samurai way of life. Realizing that the new Japanese government, under the control of Western influence, has lost its way, he dedicates himself to helping his former captors and the samurai rebellion. In preparing for war, Algren and his Japanese friend Higen (Sôsuke Ikematsu) have the following exchange:

> Higen: Will you fight the white men, too?
> Algren: If they come here, yes.
> Higen: Why?
> Algren: Because they come to destroy what I have come to love.

Sentimental dialogue often finds great expression in these films. The discourse labors to drive home the point that an authentic interracial and intercultural friendship has been established, which obscures the larger pattern of the white intruder qua savior instructing the "primitive" peoples on how to live and, in the case of *The Last Samurai*, how to die. In the end, all the samurai—including his newly found best friend Katsumoto (Ken Watanabe)—are killed. Yet Algren seems to have taught the Japanese about Western modernity as well as reminded them to be true to their own historical origins:

Emperor Meiji: You were with him [Katsumoto], at the end?
Algren: Hai. Your Highness, if you believe me to be your enemy, command
    me, and I will gladly take my life. . . .
Emperor Meiji: I have dreamed of a unified Japan, of a country strong,
    independent, and modern. And now we have railroads, and cannon,
    Western clothing. But we cannot forget who we are or where we come
    from. . . . Tell me how he [Katsumoto] died.
Algren: I will tell you how he lived.

In *Hard Ball* (2001), Conor O'Neill (Keanu Reeves) finds himself in gambling trouble and approaches a friend for a loan. His friend does not have the time or desire to coach a Chicago inner-city baseball team and tells O'Neill that he will pay off his debt if he coaches the team. O'Neill agrees and soon finds himself in the ABLA projects (named after the four main complexes there: Jane Addams Homes, Robert Brooks Homes, Loomis Courts Homes, Grace Abbott Homes) near downtown Chicago.

The nearly all-black area is clearly foreign to O'Neill. He often relies on the children to educate him about the pitfalls and perils of the area. For example, O'Neill breaks up a fight on the first day of practice but is quite obviously out of touch and cannot understand the slang used by most of his players. Serving as his racial-cultural tour guide, the nine-year-old Jarius "G-Baby" Evans attempts to tell him why the fight occurred:

O'Neill: Hey! Hey! Hey! Cool it! Cool it! What's going on?
G-Baby: All right, let me break it down to you right quick. Andre says he
    can catch any pop-up anybody can throw. Kofi say, "That's bullshit.
    You a busta." Andre say, "Roll up, bitch." Kofi say, "I'll give you all my
    gum if you can catch this ball." He threw the ball. Andre caught it. Andre say, "Pay me my money." Kofi say, "You a cheatin' bitch." No, wait.
    Kofi say, "You a motherfu—"
O'Neill (*interrupting*): Okay, I got it. Thanks.

Shortly thereafter, O'Neill gets tough with the kids and starts to find his way as their coach.

In the film *Avatar*, a paraplegic marine named Jake Sully (Sam Worthington) travels to the moon Pandora, where a mining company employs military troops to take over land from the native Na'vi people to mine unobtainium, a precious mineral. To explore Pandora's biosphere, scientists use Na'vi-human hybrids called avatars, operated by genetically matched humans who remain in machines that are psychically linked to their Na'vi avatar bodies. Sully's role on Pandora is special. He replaces his deceased twin brother as an operator of an avatar and is asked by the chief mercenary, Marine Colonel Miles Quaritch (Stephen Lang), to take on a special role unbeknownst to the scientists studying the planet's biosphere.

Quaritch: Look, Sully, I want you to learn the savages from the inside. I
    want you to gain their trust. I need you to force their cooperation or
    hammer them hard if they won't. . . . Can you do that for me?
Sully: Hell yeah, sir.

Quaritch also promises Sully that on completion of his mission the Marine
Corps will pay to fix his paralysis, giving him back the use of his legs.

Sully links to his avatar and is overjoyed to have legs. He is overconfident
and wanders off from the scientists, farther into the jungles of Pandora. Local
fauna attacks him, separating him from the scientists, and he is rescued by a native Na'vi woman, Neytiri (Zoe Saldana). Taking him back to the Na'vi village,
Neytiri is instructed to teach Sully the Na'vi ways. Soon he learns the language,
how to fight, how to ride the large birds of the Pandora jungle, and the customs
of the people. Originally sent to infiltrate the Na'vi to ultimately remove or ex-
terminate them, Sully begins (just as Algren in *The Last Samurai* and O'Neill
in *Hard Ball* do) to identify with the Na'vi and soon falls in love with Neytiri.
After revealing to the Na'vi his original mission, and with the mining company bulldozing the forest in which the Na'vi live, Sully picks the side of the
Na'vi: "I am not your enemy. . . . The enemy is out there. And they are very
powerful." Soon after, Colonel Quaritch barges into the scientists' lab where
the human body of Sully lies, psychically connected to his Na'vi avatar. Discon-
necting him from his avatar, Quaritch pulls Sully from the machine and yells,
"So, what, you find yourself some local tail and you forget what team you're
playing for?"

Sully is imprisoned but breaks free and reconnects to his Na'vi avatar. Under the guidance of Sully's military skill, the Na'vi fight the mining company
and their mercenaries. Sully's ultimate border crossing is made explicit in the
final fight between Quaritch and Sully, in which Quaritch states, "Hey, Sully.
How's it feel to betray your own race? You think you're one of them? Time to
wake up." After a close call, Sully and Neytiri triumph, the mining company is
expelled from the planet, and the Na'vi retain their lands.

Such extreme border crossing is an important aspect of these films. The
transition of the white savior from the forces of evil to good, from Western to
Eastern, from white to black, or from human to alien cements a view of whiteness as welcome anywhere and everywhere and that no boundaries need be
respected if whites wish to help.

His Saving Grace

After entering the unsettled lands of the western plains (*Dances with Wolves*),
the multicultural landscapes outside computer-simulated reality (*The Matrix*),
or the black and brown classrooms of the inner city (*The Principal, Dangerous
Minds, Half Nelson,* and *Freedom Writers*), the white protagonist must begin,
through his grace, to save nonwhite people from an impending disaster.

The transformation of the white protagonist into the white savior takes different forms. Ripe, if not over the top, religious metaphors and imagery are employed at times. For example, *Children of Men* (released in the United States on December 25, 2006) employs a litany of Christian-religious symbolism to propel the central white protagonist Theo Faron (Clive Owen) to save the key black character, a pregnant West African refugee named Kee. The film is set in 2027 United Kingdom, in which society is at the brink of collapse because of two decades of human infertility. Undocumented immigrants, mostly of color, seek sanctuary in the United Kingdom, where the government imposes oppressive, white nationalistic laws on them. Hence, Kee's pregnancy is incredibly important, as her fertility holds a possible solution to human extinction.

Faron labors through the film to help Kee, attempting, first, to deliver Kee to an immigrant rights group called the Fishes (a slightly veiled reference to the ichthys, or the sign of the fish, used by early Christians) and then to a group of scientists working on infertility.[2] Kee's pregnancy is revealed to Faron in a barn, alluding to the manger used for the birth of Jesus Christ. When Faron asks Kee about the father of the child, Kee jokes that she is a virgin—again a reference to Christianity and the Virgin Mary. Kee's safe passage from the United Kingdom is the key to humanity's salvation and continued life.

Throughout the film, Faron puts his life and safety on the line for Kee. As they enter a detention center on a bus, it is imperative that Kee's pregnancy remain hidden. However, she goes into labor. As guards come on the bus to pull suspicious-looking immigrants off for interrogation, one guard spies Kee and approaches her.

> Guard (*to Kee*): Up now. Get off.
> Faron (*in faux accent, pointing at the floor*): Caca! Caca!
> Guard: What?
> Faron: Piss. Piss. Caca. Smell.
> Guard: You smell it yourself. You fucking people disgust me. [*Guard turns and walks off the bus.*]

Just scenes later, Faron finds a safe place for Kee and delivers her child.

Other films employ these less-than-subtle religious allusions. For example, the beginning scene of *Hard Ball* finds Conor O'Neill sitting in a church pew, seemingly bowed in prayer. A Catholic priest approaches him to say, "I've got to lock up, son. You looking for faith? Forgiveness?" But in return, O'Neill states, "I'm looking for the Bulls to cover the spread." This scene places his role as incipient savior squarely in a religious context in which he is looking for both redemption and assistance, but he is looking in the wrong place (the church)

---

2. "Ichthys" hails from the Koine Greek word for "fish." The symbol is two intersecting arcs, tilted so that the ends of the right side overlap slightly and so resemble a stylized fish (i.e., ⟨×). Early Christians used it as a clandestine symbol to mark meeting places and distinguish between believers and nonbelievers.

and for the wrong thing (gambling). Such a scene prefigures that his own sins will be washed away through his help of others. And given the context of Chicago and the seedy South Side bars where he places his bets, what better place is there for O'Neill to transform into the white savior than among the downtrodden and meek, among small black children living in housing projects who wish nothing more than to play the game of baseball?

The religious imagery is overt in other films. For example, *Amazing Grace* tells the story of William Wilberforce (1759–1833), a British politician and leader of the slave abolitionary movement in the United Kingdom. Despite being based on a true story and no record of Wilberforce's supposed distaste for politics, the film portrays Wilberforce as a man disenchanted with politics and consumed by religious fervor, wishing only to live the life of a priest or monk. In a conversation with his butler, Richard (Jeremy Swift), Wilberforce (Ioan Gruffudd) confesses his apathy with politics.

> Wilberforce: It's God. I have ten thousand engagements of state today, but I would prefer to spend the day out here getting a wet arse, studying dandelions, and marveling at bloody spider's webs.
> Richard: You found God, sir?
> Wilberforce: I think he found me. You have any idea how inconvenient that is? How idiotic it will sound? I have a political career glittering ahead of me, and in my heart I want spider's webs.

Yet the film finds a way to reconcile the character's religious fervor with the historical figure of William Wilberforce. William Pitt (the youngest prime minister in U.K. history at the age of twenty-four) brings a group of abolitionists to Wilberforce's home. One of them says to Wilberforce, "We understand you're having problems choosing whether to do the work of God or the work of a political activist. We humbly suggest that you can do both." Suddenly Wilberforce sees the light.

In continuing to merge the politically pragmatic and the religiously abstract, Wilberforce then goes to his friend John Newton (Albert Finney), the former captain of a slave ship who gave up his job, sold his ship, and became a part-time monk to seek forgiveness for his sins of human trafficking. Wilberforce hopes that Newton can write about his experiences as proof of the horrors of the slave trade, but Newton claims he is too consumed with guilt:

> Newton: You of all people should know I can never be alone.
> Wilberforce: You told me you live in the company of twenty thousand ghosts. The ghosts of slaves?
> Newton: I was explaining to a child why a grown man cowers in a corner.
> Wilberforce: I need you to tell me about them.
> Newton: I'm not strong enough to hear my own confession. . . . I'm the last person you should come to for advice. I can't even say the name of any of my ships without being back on board them in my head! All I know

is twenty thousand slaves live with me in this little church. There's still blood on my hands.

Yet just as Wilberforce successfully blends politics and religion, Newton soon finds a way to write down his firsthand account of slave trading across the Atlantic. After recording all he remembers, Newton tells Wilberforce:

This is my confession. You must use it. Names, ships records, ports, people, everything I remember is in here. Although my memory's fading, I remember two things very clearly. I'm a great sinner and Christ is a great Saviour. I wish I could remember all their names. My twenty thousand ghosts, they all had names, beautiful African names. We call them with just grunts, noises. We were apes; they were human [*begins to cry*]. I'm weeping. I couldn't weep until I wrote this.

By film's end, both Wilberforce and Newton emerge as the saviors of Africans. Wilberforce, with the assistance of Newton's gripping testimony, persuades British parliament to end slavery.

This film boils down complicated and politically messy dynamics into tales of individual heroes whose moral commitments overpower and transform the ill will of oppressors. Through their art of persuasion, these beacons of hope simply appeal to the conscience of evildoers, the bad guys recognize and repent for their sins, and all is set right with the world. Such an arrangement makes for a sentimental tale, but it betrays a central tenet of radical social change that was penned by Martin Luther King as he sat in a Birmingham, Alabama, jail in 1963: "We know through painful experience that freedom is never voluntarily given by the oppressor; it must be demanded by the oppressed" (King 1963). But in the world of individual white saviors without meaningful skills or knowledge, no grassroots movement or collective demand is necessary. Only one white individual with pure thoughts and motive need appear.

In *Black Robe*, the white savior is Ariana LaForgue (Lothaire Bluteau), a French priest living in a 1634 French settlement that will one day become Quebec City, Canada. His job is to encourage the local Algonquin Indians to embrace Christianity, but he has met little success. In response, Samuel de Champlain (Jean Brousseau), founder of the settlement, sends LaForgue to find a distant Catholic mission in a Huron village. Along the way, LaForgue attempts to convert many of the Natives, despite setbacks ranging from discomfort to death.

When LaForgue enters the Huron village near the end of the film, he finds the village nearly decimated by smallpox. He discovers the priest of the church (Father Jerome) dead and then rings the church bells to beckon the Natives to him. A Huron man approaches him:

Huron man: Demon, why are you here?
LaForgue: I'm not a demon. I take the place of Father Jerome.

Huron man: He is dead?
LaForgue: Yes.
Huron man: How long do you stay?
LaForgue: All of my life.
Huron man: If we take the water sorcery [baptism], we will not be sick?
LaForgue: Baptism will not save you.
Huron man: The other black robe said so.
LaForgue: He meant only that we must ask the help of Jesus. Perhaps he will
        answer your prayers. . . .
Huron man: You must help us, black robe. Do you love us?
LaForgue: Yes.
Huron man: Then baptize us.

He then baptizes all in a ceremony, and the Hurons accept Christianity to live prosperous lives.

In *Stargate*, the white savior Dr. Daniel Jackson (James Spader) and a team of U.S. soldiers led by Colonel Jack O'Neil (Kurt Russell) travel through a mysterious star gate to land on an alien planet whose darker-skinned inhabitants all worship the ancient Egyptian deity Ra. Accompanied by an expert on ancient Egyptian theology and linguistics who possesses an ancient Egyptian necklace that sports the "Eye of Ra,"[3] Jackson and the soldiers stumble upon a village of natives who work as slaves, mining rich minerals from the desert sand. As the group approaches the village, the natives spot them and watch suspiciously.

O'Neil: All right, Jackson. You're on.
Jackson: Me?
O'Neil: You're the linguist. Try to talk to them.
Jackson: Hi. [*One of the slaves spots the Eye of Ra pendant around Jackson's
        neck, and his eyes widen.*]
Slave: Na tu de-why-ya. Na tu de-why-ya. [*The slave bows down in front of
        Jackson and the soldiers. The rest of the slaves follow suit until all bow.*]
O'Neil: What the hell did you say to him?
Jackson: Nothing.

After being treated as deities, Jackson and the team figure out that an alien force has colonized and enslaved the workers. As two saviors with scientific and military knowledge, O'Neil and Jackson do not attempt to convince the aliens to release the slaves but rather set out to lead a revolt. As thousands of slaves toil in the desert mines, a slave-owner guard dressed as the Egyptian deity Horus approaches a slave struggling with a heavy load. He scolds the slave and beats him harshly. Suddenly, members of O'Neil's team emerge and kill the guard.

---

3. The symbol in the film is actually the Eye of Horus (𓂀), an ancient Egyptian symbol of protection, royal power, and good health. In modern times, and with the Western fascination with Egyptology, the symbol has been conflated with the Eye of Ra, a symbol often displayed as a disk to represent the sun.

Yet the leader of the slaves, Kasuf (Erick Avari), is terrified at their violent resistance and immediately fears retribution from the slave-owning aliens. Jackson and O'Neil then step in to convince Kasuf of the morality and pragmatism of their revolt.

> O'Neil: Let's go.
> Kasuf: You will bring disaster to all of us, son.
> Skaara (Alexis Cruz): Father, we will not live as slaves! [*Kasuf tells his people to kneel with him, beginning to pray for forgiveness, but Skaara screams and argues with him.*]
> Jackson: Kasuf. Take a look at your gods. [*Jackson takes the Horus mask off the dead guard to reveal a human, just like the slaves.*] Take a good look.

Jackson and O'Neil form a dynamic duo of saviorhood. They together join, liberate, and ultimately control the fate of the former slave population. To cement their role as both violently powerful and forgiving and redeeming saviors to the natives, O'Neil leads the rebellion while Jackson shows mercy to those who adore him.

An extreme, yet telling, example of Jackson's compassion and unfettered power occurs near the film's end. By this moment in the narrative, it is clear that Jackson has ignited a romance with a local woman named Sha'uri (Mili Avital). But during the rebellion Sha'uri is shot and killed. Jackson is distraught and dispatches O'Neil to continue the battle against the alien overlords. Lifting Sha'uri's broken and bloody body in his arms, he travels to the heart of the alien stronghold, inside their pyramid-shaped ship. He deftly sneaks aboard, navigates the passageways and guards undetected, and lays Sha'uri's body gently in an alien sarcophagus, which he has somehow figured out how to use as a resurrection device. Moments later she is healed, and Jackson helps her escape from the ship before O'Neil uses a bomb to destroy it. Together, their blend of harbingers of death and life merge to liberate key individuals (such as Sha'uri) and the entire population from the alien slaveholders. In the end, both O'Neil and Jackson demonstrate their authority over all matters, even those seeming as unalterable as death.

The white savior's role as a leader against injustice is rarely vague. In *City of Joy*, the protagonist, Max Lowe (Patrick Swayze), is a disillusioned Texas medical doctor, who, after the loss of a patient by his hands, moves to Calcutta to find himself. After befriending a local man named Hasari Pal (Om Puri), he makes a network of acquaintances, chief among them an Irishwoman, Joan Bethel (Pauline Collins), who runs a haphazard medical clinic. But Lowe is a cynic and flees involvement in local matters, telling Bethel that he is a nonpracticing doctor because he does not like sick people.

However, Lowe's saviorhood is brought out once he discovers that a local gangster-landlord named Godfather Ghatak (Shyamanand Jalan) regularly extorts the clinic and neighborhood for protection money. After confronting the godfather and finding him unwilling to budge, Lowe calls the neighborhood to revolt. However, he finds the people not easily persuaded. Frustrated, Lowe shouts, "I don't understand you people, you act like sheep!" However, Hasari Pal's wife, Kamla Pal (Shabana Azmi), speaks up: "We must choose. Max is only trying to help all of us. I would like to stand up." As soon as Lowe is anointed the assistive savior of them all, the mood suddenly changes. A neighbor says he will rent property to the clinic that is beyond the control of the godfather. Thanks to the mere suggestion of the savior, coupled with the cooperation of one local, the problem is solved. Even when the godfather's son sends a mob to beat up the clinic volunteers for leaving the neighborhood and his control, Lowe helps the locals organize and resist. In a matter of weeks, the cynic-turned-savior restores harmony and justice to people who could not help themselves without a white Texas-bred doctor in their midst.

In *Gran Torino* Walt Kowalski plays another reluctant savior whose inner messiah is brought out to defend people of color from themselves. After a quiet and peaceful Hmong family moves in next door to Kowalski, the film quickly introduces trouble: a young cousin of the family is a gangster. He and his gang attempt to recruit the young male of the family, Thao (Bee Vang). However, after a failed initiation attempt in which Thao is sent to steal Kowalski's 1972 Ford Gran Torino, Thao and his sister Sue (Ahney Her) want no part of the violent lifestyle, and they resist their cousin's strong-arm tactics to force Thao to join their ranks. Tired of being turned down, the gang descends on the family home, where a fight breaks out and spills over to Kowalski's front lawn, breaking a ceramic garden gnome.

Kowalski emerges from his home and has the muzzle of his Korean War–era .30-06 M1 Garand rifle pointed at one of the gangsters, Smokie (Sonny Vue):

Kowalski: Get off my lawn.
Smokie: Listen, old man, you don't want to fuck with me.
Kowalski: Did you hear me? I said get off my lawn now.
Smokie: You fucking crazy? Go back in the house.
Kowalski: Yeah. I blow a hole in your face and go back in the house, and I
    sleep like a baby. You can count on that. I use to stack fucks like you five
    feet high in Korea, use you for sandbags.
Smokie (*starting to leave*): You better watch your back.
Sue: Thank you.
Kowalski (*to Sue*): Get off my lawn.

The next day, Kowalski awakens to gifts littering his front porch. Visibly annoyed by the adoration, Kowalski throws many of the gifts away in the alley. Sue approaches.

Kowalski: Why are you bringing me all this garbage anyway?
Sue: Because you saved Thao.
Kowalski: I didn't save anybody. I just kept a bunch of bumbling gooks off
    my lawn. That's all.
Sue: Well, you're a hero to the neighborhood.

Kowalski: I'm not a hero.
Sue: Too bad, they think you are. And that's why they keep bringing you
    the gifts.

The character of Walt Kowalski is atypical in his blatant racism. Generally, white saviors are kind and beneficent characters, even if their displacement among people of color was precipitated by their own moral failings. However, *Gran Torino*'s dialogue and action redeem Kowalski and invite reverence for him, even as he spills out string after string of overt racism at the very people he is supposedly helping. For example, later in the film, Sue walks home with a young white man who is clearly imitating stereotypical black styles of speech, dress, and comportment. They run into three younger black men who do not appreciate their presence. The young white man tries to defuse the tension with a handshake and a forced, "It's all good, bro." But the men are not impressed and throw him into a chain fence. They then turn their attentions to Sue, verbally and physically accosting her. Kowalski notices the interaction from across the street and approaches as though a shining knight in his white Ford pickup truck—the postindustrial, working-class man's version of a white horse:

Black guy 1: The fuck you looking at, old man?
Kowalski: The hell are you spooks up to?
Black guy 2: Spooks?
Black guy 1 You better get your ass on, honky, while I still let you. That's
    what you better do.
Kowalski (*slowly getting out of the truck*): Ever notice how you come across
    somebody once in a while you shouldn't have fucked with? That's me.
Black guy 1: Man, you fucking crazy. Get out of here, man.
Black guy 2: Look, why don't you get your ass up out of here before I kick
    your old wrinkly white ass.

In a slow, determined, and dramatic fashion, Kowalski reaches into his jacket pocket and pulls out his hand, pointed at the group of black men as if it were a gun. They snicker at him and look bewildered as he slowly points his finger at each of them and then tells Sue, "Get in the truck." But the group refuse to let Sue go and begin to laugh as black guy 1 states, "This crazy motherfucker, man. What's wrong with him? He pointed a finger at us." But Kowalski suddenly draws a real gun from his waistband, which immediately gets the attention and silence of the group as Sue escapes to Kowalski's white pickup truck.

White guy: Way to go, old man.
Kowalski: Shut up, pussy. What's with all that "bro" shit anyway? Want to
    be superspade or something? These guys don't want to be your bro, and
    I don't blame 'em. Now get your ofay paddy ass on down the road.

Kowalski and Sue then drive off into the sunset, away from the threat that Kowalski diffused.

Aside from the white savior's ability to remove the bad elements of non-white communities so that they may live in peace and tranquility, the savior also demonstrates an inexplicable talent for transforming nonwhite mindsets so that black, Latino, and Asian lives revolve around the supposed benevolence of the newfound white savior. For example, in *Hard Ball*, O'Neill attends his first baseball practice. He tells his black players to take the field, and he begins to hit balls into the outfield for them to practice catching and fielding. After repeatedly observing that the players often put one another down with harsh language and flip each other off when they make a mistake, he reaches his breaking point. O'Neill hits a line drive at Kofi Evans (Michael Perkins) that forces Kofi to quickly duck to avoid being hit by the ball. O'Neill says:

What happened? Kofi just jumped out of the way like a baby. Why is everyone so quiet? What's up, Kofi? You scared of the baaaalllll? [*Kids laugh*] New rule. No one can say anything bad to anyone else on the field. Got it?

The very next time he hits the ball, a kid catches it and a smile comes across his and the kids' faces. The rap music that underscored the previous scenes of cursing and taunting suddenly transitions to soft-playing music that is the soundtrack to the savior's moral skills: O'Neill dispels the rude and offensive behavior, accomplishing what no parent, community leader, or teacher had been able to accomplish in years past.

Such a "great white hope" in nonwhite lives is further solidified through overt dialogue that identifies the savior as the only source of purity, nobility, or morality in their lives. Once again in *Hard Ball*, one of the black players Andre Peetes (Bryan C. Hearne) asks O'Neill to drive him home. Upon arrival, Andre is scared and asks O'Neill to walk him up to his family's apartment. O'Neill agrees. Walking by an open door in the hallway, O'Neill notices a family sitting on the floor, despite furniture all over the room.

O'Neill: Everyone is sitting on the floor.
Andre: To stay below the window.
O'Neill: What?
Andre: Bullets.
O'Neill (*after a long pause*): What do you do around here for fun?
Andre: Play baseball with you.

O'Neill learns that he is the only source of stability in his players' lives. His former selfish ways of gambling begin to give way to the messianic impulse to save children of color from their culture, their environment, and themselves with the great American pastime of baseball. Despite having to pay off a gambling debt, O'Neill has the money to buy the team pizza, take them to a major league game at Wrigley Field, and buy them new uniforms—all actions for which the players seem eternally grateful.

The white savior's position in these films is a role around which the non-whites must circumambulate. And many of these films go to great lengths to solidify just how wonderful contact with the white savior is. For example, in *The Help*, Eugenia "Skeeter" Phelan (Emma Stone) is an aspiring author living in Jackson, Mississippi, during the 1960s. She decides to write a book detailing African American maids' point of view on the white families for whom they work. Near the end of the film, Skeeter recalls her own relationship with her family's black maid, Constantine Jefferson (Cicely Tyson), who raised her. Skeeter begins to wonder why Constantine left their family and doubts the veracity of the story told to her by her mother, Charlotte Phelan (Allison Janney)—that Constantine chose to go live with her family in Chicago. Instead, Skeeter discovers that her mother fired Constantine after she failed to send her daughter to the back door during Charlotte's important meeting with the all-white Daughters of the American Revolution. Skeeter then confronts her mother:

Skeeter: Constantine didn't do anything wrong. . . .
Charlotte Phelan: She [referring to an unnamed character in the film] was our president [of the Daughters of the American Revolution]! What was I supposed to do?
Skeeter: She [Constantine] did you the biggest favor of your life. She taught me everything.
Charlotte Phelan: Well, you idolized her too much. You always have.
Skeeter: I needed someone to look up to.
Charlotte Phelan: Well, I—I went to her house the next day. But she had already gone.
Skeeter: How could you not tell me all this?
Charlotte Phelan: Because I didn't want to upset you during your final exams. And I know you'd blame me, and it wasn't my fault!
Skeeter: I've got to go find her. She needs me.
Charlotte Phelan: We sent your brother up to Chicago to bring Constantine home. When he got there, she'd died.
Skeeter (*beginning to cry*): You broke her heart.

This scene demonstrates how the white savior is portrayed as nearly the entire reason for black life and agency. First, black characters are portrayed as always in need of the savior and, second, without the presence of the savior, the black character simply shrivels up and dies.

Despite 1960s Mississippi being an incredibly brutal and hostile environment for black domestic workers (a point that *The Help* itself constantly reiterates), Constantine's decision to live with family and friends (after she was fired) is framed as strange or even undesirable. In this sense, *The Help* attempts to answer the following question: Why would a black woman, employed as a service worker with no insurance or benefits, want to work alone in a racially hostile and discriminatory environment in the Deep South rather than among her family and racial community in Chicago? The answer: Because being around one ultraprivileged white girl just learning about racism keeps her heart beating. If we take the film at face value, Constantine's forced departure is what killed her, which sends an implicit yet strong message that contact with whiteness, no matter how bad, is the lifeblood of blackness.

In sum, the white savior's role is made explicit through three significant mechanisms: (1) overt religious symbolism, (2) a no-holds-barred approach to achieving peace and order for the "natives," and (3) the uncanny ability to transform nonwhite dysfunctions and cultural traditions into palatable patterns of Anglo assimilation. First, the overt religious metaphors work to associate the white protagonist with the sacrificial and redeeming message of Christ and other religious prophets. In *Gran Torino* Kowalski's intentional sacrificial death is a clear example of these religious allusions, as are many other sacrifices, such as Matthew Broderick's performance as Col. Robert Gould Shaw in *Glory*.

Second, the savior often doles out whatever violent, harsh, or destructive actions to achieve the peace and order that she or he thinks the native nonwhite people should experience. Whether setting off atom bombs in *Stargate*, unleashing round after round of gunfire in *Rambo III*, sending young black men to their state-sponsored deaths in *Monster's Ball*, or sacrificing hundreds, if not thousands, of African lives for a diamond to save one black family in *Blood Diamond*, the savior's paternalistic carnage and bloodshed is often rationalized as unavoidable, and the savior is the only one with the moral fiber to get it done. Such a pattern demonstrates the colonialist logic of these films. Simply put, (white) father knows best. Brutality and oppression are unacceptable when people of color wield these tactics but are wholly satisfactory means toward establishing a white normative order at the behest of the white savior.

Third, the savior demonstrates the ability to quickly transform bad to good. The people of color in these films are often portrayed as too desolate or captive to their own circumstances to help themselves. Accordingly, the white savior possesses a redemptive je ne sais quoi that automatically betters those nonwhites with whom he or she comes in contact. The savior inspires them and teaches them how to be more like the savior. And this implicit tale of assimilation wholly capitalizes on the woes of people of color yet tells the film through the eyes of the savior. Resultantly, the nonwhite aliens, natives, or students function as plot catalysts for the white savior to teach his or her invaluable lessons. This message is an exaggerated sense of white import coupled with a severely low estimation of the ability of people of color to sort out their own troubles.

White Suffering

Dovetailing with the dimension of explicit religious and spiritual metaphors, the white savior often experiences pain and torment. Akin to the dominant tale of Jesus's painful travel from Gethsemane to the crucifixion on Calvary, many white savior films mimic the narrative of messianic torment. The white savior's suffering is generally foregrounded in the beginning of these films and takes one of two paths: First, the character experiences early suffering but by film's end triumphs because of his or her decision to protect a group of nonwhite people. Second, after a series of twists and turns, the savior sacrifices his or her life at the end of the film so that the people of color may have better lives. Either way, the dominant Christian tradition of the suffering savior is mapped onto the film's plot and white protagonist. The paternalistic racism of the "white man's burden" is eclipsed by the supposedly pure religious narrative of one person's sacrificial redemption that allows others to live as free and noble people.

Many saviors are immediately cast as disheveled or temporarily broken people who struggle with the sins of their past. However, their contact with people of color brings out their inner savior. They rise to the occasion, overcoming their insecurities and hang-ups and dedicating their lives to saving their newfound nonwhite friends. For example, in *Amazing Grace* (2006) Wilberforce has horrible dreams that prevent his sleep. In one, he has a tortured vision in which he looks into a mirror and sees a black man in chains reaching out to him. He interprets this vision to mean that he must be the savior of enslaved Africans. In *City of Joy* (1992), Dr. Max Lowe's journey to white saviorhood is precipitated by his failure to save the life of a child on the operating table. Consumed with guilt, he quits his job and moves to India, where he soon confronts the caste system and a local overlord. In *Hard Ball* (2001) Conor O'Neill is a gambling addict and alcoholic who loses his money to bookies. When they come to collect, he is so inebriated and disappointed in his own failures that he inflicts punishment on himself. O'Neill yells, "You want to kick my ass? No one can kick my ass better than I can!" He then puts his hand through a car window and bashes his head through the window of a bar. In the next scene, O'Neill wakes up in jail. These scenes cement the soon-to-be savior's suffering.

In *Avatar* (2009) the white protagonist is Jake Sully. Paralyzed from the waist down and unable to work as a mercenary, he finds work in the Avatar laboratories. He knows that if he works hard enough, he can save the money to reverse his paralysis. Early in the film, we hear his inner dialogue: "There's no such thing as an ex-marine. They can fix a spinal if you've got the money. But not on vet benefits, not in this economy." And so Sully's cross to bear is his wheelchair, and from the film's onset he is set to overcome his burden.

In *Stargate* (1994), two white saviors combine forces to overcome their problems and save the darker-skinned humanoids from the yoke of their alien oppressor. First, there is Colonel Jack O'Neil, whose introduction makes clear his role as suffering protagonist. O'Neil sits in a room surrounded by toys, photographs, and a certificate commemorating his deceased son, Tyler. O'Neil sits on Tyler's bed, holding a pistol as he stares at the photographs. There is a knock at the slightly open door. O'Neil hides the gun under the pillow as the door opens wider, an insinuation of his depression over losing his son and his contemplation of suicide. An army officer then enters the room to state, "Excuse me, Colonel O'Neil. We're from General West's office." O'Neil blinks but does not turn around to face the man. "Sir? We're here to inform you that you've been reactivated."

The scene cuts to a suburban street. Officer 1 gets into a black sedan already occupied by Officer 2. They watch as O'Neil exits his house.

Officer 2: The guy's a mess [*referring to O'Neil*]. How'd he get like that?
Officer 1: His kid died. Accidentally shot himself.
Officer 2: Jesus.

With nothing more said, it is clear that O'Neil's depression leaves him little choice but to embark on any Army mission where he would gladly give his life not only for country but to end his suffering.

The second savior is Dr. Daniel Jackson. Jackson is a down-on-his-luck academic whose expertise is linguistics. His work has been poorly received, and he is considered a joke within the academic community. His marginality is made clear at the film's start. After he gives a lecture on which people walk out midway, he walks dejectedly outside into the pouring rain. Drenched and depressed, he is approach by a man who beckons him to speak to a woman in a nearby car. Jackson approaches the car to find Catherine Langford (Viveca Lindfors).

Jackson: What—what is this all about?
Langford: A job.
Jackson (*laughs nervously*): What kind of a job?
Langford: Translation. Ancient Egyptian hieroglyphs. Interested?
Jackson: I—I'm gonna go now.
Langford: Go where? [*laughs*]. I mean, you've just been evicted from your apartment. Your grants have run out. Everything you own are in those two bags. Want to prove that your theories are right? This is your chance.

Throughout the remainder of the film Jackson and O'Neil unite through a series of painful and violent episodes they endure with aplomb. They finally find their own sense of purpose through the liberation of dark-skinned slaves from the oppression of an evil alien menace. In the end, the slaves are freed and the universe, literally, is safe thanks to the sacrificial suffering of O'Neil and Jackson.

In *The Last Samurai*, Nathan Algren suffers nightmares for the massacres he took part in as an Army captain under General Custer. To cope, Algren took to alcohol. Hence, Algren is first introduced in the film as a man haunted by the evils of his past (murderous atrocities shown as flashbacks) who drunkenly attempts to serve as a spokesperson for the Winchester rifle company at a trade show in the 1800s.

As the scene begins, a Winchester rifle representative, played by William Atherton, steps onstage at a trade show. He says:

And now, ladies and gentlemen, the moment you've been waiting for. Winchester, America's leader in all forms of armament used by the United States Army, celebrates our nation's centennial by bringing you a true American hero. One of the most decorated warriors this country has ever known. The bloody cornfield of Antietam. The stone wall of Sharpsburg. Winner of the Medal of Honor for his gallantry on the hallowed ground of Gettysburg.

The audience politely applauds, but Algren does not step onstage, because he is backstage, drunk, and consumed with horrible memories of war. Barely conscious, Algren leans against the wall, his eyes slowly opening and closing. The representative steps behind the curtain and shakes Algren. Algren comes to life and grabs the representative by his throat.

Representative: Damn it, man, you're on.
Algren: Right. [*The representative leans in to straighten Algren's tie but sharply recoils from the smell of whiskey on his breath.*]
Representative: This company has an image to uphold, you know.
Algren: I'm upholding. I'm upholding.
Representative: Sure you are. Here's your ten dollars. Do the speech, and don't bother coming back tomorrow.

And so the audience is introduced to Captain Nathan Algren: a drunk, disheveled, dysfunctional, and unemployed man. Throughout the rest of the film, even after his capture by Japanese samurai, he struggles to overcome his alcoholism, his rude and insensitive ways, and his memories of war that impede his ability to properly function. So it is, when Algren has difficulty learning samurai swordplay, that his friend Nobutada (Shin Koyamada) goes to him:

Nobutada: Please forgive. Too many mind.
Algren: Too many mind?
Nobutada: Hai. Mind the sword, mind the people watch, mind the enemy. Too many mind. [*Long pause*] No mind.

After this advice, Algren is able to let go of his past transgressions and stops overthinking ("too many mind") his swordplay decisions. He then goes on to have his first draw, instead of a loss, with his sparring opponent. Now that Algren properly bears his cross, he sets out to protect and save his newfound samurai friends.

This theme of the savior's suffering is explicitly repeated in *The Last King of Scotland*, in which the film's white savior, Dr. Nicholas Garrigan (James McAvoy), endures a tortured crucifixion of sorts. After betraying the dictator Idi Amin, Garrigan is savagely beaten by Amin's men. He is left on the floor, covered in blood and bruises, one eye swollen completely shut. Amin then comes to Garrigan and speaks to him as he lies bruised and bloodied.

Amin: Look at you. Is there one thing you have done that is good? What you think—this was all a game? "I will go to Africa, and I will play the white man with the natives!" Is that what you thought? We are not a game,

Nicholas. We are real. This room here, it is real. I think your death will
be the first real thing that has happened to you. Listen to me, Nicholas. Listen. I know, yes. I know about you and Kay. How could you do
that to me? I am the father of this nation, Nicholas. And you have most
grossly offended her father.
Garrigan: You're a child. That's what makes you so fucking scary.

Amin then hits and kicks him, but Garrigan only laughs at him, as if taking
pity on Amin. Amin then leans down again and speaks softly to Garrigan: "In
my village, when you steal the wife of an elder. They take you to a tree and hang
you by your skin. Each time you scream the evil comes out of you. Sometimes,
it can take three days for your evil to be spent." Amin's men then pick up Garrigan and puncture his pectoral muscles with hooks, which are then used to hoist
him up so that he is suspended in the air, left to suffer for his transgressions.
He is then dropped on the ground and left to die. But as a reward for Garrigan's
suffering, a black Ugandan doctor, Dr. Junju (David Oyelowo), sneaks into the
room where Garrigan lies and revives him:

Garrigan: Why? Why are you doing this?
Junju: Frankly, I don't know. You deserve to die. But dead you can do noth-
    ing. Alive you just might be able to redeem yourself.
Garrigan: I don't understand.
Junju: I am tired of hatred, Dr. Garrigan. This country is drowning in it.
    We deserve better. Go home. Tell the world the truth about Amin. They
    will believe you. You are a white man.

Junju then helps Garrigan escape on an airplane full of Israeli hostages. The
ending scenes of the film show the plane rising into the heavens. The messianic
linear story of suffering to death to rebirth is a blatant parallel. Garrigan is
crucified, is left to die, and then rises to heaven with the "chosen people" as his
first witnesses and disciples of his new gospel—telling of the atrocities to save
Uganda from the devilish character of Idi Amin. And the attribute that allows
Garrigan to spread this gospel is, as Dr. Junju says, simply his white masculinity. His saviorhood is intimately tied to the supposed purity and privileges of
whiteness. The film the ends as it cuts from Garrigan's still bloody face to a
black screen on which the following words appear: "48 hours later, Israeli forces
stormed Entebbe and liberated all but one of the hostages. International public
opinion turned against Amin for good." Garrigan's escape and gospel against
Amin is then implicitly cited as the monumental shift toward Ugandan pros-
perity and salvation.
    Yet the white savior does not always walk off into the sunset or ascend gent-
ly into the clouds. In seventeen of these films, the savior sacrifices his life so
that the people of color can be free. The savior's death is nearly always connected to taking on the sins of nonwhite people, which allows them to be free,
safe, and redeemed. In this sense, dying becomes a selfless act of sacrifice by

which the nonwhite people owe the savior for the improved quality of their lives. For example, in *Children of Men*, the white savior Faron helps the black woman Kee and her newborn escape the authorities who would kill her and her child. Faron delivers Kee and child to a sanctuary ship where fertility scientists will work to discover how she gave birth to a natural child—thus saving all of humanity from literal extinction. However, in helping Kee and child escape, Faron is mortally shot and dies at film's end. The implication is clear: His sacrifice of life pays the price of life for all; his sacrificial death gives the world the priceless gift of life to which all will be eternally in his debt.

Such messianic sacrifices continue in other films. For example, in *Gran Torino*, much as in *The Last Samurai*, the white protagonist Walt Kowalski continually wrestles with the ghosts of his military past—specifically violence by his hand during the Korean War. Throughout the film, a Catholic priest, Father Janovich (Christopher Carley), attempts to alleviate the suffering of Kowalski, but to no avail.

> Janovich: I've been thinking about our conversation on life and death. About what you said. About how you carry around all the horrible things you were forced to do, horrible things that won't leave you. It seems it would do you good to unload some of that burden. Things done during war are terrible. Being ordered to kill. Killing to save yourself, killing to save others. You're right. Those are things I know nothing about, but I do know about forgiveness, and I've seen a lot of men who have confessed their sins, admitted their guilt, and left their burdens behind them. Stronger men than you. Men at war who were ordered to do appalling things and are now at peace.
>
> Kowalski: Well, I gotta hand it to you, Padre. You came here with your guns loaded this time.
>
> Janovich: Thank you.
>
> Kowalski: And you're right about one thing. About stronger men than me reaching their salvation. Well, halle-fucking-lujah. But you're wrong about something else.
>
> Janovich: What's that, Mr. Kowalski?
>
> Kowalski: The thing that haunts a man the most is what he isn't ordered to do.

Because of the white savior plot structure, Janovich cannot redeem Kowalski. The Catholic priest is not the white savior of the film. He only interacts with other white people. Rather, Kowalski must find a way to bear his cross and sacrifice himself for the benefit of his newfound nonwhite acolytes.

Accordingly, Kowalski sacrifices his life for his Hmong neighbors, Thao and Sue. Going to the home of Hmong gangsters who have been terrorizing Thao and Sue, Kowalski provokes them: "Now go ahead and pull those pistols, like miniature cowboys." People start emerging from their homes to witness the altercation. Kowalski then reaches into his coat pocket to retrieve a cigarette. The gangsters all cock and point their weapons at him, and Kowalski says, "Kinda jumpy, aren't we?" As in a previous scene, he points his finger at each gangster, "shooting" them one by one with his finger. In over-the-top dramatics, characteristic of a Clint Eastwood film, Kowalksi then asks, "Got a light? No? Me? I've got a light." He then reaches into his other pocket and quickly withdraws his hand, prompting the gangsters to open fire on him. He is hit several times and falls to the ground dead, still holding the Zippo lighter emblazoned with the U.S. Army Cavalry Division logo that had been in his pocket.

After the police arrive and the area is secure, Thao and Sue pull up in Kowalski's Gran Torino. Kept back from the scene, Thao spies a Hmong police officer. Speaking in the Hmong tongue, Thao approaches the officer:

> Thao: Please, it's important.
> Hmong police officer: He went for his lighter, and they shot him. He didn't even have a gun on him. This time we have witnesses. These guys will be locked up for a long time.

Kowalski's obvious sacrifice is made further evident in the reading of his will, in which he gives his house to the church and his car to Thao—to Kowalski's rude and greedy family's chagrin.

The trope of white sacrificial death for nonwhite redemption is a palpable device. Such a relationship activates a story in which one's violence, racism, paternalism, and oppressive control supposedly pales in comparison to the ultimate action of giving one's life so that others may live. This new stage in the white man's burden allows the white protagonist to experience character development, while the purpose of the surrounding people of color becomes fodder for the plot. That is, the white character's saintliness is highlighted rather than the nonwhites' struggles as seen through their eyes. The white Samaritan—whether joining the nonwhite culture in the end (e.g., *Dances with Wolves*, *Avatar*, the Matrix trilogy, *The Last Samurai*, or *Stargate*) or pulling select nonwhite members out of their dangerous and dark communities to save them (e.g., *The Blind Side*, *Amistad*, *Blood Diamond*, *Dangerous Minds*, or *Freedom Writers*)—demonstrates that only through the Samaritan's suffering and sacrifice can people of color be free. The paternalistic interactions are rationalized as less than perfect but still better than the alternative: a life of misery for people of color incapable of activating their own salvation.

The Savior, the Bad White, and the Natives

Given the common construction of over-the-top paternalism, rudeness, egotism, and subtle racism of the central white protagonists (covered in the previous sections), these budding saviors would normally be difficult to accept as benevolent redeemers. However, the white saviors are commonly positioned next to two types of other characters to distinguish them and make them all the more bearable. First, the savior is juxtaposed with racist, domineering, completely uncaring, and extremely violent white characters. Second, a nonwhite community, suffering a social malaise or ailment, surrounds the savior and contextualizes his character development. Together, we have the Savior, the Bad White, and the Natives. The effect is powerful. Relative to the dysfunctional natives and the bad whites, the white protagonist appears moderate. The savior can now be understood as only mildly rude, barely prejudiced, or even the victim of the others with whom she or he is forced to interact.

For example, in *Sunset Park*, Phyllis Saroka (Rhea Perlman) is a white physical education teacher at the predominantly black Sunset Park High School in New York City. Her dream is to open a restaurant on the Caribbean island of St. Croix, but she lacks the money. She reads a flyer advertising for a boys' basketball coach for her school, and knowing nothing of basketball, she takes the job strictly for the money. Given Saroka's selfish motivation and the very real possibility that her coaching could ruin the college prospects of many of the players, her character garners little sympathy. As a remedy, Saroka is surrounded by a host of black dysfunctions and easily vilified whites. For example, after starting to gain the basketball team's trust, one of her players, known as "Spaceman" (Terrence Howard), walks into her office crying, holding a huge knife.

Spaceman: I'm about to go kill my teacher.

Saroka: What teacher?

Spaceman: Mr. Bernstein. It's like he's always got something smart to say to me, right? It's like, I had my hair braided. And so he—so I had this wooly on my head. When I come into the classroom, he's like [*gestures as if taking hat off*], so I take it off. And he started laughin' at my braids. And the whole class just started laughin' at me. He don't know me. He don't.

Saroka: Spaceman. Spaceman, I want you to put that knife in my drawer now. Just come on over here and put it in here. [*Spaceman puts the knife in the drawer.*] Thank you. [*They walk together to class, where Mr. Bernstein stands outside the classroom.*]

Mr. Bernstein (*in sarcastic tone*): So nice to see you, and what a lovely hairstyle we're sporting today.

Saroka (*grabbing him by the tie*): What the hell do you think you're doing, Morris? This sweet, sensitive kid? Stop teasing him, and stop bullying him. Start teaching him, and start caring about his feelings. Do you understand me?

Mr. Bernstein: Yes.

Saroka: Do you have anything to add, Spaceman?

Spaceman: Science is my favorite subject, Mr. Bernstein.

Mr. Bernstein: I will keep that in mind.

Saroka: You better keep that in mind. You damn well better. Come on, Spaceman. Any other teachers you wanna talk to me about?

This scene commits a twofold action. First, it does the work of comparing the actions of Saroka against that of an irresponsible, bullying, and immature white teacher. And second, it establishes her as a savior to her black players, both on and off the court.

The creation of stark contrasts between evil white characters and the white savior is perhaps no more pronounced than in *Freedom Writers* (2007). Erin Gruwell (Hilary Swank) takes a job as teacher at Woodrow Wilson High School. She is constantly forced to confront her department head, Margaret Campbell (Imelda Staunton), and her fellow teacher Brian Gelford (John Benjamin Hickey). Their cold and overtly racist personas cast a shadow over Gruwell's know-it-all paternalism so that Gruwell is, by contrast, a kind and well-intentioned person. For example, in one scene, Gruwell tries to convince Campbell that her students should be allowed to read more sophisticated literature than what is currently prescribed.

> Gruwell: What about this? [*Holds up a copy of* The Diary of Anne Frank] We were discussing the Holocaust.
> Campbell: No, they won't be able to read that.
> Gruwell: We can try. The books are just sitting here.
> Campbell: Look at their reading scores. And if I give your kids these books, I'll never see them again. If I do, they'll be damaged. Let me explain. It's called site-based instruction. It means that I and the principal each have the authority to make these kinds of decisions without having to go to the board, who have bigger problems to solve. Do you understand how it works now?
> Gruwell: I'm sorry. I didn't mean to overstep your authority. I would never do that. I just—I don't know how to make them interested in reading with these.
> Campbell: You can't make someone want an education. The best you can do is try to get them to obey, to learn discipline. That would be a tremendous accomplishment for them.

In the next scene, Gruwell pleads her case to fellow teacher Brian Gelford:

> Gruwell: I really think that the stories like *The Diary of Anne Frank* and— that they'd be so great for them, and she doesn't seem to understand that they could relate to these stories considering all that they face.
> Gelford: Oh, of course. It's a universal story. I mean, Anne Frank, Rodney King, they're almost interchangeable.
> Gruwell: Are you making fun of me?
> Gelford: Yeah. God, listen to what you're saying. How dare you compare them to Anne Frank? They don't hide. They drive around in the open with automatic weapons. I'm the one living in fear. I can't walk out my door at night. And you blame these kids? This was an A-list school before they came here. And look what they turned it into. I mean, does

it make sense that kids who want an education should suffer because their high school gets turned into a reform school? Because kids who don't want to be here, and shouldn't be here, are forced to be here by the geniuses running the school district? Integration's a lie. Yeah, we teachers, we can't say that or we lose our jobs for being racist. So, please, stop your cheerleading, Erin. You're ridiculous.

As shown, Gruwell's growing paternalism pales in comparison to that of the teachers and administrators, who seem to care only about test scores and obedience.

The parceling of good and bad whites to make the savior shine continues in films about sports (*Hard Ball*), the attempted colonization of aliens (*Avatar*), revisionist histories about dictators (*The Last King of Scotland*), South African apartheid (*A Dry White Season*), or Mississippi in the 1960s (*The Help*). In *Hard Ball*, O'Neill's South Side Chicago team, the Kekambas, begins to win games, which draws the ire of other white coaches who are accustomed to sitting atop the baseball league. Thus, during games the opposing coaches maneuver to remove the good players from the Kekambas. During one game, and after seeing his players struck out one after another, the opposing team's coach, Matt Hyland (D. B. Sweeney), along with the umpire (Andre Morgan) and the league's president Darryl Mackey (Freeman Coffey), decides that O'Neill's pitcher cannot play because he wears headphones. However, O'Neill knows that the headphones keep his pitcher, Miles Pennfield II (A. Delon Ellis Jr.), calm and focused; he cannot play without them. O'Neill approaches home plate, where Hyland, the umpire, and Mackey stand.

O'Neill: What now?
Hyland: Coach, we're in agreement that the pitcher can't wear headphones.
Mackey: Matt makes a good point about safety.
O'Neill: C'mon, you're kidding me, right?
Hyland: Think about it. What if he gets hurt because he couldn't hear in a dangerous situation? There's liability issues.
O'Neill (*turning to his team*): Bring it in, guys.
Hyland: What are you doing?
O'Neill: I want you guys to explain why they lost Jamal, and why Miles can't wear headphones, and why the Bua Was and Waa Tas have nice uniforms and we have shitty T-shirts.
Mackey: Now easy, coach, you're already on a warning.
O'Neill: Kekambas, this is the president. And that is the coach of the goofiest team in the league. And they kicked Jamal off the team because he was born two weeks early, and now they're making Miles take his headphones off because he's *pitching too good.*

Here coach O'Neill demonstrates to his team the dirty tactics employed by the league and its coaches to marginalize the Kekambas and make their defeat more likely. This device is important, because just minutes later, O'Neill decides to quit the team and go back to gambling, an action that invites the displeasure of his team, which has come to depend on him.

In *Avatar*, even though the protagonist Jake Sully is asked by his commanding officer to infiltrate the Na'vi and expose their weaknesses, their entire presence on Pandora is orchestrated by the RDA, or Resource Development Administration—a company with monopoly rights to all products shipped, derived, or developed from Pandora. Parker Selfridge (Giovanni Ribisi) is the RDA administrator in charge of mining the mineral unobtainium. As he tells one scientist, "This is why we're here: unobtanium, because this little gray rock sells for 20 million a kilo. That's the only reason. It's what pays for the whole party. It's what pays for your science." Selfridge's greed and corruption are extensive. As Jake Sully becomes increasingly uncomfortable with his role as a mole with the Na'vi people, he confronts Selfridge, yet Selfridge is unyielding in his colonial superiority and capitalist lust:

> Sully, Sully. Just find out what these blue monkeys want. You know, I mean, we—we tried to give them medicine, education, uh, uh, roads, but no, no, no. They like mud. And that wouldn't bother me; it's just that their, uh, their damn village happens to be resting on the richest unobtainium deposit within two hundred klicks in any direction. I mean, look at all that cheddar. Look, look, look. Killing the indigenous looks bad, but there's one thing that shareholders hate more than bad press, and that's a bad quarterly statement. Just find me a carrot to get them to move, or it's going to have to be a stick, okay?

In *The Last King of Scotland*, the white savior Dr. Nicholas Garrigan is constantly juxtaposed against the conniving, secretive, and racist British agent Nigel Stone (Simon McBurne). This relationship is set from the beginning. In their first on-screen meeting, Stone turns to Garrigan and says, "He's [Amin] got a firm hand. The only thing the African really understands." To which Garrigan—a Scottish expatriate—mutters under his breath, "Bloody English."

In *A Dry White Season*, a black child is badly beaten by the South African apartheid police. The child's father takes him home to the white character of Ben du Toit (Donald Sutherland) to find out what recourse they have. After du Toit tells him nothing can be done about the police maltreatment and that the child's wounds would heal, the father, Gordon Ngubene (Winston Ntshona) states, "I'm not worried about those wounds. I know they'll get better. It's the wounds here [pointing to his heart]. These are the ones I worry about." After Ngubene and his son are turned away from the du Toit house and left to nurse their physical and psychological wounds alone, Sutherland's eldest son says, "These kids are going mad. Bloody savages. The only language they understand is force." As Ben du Toit gains a critical consciousness of the atrocities of the South African apartheid system, his paternalism is counterbalanced by the constant stream of overtly racist whites who prop up the apartheid system through lies, coercion, and murder.

The Help (2011) concentrates on the relationships between the white savior Skeeter Phelan and black female domestic servants in 1960s Jackson, Mississippi. Skeeter's cinematic modus operandi is to interview the maids about their lives so as to get a job as a journalist in New York City. But to do so, she has to bring attention to the plight of these black domestic servants by writing about their working conditions under the noses of racist white housewives and publishing these interviews as a kind of tell-all exposé. *The Help*, much like many a white savior film, trades explicitly on the careful parceling of good and bad whites. In one scene, Hilly Holbrook (Bryce Dallas Howard) explains her reasoning behind supporting an initiative to ban black servants from using the indoor toilets of white homes:

> Everybody knows they [African Americans] carry different diseases than we do. That's exactly why I've designed the Home Help Sanitation Initiative, as a disease preventative measure. A bill that requires every white home to have a separate bathroom for the colored help.

In another scene, Holbrook again explains her initiative, but this time to Skeeter, who pokes fun at her prejudiced attitude:

> Holbrook: That's why I drafted the Home Help Sanitation Initiative.
> Phelan: The what?
> Holbrook: A disease preventative bill that requires every white home to have a separate bathroom for the colored help. It's been endorsed by the White Citizens Council.
> Phelan: Maybe we should just build you a bathroom outside, Hilly.
> Holbrook: You ought not to joke about the colored situation. I'll do whatever it takes to protect our children.

By scapegoating Hilly Holbrook as the evil racist housewife of Jackson, Mississippi, audiences are free to sanction Skeeter to usurp control of black women's voices under the guise of freeing them from their state of economic and racial servitude. Skeeter is then easily framed as a savior who breaks free of the constraints of white racist normativity. Her job offer from a New York publishing company is thus seen as just deserts for her racial "activism."

The Color of Meritocracy

Another common dimension of the white savior film is the patterned conflation of whiteness with an ethic of hard work, delay of gratification, and a mindset wholly focused on the individual triumph over obstacles. This dimension is particularly flexible and grounds the white savior as the source of social uplift and redemption through an array of characters and cinematic plots.

One particularly fruitful intervention of the hardworking white savior occurs in the urban classroom. Several of the films in this sample highlight a white teacher plunging into an abyss of apathetic and at-risk students of color that plod through an uncaring and racist educational system that has all but abandoned them, such as *The Principal* (1987), *Dangerous Minds* (1995), *The Substitute* (1996), *Half Nelson* (2006), and *Freedom Writers* (2007). In these films, white teachers enter their classrooms as timid tenderfoots but soon turn into pedagogical behemoths, vanquishing bad grades and bad attitudes with a single wave of their ruler. This transformation takes a three-step approach.

First, the students represent a cacophony of racial stereotypes: unwed teenage mothers, Latino gangsters and their hand-wringing girlfriends, and black drug dealers and break-dancers. Second, in trying to transform and inspire them, the white teacher first fails. The mandated lesson plans fall short and the students ridicule the teacher. Soon, after putting the savior's educational acumen and hard work to the test, the teacher instructs them to write about their own experiences, thus giving them agency to think more critically about their lives via pen and paper. Without explanation, the students are soon transformed into bards of the ghetto—composing soliloquies on the murder and mayhem that surrounds them. Third, these students, because of the white savior's instructions, prove themselves exceptions to the other nonwhites around them. They go on to leave their culture of poverty behind, demonstrating that if people of color would just emulate the work ethic of their white teachers and act right (read, white), then racial and class inequality would be a thing of the past.

In *Dangerous Minds*, LouAnne Johnson (Michelle Pfeiffer) is a recent divorcée and retired U.S. marine who applies for a teaching position at Parkmont High School in California. She is hired and immediately thrust into an academy course that she assumes is full of bright and successful students. But as she enters the classroom, she finds it in disarray and full of black and brown faces who are rapping, throwing objects at one another, talking loudly, listening to music on their headphones and stereos, and doing anything but paying her attention—except for the one black girl who shouts out, "White bread!" as she enters the room. In an attempt to corral their attention, Johnson asks about her predecessor, Miss Shepherd. The class responds by intimidating her, led by the alpha male of the classroom, Emilio Ramirez (Wade Dominguez).

> Student: Ooh, no, she ain't asking about Miss Trifling-Ass Shepherd. Yo, yo, yo, yo, yo! Listen up! Yo, listen up! White Bread wanna know what happened to Miss Shepherd. . . .
>
> Raul Sanchero (Renoly Santiago): Ohh! No, no, no. Everybody, everybody. Emilio ate her.
>
> Ramirez: Bullshit. That bitch was too ugly to eat. I fed her to my dogs. [*Long pause. Ramirez walks up to Johnson and leans close to her.*] But I'll eat you.
>
> Johnson: What is your name?
>
> Ramirez: Emilio Ramirez.

Johnson then writes Emilio's name on the board in an attempt to discipline him, but Ramirez does not back down. The entire class begins to chant, "Emilio!" and Johnson is driven from the room, close to tears. She then asks her friend and colleague who teaches in a nearby classroom, "Who are these kids? Rejects from hell? . . . I can't teach them!" Her colleague, Hal Griffith (George Dzundza), responds, "Yes, you can. All you got to do is get their attention. Or quit."

Johnson hits the books, reading about pedagogical strategies and teaching techniques. Lying in bed that night, she suddenly sits up, heads for her closet, and says to herself, "Okay, you little bastards." At that moment the background music shifts from elevator music to a loud rap song whose chorus includes the line, "put your back into it." A jump cut then shows Johnson at her desk the next morning, clad in jeans, plaid shirt, and a black leather jacket, with her feet kicked up on the desk and a nonchalant expression on her face. The bell rings and students enter the classroom. We overhear student intimidations and jokes, from "Yo, you didn't get enough yesterday?" to "Hey, everybody, everybody, look, a cowboy." She gets up and writes on the board, "I AM A U.S. MARINE. Does anyone know karate?" This immediately gets the attention of the classroom, and she begins to teach them throws and martial arts moves. The class temporarily pays attention, and she seizes the moment:

> Well, that was A work. You'd make good marines. In fact, from this moment, each one of you is like an inductee. With a clean record. So if you want to pass, all you have to do is try. Because at this point. Everyone has an A. [*Some students murmur in shock and disbelief.*] But it's up to you to keep it.

One student then yells out, "Bullshit!" to which Cornelius Bates (Marcello Thedford) responds, "Yo, why don't you shut up, man? What if it ain't bullshit? I ain't never had no fucking A before." The students seem captivated by their newfound chance, and the next scene displays happy and relaxed kids playing and dancing during recess. The first battle has been won, as the white savior gives them the opportunity to work hard and manage their own destiny, all with the meritocratic phrase "But it's up to you to keep it."

Throughout the rest of the film, Johnson teaches the class to work hard on their studies, but she also weaves moral instruction about individual bootstrapping into lessons about English literature and grammar. In one classroom scene, Johnson teaches them to conjugate a verb but becomes a kind of Ayn Rand–like philosopher, instructing them that they always have individual choice even in the face of certain death.

> Johnson: Okay, "We must die." Is "must" a verb? Can you, uh, can you "must" something? . . . Okay, what verb that we used today is the most powerful?
> Student 1: Die!

Student 2: Piss!

Callie Roberts (Bruklin Harris): Choose.

Johnson: Choose. Callie, why?

Roberts: Because that's the difference between owning your life and being afraid. Saying, "I choose," no matter what.

Sanchero: You mean, like a guy's got a gun to your head and he's pulling the trigger and you say, "I choose to die"?

Roberts: No, you ain't choosing to die, but you can choose to die without screaming, right? I mean, you could always choose something.

Sanchero: Not where I live. Shit.

Similar techniques are repeated in white savior films such as *The Principal* (1987), *The Substitute* (1996), *Half Nelson* (2006), and *Freedom Writers* (2007). In *Freedom Writers*, Erin Gruwell teaches at Woodrow Wilson High School in Long Beach, California. The school is a formerly high-achieving school that has recently put an integration plan in place, and the students of color are blamed for lowering the test scores. The department head, Margaret Campbell, after hiring Gruwell, asks her, "You're from Newport Beach?" to which Gruwell replies, "Yes." Campbell says, "It's too bad you weren't here even two years ago, you know. We used to have one of the highest scholastic records in the district, but since voluntary integration was suggested we've, um, lost over 75 percent of our strongest students."

In many ways, *Freedom Writers* is *Dangerous Minds 2.0* because it takes the same recycled stereotypes about race, class, and Southern California's troubled schools and magnifies their racialized tension to such an extreme that superteachers like Gruwell are portrayed as the right individual solution to structural problems. To rationalize this individualistic and paternalistic intervention, Gruwell draws an analogy between the students' racial discord and that of the twentieth century's most agreed-on evil—Nazism. One day in class, a Latino student named Tito (Gabriel Chavarria) draws a racist caricature of a black student in the class, Jamal Hill (Deance Wyatt). Upon receiving the note, Hill is visibly shaken and the Latino students begin to laugh. Gruwell notices the disruption and seizes the note from Hill, which is a side portrait of Hill with extremely oversized lips and the mocking words "PASS ME" (the note is meant to characterize Hill as a "kiss up" to Gruwell by using the racist image of oversized lips). Gruwell is disturbed by the image and says to the class, "What is this?"

Hill: Just leave it alone.

Gruwell: You think this is funny? Tito, would this be funny if it were a picture of you?

Tito: It ain't.

Gruwell: Close the workbooks. Maybe we should talk about art. Tito's got real talent, don't you think? You know something? I saw pictures just like this once. In a museum. Only it wasn't a black man. It was a Jewish man. And instead of the big lips he had a really big nose. Like a rat's nose. But he wasn't just one particular Jewish man; this was a drawing of all Jews. And these drawings were put in the newspapers by the most famous gang in history. You think you know all about gangs? You're amateurs. This gang would put you all to shame. And they started out poor and angry, and everybody looked down on them, until one man decided to give them some pride. And identity. And somebody to blame. You take over neighborhoods? That's nothing compared to them. They took over countries. You want to know how? They just wiped out everybody else. Yeah, they wiped out everybody they didn't like and everybody they blamed for their life being hard. And one of the ways they did it was by doing this [*holds up Hill's caricature*]. See, they'd print pictures like this in the newspapers. Jewish people with big, long noses. Blacks with big, fat lips. They'd also publish "scientific evidence" that "proved" that Jews and blacks were the lowest forms of human species. Jews and blacks were more like animals. And because they were just like animals, it didn't really matter whether they lived or died. In fact, life would be a whole lot better if they were all dead. That's how a Holocaust happens. And that's what you all think of each other.

But the students do not buy into Gruwell's racial evangelizing. They tell her that she has no idea what she is talking about because she does not know their harsh, everyday realities. One student named Eva Benitez (April L. Hernandez) chastises her for oversimplifying their racialized lives.

> Benitez: It's all about color. It's about people deciding what you deserve. About people wanting what they don't deserve. About whites thinking they run this world no matter what. You see, I hate white people.
> Gruwell: You hate me?
> Benitez: Yeah.
> Gruwell: You don't know me.
> Benitez: I know what you can do. I saw white cops shoot my friend in the back after reaching into his pocket. His pocket! I saw white cops break into my house and take my father for no reason except for because they feel like it. Except because they can. And they can. Because they're white. So I hate white people on sight.
> Gruwell: . . . You know what's gonna happen when you die? You're going to rot in the ground, and people are going to go on living, and people are going to forget all about you. And when you rot, do you think it's going to matter whether you were an "original gangster"? You're dead. And nobody—nobody—is going to want to remember you, because all you left behind in this world was this [*holds up the caricature*].
> Tito: . . . That thing you said before, the Holocaust? . . . What is that?

Gruwell soon realizes that only one student (the lone white face in the classroom) has ever heard about the Holocaust but that nearly everyone has been shot at. The bell then rings, the students vacate the room, and Gruwell stands alone in disbelief.

But soon her savior mentalities kick in, and Gruwell begins teaching them about their social commonalities that cut across the color line. She gives each student a notebook in which they are required to write about their lives. Over the course of the film, the cognitive and emotional writing exercises transform the students. In scene after scene, Gruwell conditions her students that their structural situations are unfortunate but matter little to their destiny in the end. Gruwell's message is simple: race does not matter as much as individual willpower.

At times, such messianic teachers need not enter an official classroom but can mentor their students through sports, as in *Sunset Park* (1996), or even from the comfort of their living rooms, as in *Finding Forrester*. In *Sunset Park*, Phyllis Saroka starts coaching the basketball team to earn extra money. She knows nothing of basketball but studies the game by sacrificing her extra cash to buy a TV and VCR to watch countless hours of basketball. With little more than determination, and in a matter of weeks, she transforms herself into a coach who takes the team to the title game. In one poignant scene, Saroka instructs her star player, Shorty (Fredro Starr), on how to succeed in life and leave the ghetto behind. In so doing, she gives him the quintessential, if-you-work-hard-enough-you-could-do-anything speech:

> Shorty: I stay up at night sometimes knowing basketball don't mean nothing. School don't mean nothing. If I work, if I don't work, it don't mean nothing. I'm gonna end up dead in the same projects anyway. So why even bother, right?
> Saroka: You could do something, you know. I mean, you could go to college.
> Shorty: Ain't none of my people stupid, Coach, but ain't none of us think about college.
> Saroka: Why is that?
> Shorty: I don't know. Do white people have that same mentality?
> Saroka: I always thought I'd go to college. You know, that's just part of what everybody around me did. I could grow up and be a woman president, the first woman president. I believed it.
> Shorty: You crazy, Coach.

The scene provides an implicit comparative message about black and white cultural expectations. Whites provide a culture in which they all "always thought" they would go to college, while blacks never "think about college."

After a scene in which she chastises her players to study harder, another scene depicts Drano (Antwon Tanner) trying to mentor Butter (Talent Harris) in algebra. The two had earlier discussed a trip down south, in which Butter described southern black women as unwilling to sleep with men unless they were given a chicken. Drano recalls the conversation and uses it to teach Drano a math lesson.

Drano: If $2x$ equals 42, then what does $3x$ plus 5 equal?

Butter: How a letter gonna equal a number?

Drano: Look, look, look, look. Okay, I got it. Check this out. Say you got two honeys, right?

Butter: Right.

Drano: And you gotta buy both of them a chicken, right? Now you gonna buy these two chickens, and for two chickens, it costs forty-two dollars, right? So, what is three chickens plus five dollars?

Butter: What's the five dollars for?

Drano: The hotel.

Butter: Right, right! All right. Okay, hold on. I'm with you here. Three chickens. And a hotel. That's sixty-eight dollars!

The scene relies on the violently stereotypical myths about black male hypersexuality, black people's attraction to chickens as food, and black women's willing prostitution of their sexuality for material gain. Yet the entire scene is couched within the larger rubric of Coach Saroka's demand that they study harder and pull their grades up. And by the end of *Sunset Park*, after taking her team to the championship game, Saroka informs the team she will return to coach them next year. Moreover, given that her players are now academically successful, she tells her team, in a melodramatic fashion, that they will go to college "not for basketball. For life."

In *Finding Forrester* (2000), William Forrester (Sean Connery) is a reclusive white writer who takes on the mentorship of a young African American boy named Jamal Wallace (Rob Brown). The film begins by highlighting Jamal's love of reading and his prowess on the basketball court, the latter of which wins him a scholarship at a prestigious private prep school. Yet Jamal's neighborhood peer group convinces him to break into Forrester's apartment. Entering the apartment, Jamal is made uneasy by Forrester's strange reclusiveness and flees. However, in his flight, he leaves behind his backpack, filled with his personal journals. Shortly thereafter, Forrester drops Jamal's backpack to the street from his window, where he has been watching Jamal. Jamal retrieves his bag to find that Forrester has edited his journals with a red pen. Jamal then returns to Forrester's apartment: "I came back to see if you could help me out with my writing." Forrester replies curtly, "Here's one: 5,000 words on why you'll stay the fuck out of my home." Surprising Forrester, Jamal completes the assignment and wins a modicum of respect from Forrester.

Throughout the remainder of the film, William Forrester and Jamal Wallace grow close through Forrester's literary guidance and critiques of Jamal's writing, to which Jamal responds with aplomb:

Forrester: Paragraph three starts with a conjunction, "and." You should never start a sentence with a conjunction.

Jamal: Sure you can.

Forrester: No, it's a firm rule.

Jamal: No, it *was* a firm rule. Sometimes using a conjunction at the start of a sentence makes it stand out. *And* that may be what the writer's trying to do.

Forrester: *And* what is the risk?

Jamal: Well, the risk is doing it too much. It's a distraction. *And* it could give your piece a run-on feeling. *But* for the most part, the rule on using "and" or "but" at the start of a sentence is pretty shaky. Even though it's still taught by too many professors, some of the best writers have ignored that rule for years, including you.

Later, Jamal's school accuses him of plagiarism because he revised an unpublished manuscript of Forrester's, which Forrester had given him permission to use. Forrester then emerges from his reclusion to defend Jamal at an essay contest; he vindicates his writing and then disappears. A year later, it is Jamal's senior year in high school, and he is fielding college offers from prestigious universities because of his exceptional writing. Forrester's lawyer contacts Jamal and reveals that Forrester has died from cancer and willed the rights of his second novel, "Sunset," to Jamal and that Jamal is to write the foreword.

Finding Forrester tells a story of intellectual bootstrapping, whereby Jamal writes his way out of the ghetto and into the Ivy League, a story that recalls the ever-popular narrative of hard work as a cure-all. This film, like the others, subtly makes invisible and dismisses the structural causes of racial and class inequality through its focus on the exceptional black actor. The message is simple. If he can do it, then anyone can and should. Yet folks of color do not pull themselves up in these films. And that is what motivates the need for the white savior in the first place. The white savior is black motivation personified in a white body. Simply by cross-racial osmosis, black and brown characters soak up the ability to work hard, learn patience, and pursue the dreams they never before thought possible to achieve. Through minimal contact with the white savior, patterns of nonwhite dysfunction become lily-white Horatio Alger stories, while dysfunctional lazy and ignorant black and Latino characters morph into WASP-like workers building their American Dream.

White Civility, Black Savagery

Another dimension of these films is the colonialist fantasy that situates whiteness (especially U.S. and European whiteness) as the par excellence manifestation of civilization and rationality relative to the construction of blackness (especially African, West Indian, South American, and U.S. inner-city American) as savage, emotional, and even exotically magical in its quaint and premodern folkways.

For example, *A Dry White Season* (1989), *Cry Freedom* (1987), *Tears of the Sun* (2003), *The Constant Gardener* (2005), *Blood Diamond* (2006), and *The Last King of Scotland* (2006) conjure images of an Africa in despair and turmoil that must be saved by the colonialist, religious, and capitalist interventions of a white do-gooder. These films align with other recent movies, such as *Black Hawk Down* (2001), *Hotel Rwanda* (2004), and *Shake Hands with the Devil* (2007), that portray Africa as a Wild West to be settled by the white cowboys and their six-shooters. These representations hinge on a popular assumption that violence and lawlessness are an essential quality of African peoples across the vast diversity of the continent, which then encourages popular support for Western powers' intervention through the supply of crippling loans, overt military and intelligence actions, and globally asymmetrical labor and trade policies that benefit the economies of the West.

Peter Davis writes in *In Darkest Hollywood* that the patterned stock-and-trade representations of Africans as savages (and Europeans and Americans as the quintessential civilized) have a "devastating impact" because much of Hollywood film is marked as "apolitical, even while it stamps stereotypes and projects behavior that is as profoundly political as it is influential" (1996: iv). Davis contends that these representations are akin to an opiate for which there may be no medication: "People everywhere were not coerced into going to the cinema . . . [but] eagerly allowed themselves to be seduced into an addiction that is well-nigh incurable" (4). That is, the African-as-savage trope has become so expected and so commonsense—what sociologists call hegemonic—that deviations from the image now come across as fictional and out-of-place or are condemned as liberal ideology.

In *Tears of the Sun* (2003), Lieutenant A. K. Waters (Bruce Willis) leads his Navy SEAL team into Nigeria to extract Dr. Lena Fiore Kendricks (Monica Bellucci), a U.S. citizen by marriage. However, the mission's twists and turns from Nigeria to Cameroon reveal scene after scene of atrocities at the hands of African rebels. Waters is the premier white savior. Possessing the moral and cognitive aspects of civilization, he takes it on himself to deviate from his military instructions to save innocent Africans from rebels, tyrants, and despots. Near the end of the film, and thanks to the actions of Waters, Arthur Azuka (Sammi Rotibi) is installed as tribal chief and the proper heir of his father's vision of a democratic Nigeria. The end of the film shows Azuka raising his arms in exaltation of Waters's actions as he exclaims, "Freedom!" The film then fades to a quotation from Edmund Burke: "The only thing necessary for the triumph of evil is for good men to do nothing."

Burke's statement properly frames the savior within the rubric of classic liberalism. This philosophy advocates individual liberty and reform as the best vehicle for social change rather than the recognition of, and impetus to modify, structural forms and causes of inequality and violence. Hence, *Tears of the Sun* valorizes the individual rationality of white men, as embodied in the character of A. K. Waters, as rugged, individualist, and civilized warrior-poets who police the African jungles because the natives either do not know how or are unwilling to do so. Africa and Africans become akin to the Western plains and Native Americans in the Hollywood Westerns of yesteryear. Today's white savior films simply replace the white horse and cowboy hat with an Mi-17 helicopter and camouflage paint.

This same dynamic is repeated in *The Constant Gardner* (2005). Justin Quayle (Ralph Fiennes) is a horticulturalist in love with his wife, Tessa Quayle (Rachel Weisz), an outspoken human rights activist who persuades Justin to go to Kenya. Early in the film, Tessa is murdered, and the formerly timid Justin decides to find her killers. As he searches, he is slowly transformed into a savior, not only of his wife's memory and her vindication but of Kenyans writ large. The film is fragmented in its style, and soon the audience learns that Tessa's death was a part of a larger conspiracy in which a Western drug company (known as DHS) conducts fraudulent testing of a tuberculosis drug called Dypraxa, a medication known to possess harmful side effects. Still, the company tests it on Africans. The movie then details the extremes to which Justin goes to stop DHS from inflicting any more pain on Kenyan test subjects. In the end, Justin has outed all complicit parties and is killed by three men, presumably hired guns of DHS. Accordingly, Justin correctly synthesized his pure love of Tessa with expert cognitive sleuthing skills, which allowed his slow emergence as a balanced white savior of Kenyans—saving them from evil British parliamentary bureaucrats, greedy pharmaceutical companies, and savage Africans complicit in the cover-up.

Even the films whose stories do not go well for the white savior or explicitly critique the white savior trope end up reestablishing the narrative. For example, in *The Last King of Scotland*, Dr. Nicholas Garrigan, a Scottish doctor, conjures the specter of Dr. Stanley Livingston, but he is flawed from the onset and ends up playing a bit of an imperfect savior. While he continually critiques British imperialism in Uganda as an unfair and meddling colonialist influence (that he all too well understands as a Scot), by film's end he pleads with British forces to rescue him from under Idi Amin's boot. This dynamic reproduces the notion that while Western intervention is far from perfect, Africa would spin out of control into absolute despotism (and hurt the well-meaning white people who went there to save it (e.g., Dr. Garrigan) without the white civilizing influence.

In another example, *Blood Diamond* (2006) allows Danny Archer (Leonardo DiCaprio) and Maddy Bowen (Jennifer Connelly) to meet at a peaceful bar in the middle of the Sierra Leone civil war (1996–2001). The two engage in a playful but spirited introduction of their purposes in Africa:

Archer: American, huh?
Bowen: Guilty.
Archer: Americans usually are.
Bowen: Says the white South African.
Archer: Tsk-tsk-tsk. I'm from Rhodesia.
Bowen: We say "Zimbabwe" now, don't we?
Archer: Do we?
Bowen: Last time I checked.
Archer: So don't tell me, you're here to make a difference, huh?
Bowen: And you're here to make a buck?
Archer: I'm here for lack of a better idea.

Bowen: That's a shame.

Archer: Not really. Peace Corps types only stay around long enough to realize they're not helping anyone. Government only wants to stay in power
until they've stolen enough to go into exile somewhere else. And the
rebels, they're not sure they want to take over; otherwise they'd have to
govern this mess. "TIA," right?

Bowen: What's TIA?

Archer: "This is Africa."

This exchange sets the stage for the two central white characters of the film.
Archer and Bowen come across as interlopers in a foreign land that is unequiv-
ocally damaged and broken. One, Archer, wants to profiteer from it, and the
other, Bowen, naively wants to save it. Despite exposing their respective utter
greed and misplaced idealism, they unite against the dysfunction of Africans.
Whether democratically elected or put in power by revolutionary change, Africans are doomed to run Sierra Leone into the ground. The film contextualizes
the story by situating it in the tragedy of the human rights violations of blood
diamond mining, giving it not only the glitter of precious stones but also the
sensation and sentiment of Hollywood. It is hard not to root for the white savior
when child soldiers, slavery, and genocide—all furthering the material wealth
of multinational corporations and individual soldiers of fortune—undergird
the film's plot.

Science fiction–based savior films also conflate nonwhite people with un-
civilized savages incapable of technological thought or scientific invention.
Stargate (1994) takes a disturbing approach to a conspiracy theory that has entered popular culture and academic circles alike. As Egyptology and historiography converged, many began to wonder how the ancient Egyptians built the
pyramids. Soon conspiracy theories tinged with racism emerged. For example,
some maintain that alien visitors built the structures because the ancient Africans did not possess the civilization to do so.[4]

Stargate starts off with a scene of archeologists digging in the Giza Plateau
in 1928. Professor Langford (Erik Holland) is shown discovering a large metal
and stone circle. The next scene skips forward to the 1990s. The film's protagonist, Egyptologist Dr. Daniel Jackson, is giving a lecture to a white academic
community. In the lecture, he argues that Egyptians did not build the pyramids, specifically, the Pyramid of Khufu (or Cheops), which is the oldest and
largest of the three pyramids in the Giza Necropolis. Dr. Jackson claims a prior

---

4. See, for example, *Architects of the Underworld: Unriddling Atlantis, Anomalies of Mars,
and the Mystery of the Sphinx* (Rux 1996) and *Gods of the Dawn: The Message of the Pyramids
and the True Stargate Mystery* (Lemesurier 1999). As recently as 2011, a viral e-mail recalled
a 2010 lecture by a Dr. Ala Shaheen, the supposed head of the Cairo University Archaeology
Department, in which Dr. Shaheen purportedly said, "There is something inside the pyramid
that is 'not of this world.'" The only problem with this story is that it was a hoax article and
that an actual Dr. Alaa el-din M. Shaheen, minister of archeology for Egypt, denied any such
statement. See Collins, n.d.

discovery by Egyptologists was fraudulent and contends that Egyptian civilization was unevolved at the time of building the Great Pyramid of Khufu.

> Jackson: Every other architectural structure at the time was covered with detailed hieroglyphics. When is the academic community going to accept the fact the pharaohs of the Fourth Dynasty did not build the great pyramids? [*Many of the audience begin to mutter among themselves.*] Look, look inside the pyramid, the most incredible structure ever erected. There are no writings whatsoever. And—
>
> Professor: Doctor Jackson, you've left out the fact that Colonel Vyse discovered inscriptions with Khufu's name—
>
> Jackson: Well, his discovery was a fraud. [*Outraged mutterings come from the audience. Some start to laugh.*] I—I mean, I've been able to show that a fully developed writing system appeared in the first two dynasties, you know, which—you know, almost as if it was based on an even earlier prototype.

This exchange represents the lone, rational, rebel voice of Dr. Jackson being pitted against the politically correct academic community. Importantly, this film was released at the height of the culture wars in the mid-1990s and is an eddy of the rising ride of Afrocentric and multicultural ideology that defended the assertion that Africans built the pyramids.

But Dr. Jackson soon discovers he is right. The discovery by Professor Langford is a star gate that allows travel from Earth to a planet across the universe that resembles the desert region of Africa. Upon visiting the planet, Jackson and his team discover a darker-skinned community of slaves, held captive by an advanced alien race that built pyramids on earth as well as on the newly discovered desert planet. The film thus presents an overt comparison: the newly found darker-skinned people who dress in tattered cloth, are barely literate, live in huts, and believe in a god named Ra are supposed to represent ancient Egyptians—unskilled savages attached to mythologies and kept in check by brutal oppressors.

In some films the darker-skinned people possess a noble and moral magical power. For example, in *The Help*, Skeeter has a flashback of her time with her black maid, Constantine, in which Constantine imparts a kind of otherworldly folk wisdom on how to live a moral life full of self-esteem:

> Constantine: What you doin' hidin' out here, girl?
>
> Skeeter: I just couldn't tell Mama I didn't get asked to the dance.
>
> Constantine: It's alright. Some things you just got to keep to ourselves, right?
>
> Skeeter: All the boys say I'm ugly. Mama was third-runner-up in Miss South Carolina, and I just—
>
> Constantine: Oh, you quit feelin' sorry for yourself. Now, that's ugly. Ugly is somethin' that grows up inside you. It's mean and hurtin', like them

boys. Now, you're not one of them, is you? [*Skeeter shakes her head.*] I didn't think so, honey.

Sometimes the magical exoticism is subtle and reflected in only a line or two, as in one such case in *The Last Samurai*. Captain Algren comes to view his Samurai captors as possessing a basic form of mysticism: "There is indeed something spiritual in this place," he states matter-of-factly. In many of these films, the white savior must interact with at least a few noble savages so that the nonwhite culture at hand is demonstrated to be worth saving.

Birthed from the *bon sauvage* character of seventeenth-century French literature, the term "noble savage" personified European discontent with modernity. As European colonialism gained momentum, Africans and indigenous New World peoples were said to possess the noble qualities of harmony with nature, generosity, childlike simplicity, happiness under duress, and a natural, innate moral compass. Contact with the noble savage was encouraged, as the Romantics of the eighteenth century propagated the belief that preindustrial society had moved away from its traditional roots, thus losing touch with the necessary precepts of humanity's true and primitive condition of passion, emotion, and moral instinct (Hughey 2009).

The character of the noble savage remained relatively static until the midnineteenth century, when writers, most notably Charles Dickens, began to critique and disassociate themselves from the genres of Sentimentalism and Primitivism. In the United States, Native peoples, certain Asian groups, and certain aspects of African American culture were viewed as having natural authenticity—a closer relationship with those things thought premodern: the land, spirituality, animals, and exotic phenomena yet unexplained by scientific inquiry (Deloria 1999). Now, in modern white savior films, the nonwhite characters are often framed as worth saving because of their custody of unexplainable magical or spiritual quality that is valued but not fully understood by the logic and materialism of the white savior. By saving the people of color, the white savior takes possession of the primordial morality, making him- or herself more complete as a person, all under the guise of rescuing and protecting nonwhite others.

"Based on a True Story": Racialized Historiography

Many of these films (nineteen out of fifty, or 38 percent) claim they are based on a true story or directly refer to historical events of a highly racialized nature such as the U.S. Civil War, the atrocities of Nazi Germany, apartheid in South Africa, the incident at Wounded Knee, or the U.S. civil rights movement.[5] For

---

5. The nineteen films are *Cry Freedom* (1987, based on antiapartheid activists); *Mississippi Burning* (1988, based on the murder of three civil rights workers in 1964 Mississippi); *Rambo III* (1988, based on the United States supplying weapons and training to the Afghan mujahideen during the Soviet-Afghan War); *A Dry White Season* (1989, based on South African apartheid);

example, *The Constant Gardener* (2005) is based on the real-life Pfizer drug trial of Trovan in Kano, Nigeria; *Music of the Heart* (1999) is based on the Opus 118 Harlem School of Music; and *The Long Walk Home* (1990) recalls the Montgomery, Alabama, bus boycott of 1955.

Many defend the supposed lack of ideological slant or racial politics in these films by noting that they are based on actual, historical events. Such reenactments may seduce audiences into an uncritical appraisal of these films. How could one critique the film if it is real life? However, these films link the supposed authenticity of history with the standpoint of the white savior rather than with the points of view of the people of color supposedly being helped. These films do not simply retell history from an apolitical and ideologically neutral place but subtly rewrite historical events so that white colonizers, paternalistic controllers, and meddling interlopers seem necessary, relevant, and moral.

Such an approach is tricky, as many have become savvy to the white savior trope in recent years (see Chapters 3 and 4 on critics and audiences, respectively) and are wary of an overdrawn plot device that makes characters of color little more than background props for the heroic action of the central white protagonist. Accordingly, many films go to great lengths to portray the story as anything but a white savior film, instead framing it as a needed exposé of the supposedly hidden or exotic lives of people of color. For example, in *The Help* (2011) Skeeter tells her New York book editor Elaine Stein (Mary Steenburgen):

> I'd like to write something from the point of view of the help. These colored women raise white children, and in twenty years those children become the boss. We love them, and they love us, but they can't even use the toilets in our houses. Don't you find that ironic, Miss Stein?[6]

Glory (1989, based on the personal letters of Civil War Colonel Robert Gould Shaw); *The Long Walk Home* (1990, based on the 1955 Montgomery, Alabama, bus boycott); *Thunderheart* (1992, based on the events of the Wounded Knee incident in 1973); *Schindler's List* (1993, based on German businessman Oskar Schindler); *Ghosts of Mississippi* (1996, based on the 1994 trial of Byron De La Beckwith, the man accused of killing civil rights activist Medgar Evers); *Amistad* (1997, based on the 1839 uprising on the slaveship *La Amistad*); *Music of the Heart* (1999, based on the Opus 118 Harlem School of Music); *Tears of the Sun* (2003, based on the Nigerian civil war); *The Last Samurai* (2003, based on the Meiji Restoration and 1877 Satsuma Rebellion led by Saigō Takamori); *The Constant Gardener* (2005, based on the Pfizer drug Trovan and its clinical trials in Kano, Nigeria); *Amazing Grace* (2006, based on William Wilberforce's antislavery crusade); *Blood Diamond* (2006, set in the Sierra Leone civil war of 1992–2002); *The Last King of Scotland* (2006, based on events involving Ugandan dictator Idi Amin); *The Blind Side* (2009, based on the life of NFL football player Michael Oher); and *The Help* (2011, based on the lives of domestic servants in 1960s Mississippi).

6. *The Help* (2011), a film based on the 2009 best-selling book of the same name by Kathryn Stockett, grossed over $166 million within a few months and gave not a penny to the real-life characters on which it was based. Early in 2011, Abilene Cooper, a sixty-year-old black woman who long worked as a maid to Kathryn Stockett's brother, sued Kathryn Stockett for $75,000, based on the complaint that the book's principal character (named Aibileen Clark) was an unpermitted appropriation of her name and image. Stockett replied by filing for

In an era of backlash against civil rights and in which increasing numbers of people (including nonwhites) believe racism and racial inequality are things of the past, these films assist in a watered-down retelling of history. Such films reengineer the past to fit within our contemporary moment of conservative racial politics. White savior tales of interracial interaction and supposed cooperation become hollow narratives of racial reconciliation that warn people of color to be thankful for their select white allies while helping whites alleviate feelings of white guilt for their racist past. Stories about apartheid, slavery, colonialism, war, and many forms of racial inequality are distilled into romantic and sentimental tales of one person's heroic and well-intentioned actions rather than the actual legal, political, and social structures that reproduced racial inequality and oppression in the face of good intentions and individual heroic deeds. In so doing, these films tell a dangerous myth—that racial inequality would simply go away if more white people simply tried to save black people from themselves (read, assimilate) rather than examine and challenge the laws, customs, and traditions of a white supremacist nation-state with still-entrenched racial inequality and discrimination.

For example, *The Blind Side* (2009) stars the white savior Leigh Anne Tuohy (Sandra Bullock) and the to-be-saved Michael Oher (Quinton Aaron). The film is based on Michael Lewis's book *The Blind Side: Evolution of a Game* (2006), which examined the real life of Michael Oher, from his humble beginnings in an impoverished area of Memphis, Tennessee, to his becoming offensive tackle for the Baltimore Ravens in the NFL. In the film, Oher is depicted as a mute, docile, slow (yet ever-grateful) black boy who was homeless until a white Republican family (the Tuohys) from Mississippi took him in.

Interestingly, the real-life Michael Oher took issue with his representation in the film in his own book, *I Beat the Odds: From Homelessness, to "The Blind Side," and Beyond* (2011). While Oher maintains his appreciation for the Tuohys, he writes of the film:

> I felt like it portrayed me as dumb instead of as a kid who had never had consistent academic instruction and ended up thriving once he got it. Quinton Aaron did a great job acting the part, but I could not figure out why the director chose to show me as someone who had to be taught the game of football. Whether it was S.J. moving around ketchup bottles or Leigh Anne explaining to me what blocking is about, I watched those scenes thinking, "No, that's not me at all! I've been studying—really studying—the game since I was a kid!" That was my main hang-up with the film. (2011: 205)

Hollywood ignores the intersection of educational and racial inequality (Oher's lack of "consistent academic instruction") while the white savior motif emerges

---

summary judgment, citing a one-year statute of limitations on the lawsuit. Just after the film's release in August 2011, a Mississippi judge agreed and threw out Clark's suit because it was filed too late (Robertson 2011).

in terms of saving Oher from homelessness and creating a fictional dolt of a character for whom white children such as S.J. (Jae Head) had to instruct Oher on the basics of football. With that narrative in place, there was no aspect of his life left unsaved by his white, messianic adopted family.

Such a drastic lie was necessary for *The Blind Side* (2009) to work—and for Bullock to win an Oscar, a Golden Globe, and a Screen Actors Guild Award. If the film had stuck closer to the truth, depicting Oher as a talented, intelligent football player who did not receive consistent educational resources growing up, then the only savior role for the Tuohys (especially for Leigh Anne) would be to pay for his tuition at a private boarding school at most or a morning ride to public school at the least. Instead, Oher was recast as a gentle giant who struggled with logical problem solving but who possessed nearly animalistic and primordial protective instincts despite his origins in the crime-ridden ghetto with a nearly absentee mother. With this racialized deficiency in place, the Tuohys could easily step in to provide material resources and a safe place to live, a stable home complete with a steel-magnolia-meets-June-Cleaver mom, and a learning environment in which a white child, nearly a decade younger than Oher, teaches him the knowledge and thinking skills necessary to trans-late instincts into logical on- and off-the-field decision making. Such saving graces adorned the film throughout. In one particular scene Leigh Anne Tuohy gives Oher his own bed:

> Tuohy: John says all the pro athletes use futons if they can't find a bed big enough, so I got you one of those. Of course, the frame was heinous; was not about to let that in my house, but I got you something nicer.
> Oher: It's mine?
> Tuohy: Yes, sir. What?
> Oher: Never had one before.
> Tuohy: What, a room to yourself?
> Oher: A bed.

The sentimentalism is ripe, if not over the top. Who could not feel respect and empathy for a person who gives an adult his first bed and safe place to sleep?

Messages of racial difference and tension are constant, yet implicit, plot de-vices throughout the film. And *The Blind Side* trades on its supposed authentic-ity as a vehicle for these potent racial messages. After Oher is taken in by the Tuohys, he remarks, "I look, and I see white everywhere. White walls, white floors, and lots of white people." The Tuohys are racially signified through an array of southern, good-ole-boy white stereotypes that border on racist: they are Republican politically, Tennessean geographically, and Baptist religiously; the patriarch of the family, Sean Tuohy, is played by the country music star Tim McGraw; and they believe that their son did not get a role in the school play because of antiwhite multicultural bias (Sanneh 2010).

Despite these references to a staid and narrow-minded whiteness that generally follows the cinematic arc in which the racist whites unlearn their ignorant ways through contact with their newfound nonwhite friend by film's end, *The Blind Side* does not portray an apologetic or remorseful whiteness. Rather, the superiority of their saviorhood carries them throughout. When a nameless black male character in Oher's old neighborhood threatens Leigh Anne Tuohy, she fires back that he had better not come into her neighborhood because she knows the district attorney and is a member of the National Rifle Association. As Kelefa Sanneh remarks of this scene in the *New Yorker* (2010):

> This kind of threat, a Southern white woman telling a black man to stay in his own neighborhood, has a long and dismal history, but Bullock delivers it with verve, and without a trace of self-consciousness. (No doubt the scene helped her win her Academy Award.) Leigh Anne is refreshing, because there's no trace of anxiety in her white identity—for her, it's neither something to live down nor something to live up to.

In this light, whiteness as savior rewrites history to such an extent that blatant representations of the methods of racial segregation and superiority—acts and threats of physical (NRA) and institutional (district attorney) violence—are transformed into acceptable and heart-warming maternal care across the color line.

With such cinematic fiction masquerading as fact, does Hollywood ever draw the line? Sadly, the answer is rarely. For example, in *Glory* (1989), the historical figure of Civil War colonel Robert Gould Shaw—commander of the all-black 54th Massachusetts Infantry Regiment—is played by Matthew Broderick. While Shaw is depicted as whipping the black soldier Private Trip (Denzel Washington) for disobeying orders, by film's end he is shown giving his life with his black regiment, as both Trip and Shaw fall dead on the beach at Fort Wagner, South Carolina. Very little is made of Shaw's actual abolitionist ideology or his organization of a successful military boycott over equal pay for his black soldiers (although this activism is briefly referred to in one scene). Rather, he is seen as just a kind-hearted white man who decided that black men were equal to him.

In *Amistad* (1997), a film based on the 1839 slave uprising aboard the slave ship *La Amistad*, the U.S. Supreme Court rules that the slaves aboard *La Amistad* are free men. The impassioned argument before the Supreme Court by white saviors, property law attorney Roger Baldwin (Matthew McConaughey) and former president John Quincy Adams (Anthony Hopkins), supposedly begins a wholesale shift in U.S. attitudes toward slavery, which upends the South's peculiar institution and plunges the country into Civil War. Without this case and the messianic lawyering it portrays, so the film subtly conveys, the United States might have retained the legality of slavery for many more years. The problem is that these same justices did retain slavery for years to come and then worked to establish the bulwarks for Jim Crow. As the historian Eric Foner writes:

> Most seriously, *Amistad* presents a highly misleading account of the case's historical significance, in the process sugarcoating the relationship between

the American judiciary and slavery. The film gives the distinct impression that the Supreme Court was convinced by Adams' plea to repudiate slavery in favor of the natural rights of man, thus taking a major step on the road to abolition. In fact, the *Amistad* case revolved around the Atlantic slave trade—by 1840 outlawed by international treaty—and had nothing whatever to do with slavery as an [*sic*] domestic institution. Incongruous as it may seem, it was perfectly possible in the nineteenth century to condemn the importation of slaves from Africa while simultaneously defending slavery and the flourishing slave trade within the United States. . . . Rather than being receptive to abolitionist sentiment, the courts were among the main defenders of slavery. A majority of the *Amistad* justices, after all, were still on the Supreme Court in 1857 when, in the Dred Scott decision, it prohibited Congress from barring slavery from the Western territories and proclaimed that blacks in the United States had "no rights which a white man is bound to respect." (1998)

Moreover, the crescendo of the film, arguably the closing arguments of Adams before the Supreme Court, bear no resemblance to Adams's actual words but instead tell audiences that the sentimental and moral words of Adams must have swung the Court justices, who in their ultimate wisdom saw the light of abolition. As the History Place (a website dedicated to "Students, Educators, and all who enjoy History") wrote of the film, "When Adams appears before the Supreme Court, he delivers a quiet, dignified argument for freedom with the power to set men free, both then and now" (Harvey 1997). With the moral authority of being based on a true story, the reverence for Founding Fathers, and the rising libertarian strand of thought that any form of government is, ipso facto, oppressive, *Amistad* becomes a dangerous vehicle for the sanctification of paternalistic whiteness in relation to U.S. politics, law, slavery, and the abolitionist movement.

By the end of *Blood Diamond*, not long after the white savior Danny Archer (Leonardo DiCaprio) dies after saving Solomon Vandy (Djimon Hounsou), the screen fades to black to show the following epilogue:

> In January 2003, forty nations signed
> "The Kimberley Process"—an effort to
> stem the flow of conflict diamonds.
> But illegal diamonds are still finding their way to market.
> It is up to the consumer to insist
> that a diamond is conflict-free.
> Sierra Leone is at peace.
> There are still 200,000 child soldiers in Africa.

The message is clear: if more white people like Archer cared, African child soldiers and blood diamond trade would be no more.

The problem with conflict diamonds is framed as neither the predatory relationship between European colonialists that own the diamond mines and their exploitation of African labor nor the fetishization of material objects over the bodies that find and create them—as is the case in legal mining of precious stones in Africa, South America, and Asia. Rather, we are told that the problem can be fixed with audience members' capitalist consumption habits. Even though the film itself explains that conflict diamonds easily masquerade as conflict-free stones so that the distinction is forever lost once a stone reaches the market, the audience is told that the way to keep Sierra Leone "at peace" (and to end child slavery and child soldiering) is to be a careful consumer.

Depictions of supposedly real-life white-nonwhite interactions are almost always mediated by a neocolonialist framework of, respectively, helper-helpless, the knower–the ignorant, and civilized-savage that in the end form a powerful collective memory. Defined by Hugo von Hofmannsthal in 1902 as the "dammed up force of our mysterious ancestors within us" (quoted in Schieder 1978: 2), a definition refined in 1925 by Maurice Halbwachs in *Social Frameworks of Memory* ([1925] 1992), the term "collective memory" conceptually separates individual (psychological) and collective (sociological) memory (Olick and Robbins 1998: 106). The concept relates to Emile Durkheim's theory of ritual and collective representations through an analysis of the social practices of commemoration, which he articulated in *The Elementary Forms of the Religious Life* ([1912] 1995). Control over historical events' meaning may seem incredibly distant from racial filmmaking. History profoundly affects the metanarratives and common sense of our present culture (Bodnar 2001). While some argue that collective memory is largely reproduced through the construction of memorials and national monuments (Irwin-Zarecka 1994; Schwartz 2000; Wagner-Pacifici and Schwartz 1991), others note how visual media sustains memory through a continuous production of representations (Bodnar 2001; Griffin and Hargis 2008; Monteith 2003; Morgan 2006). Michel Foucault observes:

> Since memory is actually a very important factor in struggle . . . if one controls people's memory, one controls their dynamism. And one also controls their experience, their knowledge of previous struggles. . . . It's vital to have possession of this memory, to control it, administer it, tell it what it must contain. And when you see these films, you find out what you have to remember. ([1975] 1995: 25–26)

It is germane to consider how film and culture intersect to see both *which* pasts are remembered over others, and *how* pasts are selected as worthy of remembrance in the present. The media scholar David Grainge writes, "The balance of memory and forgetting in American culture—what is remembered, by who and for who—has in recent years become entwined in hegemonic struggles fought and figured around the negotiation of America's national past" (2003: 3). Conflict over interpretation of the past is an always-present dimension of social life. Cinematic representations of interracial contact and supposed across-the-color-line friendship obfuscate that Western history is a tale of white domination. These films, "based on true stories," are an easy-to-access reservoir of "authentic" history. The historiography of the film is taken for granted and audiences need not be coerced to accept their story lines but more readily consent to their mythology of white and nonwhite cooperation.

Given that Hollywood elites must highlight select elements of the past for particularly memorable and emotionally charged stories, racial redemption stories that center on white racism, black dysfunctions, and a white do-gooder to make it all better fit the criteria. In this sense, the content of white savior films helps promote a kind of collective memory consensus. William D. Routt thus argues in *The Film of Memory*:

> To put it baldly, I am saying that films, and especially popular films (for of all films, popular films are those made most surely for showing in public), constitute history. Not that they interpret history or substitute for it, but that they are history. Not the past, but history. And not the only history, but, if you like, in some sense the truest sort. (2006)

With the understanding that film can masquerade as the truest form of history, we can now more easily understand why white savior films such as *Dances with Wolves* (1990) and *Schindler's List* (1993) were selected for preservation in the National Film Registry in the Library of Congress for having "cultural, historical, or aesthetic significance" ("'Schindler's List' added to film registry" 2004; National Film Registry 2011).

Conclusion

The content of these films demonstrates a twofold dynamic: they collectively *reflect* the dominant ideological currents and unsettled racial times of each decade, and they demonstrate their creators' attempts to design products that will *resonate* with audiences' differing tastes and understandings of race relations. While I situate these films within three prevailing racial moments in recent history, what this chapter leaves unanswered is both a deeper specification of these three racial eras and how the diffuse and multiple meanings of these films are organized and interpreted for easy and comfortable public consumption within those time spans. That is, beyond their content and in the context of three racial currents in the United States, how do authoritative voices assist audiences to view these white savior films as little more than entertainment, neutral retellings of history, and maudlin acts of interracial cooperation? I attempt to answer these questions in the next chapter by examining how film reviewers and critics make sense of these films amid the undulations of the American racial landscape.

3

Reviewing Whiteness

Critics and Their Commentary

Reviewers' failure to discuss the gratuitous and unconscious
racial material provides a useful indicator of the mainstream
culture's concerns—and obliviousness.

—Robert M. Entman and Andrew Rojecki, *The Black Image in the*
White Mind: Media and Race in America

In July 2000 the film critic David Manning hit the scene. In the *Ridgefield Press*, a small Connecticut weekly, Manning praised Columbia Pictures films such as *Hollow Man*, *The Patriot*, and *A Knight's Tale*. In his review of *A Knight's Tale*, he branded relatively unknown actor Heath Ledger as "this year's hottest new star!" (Horn 2001). A year later, during a citation check of Manning's quotations, *Newsweek* reporter John Horn uncovered a mysterious detail: the *Ridgefield Press* had never heard of Manning. Upon further investigation, Horn discovered that David Manning did not exist. He was nothing more than a fictional sobriquet created by the Sony Corporation (Columbia Pictures is a subsidiary of Sony) to dole out high marks to its own films (Horn 2001). After media outlets from the BBC to *Wired* decried the immorality of faux praise, Sony agreed to an out-of-court settlement to refund $1.5 million to dissatisfied customers who saw *Hollow Man*, *The Animal*, *The Patriot*, *A Knight's Tale*, or *Vertical Limit* in American theaters, on the logic that Manning's reviews influenced audience choice.

Fast-forward ten years to February 2010. The renowned film critic Roger Ebert graces the cover of *Esquire*. A front-page cover for Ebert, described by *Forbes* as "the most powerful pundit in America" (Van Riper 2007) and the first film critic to win a Pulitzer Prize, seemed unremarkable in its own right. However, the front page distinguished itself from Ebert's previous media exposure. The cover revealed a close-up shot of Ebert, sans lower jaw—the effect of multiple surgeries to fight thyroid cancer. As *Esquire* writer Chris Jones said of Ebert, "Following more surgery to stop a relentless bloodletting, he was left without much of his mandible, his chin hanging loosely like a drawn curtain, and behind his chin there was a hole the size of a plum" (2010). Immediately after publication, the blogosphere and Twitterverse erupted. Online commentators questioned using the shock value of Ebert's face to sell magazines and expressed a great deal of concern that his image was prostituted. However, not all discourse was sympathetic. Referring to Ebert's left-wing film criticism, a self-proclaimed Tea Party member and writer for *RedState*, tweeted, "I mean, honestly. How many pieces need to fall off @ebertchicago before he gets the hint to shut the fuck up."

The divergent reactions to Manning and Ebert are telling. Through either castigation or compassion, the discourse reflects the central place and import of our cinematic interpreters. Perhaps because of our present moment of info glut, in which we are drowning in a sea of (mis)information, we desire experts to tell us how and why to separate the wheat from the chaff. Without our cinematic tour guides, how would those in the United States, and around the world, make sense of the nearly six hundred U.S.-produced Hollywood films released every year in American theaters, to DVD, and by digital download?

Film Reviewers and the Film Industry

In 1916 the German psychologist, Harvard professor, and amateur film critic Hugo Münsterberg wrote of film, "How can we teach the spirit of true art by a medium which is in itself the opposite of art? How can we implant the idea of harmony by that which is in itself a parody on art?" As Münsterberg's frustrations detail, the beginning of film criticism was marked by an ominous pessimism and fear: movies were a popular, rather than elitist, activity that democratized and challenged the old guard's strict hold on what properly constituted art and art's role in society. Movies, Münsterberg continued,

> must be fraught with dangers. The more vividly the impressions force themselves on the mind, the more easily must they become starting points for imitation and other motor responses. The sight of crime and of vice may force itself on the consciousness with disastrous results. . . . The possibilities of psychical infection and destruction cannot be overlooked. (1916: 71)

And so some began to worry that without the guidance of trained and watchful gatekeepers, the rising tide of moviegoers might corrupt society.

The sociologist Shyonn Baumann (2002) argues that over the twentieth century film slowly moved from being popular entertainment, leisure pastime, and amateur artistic expression to being a legitimate form of art. By the 1950s, especially in the United States and Europe, movies and their interpretation took a larger and larger share of the public's discussion, time, and pocketbooks. The film industry, both in terms of production and its interpretation by cultural critics, had developed into an art world—or what the sociologist Howard Becker calls a "network of people whose cooperative activity, organized via their joint knowledge of conventional means of doing things, produces the kind of art works that an art world is noted for" (1982: x). During this period one of the most influential studies on film critics, by the sociologists Paul Lazarsfeld and Elihu Katz, found a significant flow of influence from movie experts to their advisees. People actively sought out opinions from those they felt were well informed about the art worlds of film and popular culture (Katz and Lazarsfeld 1955). Accordingly, Baumann (2002) finds that film advertisements with reviewer blurbs significantly increased over time: from only 7 percent in 1935 to 47 percent in 1980. Since the recognition of the import of film critics, much scholarly ink has been spilled in the pursuit of understanding film critics' roles in movie markets (Cameron 1995).

For example, the communications scholar Bruce Austin (1983) finds that critics assist the public in making film choices, understanding film content, and perhaps most importantly, communicating thoughts about film in social settings. The economist Samuel Cameron (1995) argues that critics are vital for enjoyable consumption experiences, in that reviews can be fun to read in and of themselves. This effect is far from isolated. In the United States more than one-third of filmgoers report seeking the advice of film critics and approximately one-third say they choose films based on favorable reviews ("Town & Country" 2001). In fact, Baumann (2002) finds that the marketing of film relies on quotes from film critics to such an extent that their omission may raise suspicions among potential audience members. Accordingly, the marketing scholars Suman Basuroy, Subimal Chatterjee, and S. Abraham Ravid (2003) find that film reviews correlate with weekly box office revenue, suggesting that critics play a dual role: reviewers both influence and predict box office revenue.

A slew of empirical studies have since examined the relationship between film reviews and box office performance (De Silva 1998; Jedidi, Krider, and Weinberg 1998; Litman and Ahn 1998; Ravid 1999; Sochay 1994). For example, Jehoshua Eliashberg and Steven Shugan (1997) find that critics correctly predict box office performance but do not influence it. However, other research indicates that film reviews influence a film's theater appearance. For example, Gerda Gemser, Martine Van Oostrum, and Mark Leenders (2007) find that the number and size of film reviews in newspapers directly influences which films audiences decide to see, how long the movies last in theaters, and how much movies gross. In addition, Peter Boatwright, Suman Basuroy, and Wagner Kamakura (2006) find that positive reviews positively influence box office performance. Hence, Basuroy, Chatterjee, and Ravid report, "The desire for good reviews can go even further, thus prompting studios to engage in deceptive practices" (2003: 103). Recall Sony Pictures inventing David Manning and his glowing reviews.

From this large corpus of work, two consistent principles emerge: First, there is a strong correlation between film reviews' assessment of a film and its box office sales. Second, evidence is sufficient that reviewers actively mediate the meanings of films for the public (Cloud 1992; Cooper 2000; Holbrook 1999; Prince 1997). The latter point is especially important when considering films that showcase the hot-button topics of interracial interactions, such as the genre of the white savior film. Film reviewers and critics, as cultural authorities that navigate our racial tempest, are increasingly perceived as valuable voices (Duan, Gu, and Whinston 2008; Holbrook 1999). After all, filmgoing and its subsequent interpretation are ritualized social activities (Lyden 2003; Stempel 2001). One may rely on the evaluations of film critics so as not to lose face (Goffman 1963) or accrue the label of racist (Bonilla-Silva 2010) when discussing racialized films in public or sensitive social settings.

For the majority of scholars researching white savior films, their point of intervention has been the content of the movie genre itself (Bernardi 2007; Chennault 1996; Giroux 1997; Moore and Pierce 2007; Rodríguez 1997; Stoddard and Marcus 2006; Vera and Gordon 2003). This approach often places white savior films in a historical trajectory whereby the film serves as a reflection of the paradoxical mix of progress and stasis in Hollywood's representation of racial identities and race relations. And while much of the aforementioned work remains astute in the evaluation of white savior films' genre conventions, it does not examine how reviewers decode these films. That is, while films are cultural objects (Griswold 2002) that resonate with the larger society because of their aura (Schudson 2002), we often ignore how film reviewers construct and reform that aura. By tackling this side of the equation, we can enter the circuit of meaning by asking how the polysemy of film is settled through the labor of film critics, not as atomistic and disconnected actors, but as a coherent interpretive community, itself influenced by the dominant discourse and imperatives of current race relations.

Film Reviewers as an Interpretive Community

Film criticism is typically associated with individual aesthetic judgment rather than socially shared scripts of explanation. We commonly view a thumbs-up or thumbs-down from Roger Ebert, Stanley Kauffman, Rex Reed, or the indomitable Pauline Kael as the result of their individual expertise, particular interests, and wisdom gained over their careers. Yet this is a facile understanding of film critics, as it portrays them as solitary beings disconnected from one another and as lonely actors that partition their noble and intellectual appraisals from the lowbrow dominant ideologies, social currents, and cultural trends in which they live. Accordingly, I enjoin the reader to resist the temptation to view film reviewers (and their products, film reviews) as if they exist as singular entities above the fray of culture. As the management professors Greta Hsu and Joel Podolny write:

> Viewed in isolation, a critic's review is simply a judgment about qualities of an individual act or work. However, reviews do not exist in isolation. . . . The slot into which the critic places the work strongly shapes the expectations, perception, and—at a more basic level—the attention of that broader audience. [Some reviews] . . . may have more of the character of a social movement, with different individuals making partial contributions to a broader whole. (2005: 191)

Film reviewers constitute an "interpretive community" (Fish 1976). While a film's meaning certainly includes authorial intent, which a critic may (or may not) bring to the fore, no film possesses meanings outside a set of cultural assumptions regarding both what the characters signify and how they should be interpreted. Hence, critics interpret films within a specific community that structures a particular understanding and appraisal. The communication scholar Philip Vannini writes:

> Interpretation is thus a social practice—a practice that in the late capitalist era works as a form of decoding of the ideological meanings inscribed into the art-turned-commodity by its commercial producers. . . . A political aesthetics of interpretation is thus a cultural practice rooted in a specific interpretive community. (2004: 48, 49–50)

Reviewers draw on specific, shared cultural frameworks to interpret films with strong and repeated racial content. And given that reviewers operate as mediating voices between the film's production and its consumption, their interpretations must find expression between the rock of an accurate product appraisal and the hard place of people's commonsense racial interpretations and expectations. While the former is a bit more straightforward, the latter begs a crucial question: What constitutes racial common sense in any given historical period?

The Discourse of Racial Neoliberalism   •

The past half century has been marked by a growing backlash against laws, policies, customs, and language that would promote racial diversity and racial equality. In the scope of U.S. history, this is far from new. Progress toward racial equality and heterogeneity has been regularly followed by vituperative moves to erase that progress, ironically by those claiming to pursue color blindness and equality (Bell and Hartmann 2007; Taylor 1994). For example, the Reconstruction Era (1865–1877) saw significant pushback against laws and programs that sought socioeconomic uplift for newly freed slaves, a fact detailed in W.E.B. Du Bois's landmark study *Black Reconstruction* (1935). And many fighting against the gains of Reconstruction did not frame their resistance in overt racism terms but couched their rhetoric in the supposedly color-blind protection of American values, culture, and civilization from those less intelligent, less patriotic, or less evolved. Even the Ku Klux Klan denied racial animus; they often explained that they desired only the color-blind improvement of the nation (Hughey 2012).

After the great migration of African Americans from the U.S. South to northern urban centers (1910–1930)—a move that partially resulted in increased black socioeconomic mobility—some white American workers began to resent their black coworkers. Many white-dominated labor unions banned black members under the assumption that those "unskilled" black workers did not deserve the same privileges as whites. It was skill, not race, those all-white unions argued, that governed their decision. And they resented the charge that race had anything to do with their racial segregation.

After the U.S. civil rights era (1955–1968), many looked forward to the end of discrimination. Accordingly, with the passage of civil rights legislation, many declared Jim Crow dead. Since the 1970s, the discourse that race no longer matters has strengthened in frequency and intensity. This is a remarkable attitude and discourse given that the post-civil-rights era has been marked by overt and subtle forms of racial discrimination against people of color, the continued salience of racial identity for all age cohorts across the color line, and either stalled trends toward racial equality or the outright widening of racial inequality gaps between whites and nonwhites.[1] Moreover, media representations are far from racially diverse. The big-three cable news networks (CNN, MSNBC, and Fox News) consistently ignore the voices and faces of people of color. Eighty-eight percent of Fox's prime-time guests are white, followed by 83 percent for both CNN and MSNBC. Also, despite Latinos now constituting 15 percent of the U.S. population, they were less than 3 percent of the guests on these cable news networks (Media Matters 2008).

Despite these prowhite realities, many whites have opposed the programs, policies, and laws that would curtail the growth of racial discrimination and inequality under the logic that these measures are antiwhite attacks on their jobs, their positions, and their rights. Following this worldview, society should abandon attention to these racial inequities and race to treat everyone as an individual. The sociologist Eduardo Bonilla-Silva says that such "color-blind racism" functions to justify the second-class status of people of color without sounding or appearing traditionally racist. Such postracial and color-blind narratives are exemplified by the assertion "I am all for equal opportunity, that's why I oppose affirmative action," which enables one to argue against all measures to eradicate de facto racial inequality while seeming reasonable, moral, and appropriately color-blind (Bonilla-Silva 2010: 28). The problem with this worldview is that extant racial inequalities and discriminatory systems already at play do not treat the members of different racial groups as individuals but afford one group better chances than others on the basis of race.

---

1. For example, in 1995 the median wealth of a white household was seven times the median wealth of black and Latino households. But by 2010 the median wealth of a white household was nineteen times that of blacks and fifteen times that of Latinos (Kochhar, Fry, and Taylor 2011). In the early 2000s, audit (or paired testing) studies of job discrimination found a high prowhite bias, but even more shocking was the finding that whites *with* criminal records received more favorable treatment in the search for employment (17 percent) than blacks *without* criminal records (14 percent) (Pager 2003). Moreover, résumés with stereotypically white-sounding names (e.g., Emily or Greg) receive 50 percent more callbacks for interviews for various occupations and industries than résumés with stereotypically black-sounding names (e.g., Lakisha or Jamal) (Bertand and Mullainathan 2004). And in part because of racial profiling, biased court systems, and unequal sentencing laws, blacks and Latinos go to prison at much higher rates than whites; African Americans are incarcerated at nearly six (5.6) times the rate of whites, and Latinos are incarcerated at nearly double (1.8) the rate of whites (Mauer and King 2007).

As a consequence of this cultural logic, funding to civil rights initiatives has been assailed as special-interest earmarks and handouts for the undeserving, public welfare programs have been privatized or dramatically underfunded, and policies designed to uplift nonwhite racial groups (e.g., affirmative action and busing) have been assailed as discriminatory to whites. In fact, a recent study found that whites believe that racism against them has significantly increased and that racism against blacks has deceased by the same margin. That is, more and more whites see racism as a zero-sum game they are now losing, despite the aforementioned privileges they enjoy (Norton and Sommers 2011). This white-victimization narrative translates into a rise in neo-Nazi, Ku Klux Klan, neo-Confederate, and white nationalist groups—organizations that increased by 66 percent from 2000 to 2010 (from 602 such groups in 2000 to 1,002 in 2010) (Potok 2011). Such reactions are a dominant characteristic of racial discourse today: an insidious form of racial neoliberalism that rationalizes inequality and discrimination, not through collective appeals to racial domination or racial consciousness, but through appeals to individualism and color blindness.

The strictures of this racial discourse are not one dimensional, and they have not remained static over the past quarter century (1987–2011). Yet this dominant racial discourse has become, in key moments, durable and inflexible. As the sociologist Troy Duster writes:

> Race, like H_2O, can take many forms, but unlike H_2O it can transform itself in a nanosecond. It takes time for ice to boil or for vapor to condense and freeze, but race can be *simultaneously* Janus-faced and multifac(et)ed—and also produce a singular dominant social hierarchy. Indeed, if we make the fundamental mistake of reifying any one of those states as more real than another, we will lose basic insights into the nature and character of racial stratification in America. (2001: 115)

In key moments, a national discussion on race can spark, grabbing hold of the nation's consciousness, and briefly expand or narrow the types of comments and logics allowed as acceptable, moral, and American. Events such as the 1988 congressional passage of the Civil Rights Restoration Act, the 1992 Los Angeles race riots, the 1995 acquittal of O. J. Simpson, the 2001 attacks on the World Trade Center, the U.S. Supreme Court affirmative action decisions of *Grutter v. Bollinger* and *Gratz v. Bollinger* in 2003, and the election of Barack Obama in 2008 were such moments. But what effect do these events have on racial neoliberalism qua common sense, and in turn, how does this discourse guide the racialized evaluations of film reviewers in the public sphere?

Dominant Racial Discourse as Common Sense

In any given period and context, a set of ideologies, values, and worldviews become accepted not as constructs of human invention, but as a priori, natural ways of being, as manifest in the common tautological expressions "That's just the way things are" or "It is what it is." These accepted understandings of the world are not neutral, but subtly justify and legitimate the interests of dominant groups and their attending systems, whether that of capitalism, patriarchy, heterosexism, or white supremacy. "Common sense" is then, in the words of the social theorist Antonio Gramsci, "hegemony," a taken-for-granted process in which people consent to, and willingly participate in, a nexus of institutions, social relations, and ideas that work against their own interests (Gramsci 1971).

Accordingly, film critics interpret racial content through a specific ideological lens that masquerades as common sense, just as an actual lens must render itself transparent to do its job of focusing one's sight. For example, in 2011 the *New York Times* started a monthly column, Ask the Film Critics, in which reviewers respond to questions mailed to them. In the April issue, the film critics Manohla Dargis and A. O. Scott wrote of the substance and worth of "understanding cultural differences in reviewing movies" (2011b). Dargis and Scott (like many other film critics) argued the abstract point that attention to ethnic, racial, or cultural differences are important in film reviewing. But they did not specify why attention to these differences matter and they certainly avoided the topics of power, injustice, and racism—the latter remaining the third rail of American culture. Rather, they couched their remarks within the comfort of individualism and used a safe culinary metaphor: "The analogy to food is imperfect, but somewhat apt. Our first taste of chimichurri or vindaloo or gefilte fish may be off-putting and strange, but that initial frisson of strangeness can also be a spur to further exploration" (2011a). I do not fault Dargis or Scott in particular but refer to their words as an example that film review discourse is mutually constrained and enabled by today's racial common sense. If one breaks from the color-blind script by bringing up racism, the response will generally be—pardon the pun—a bit more colorful.

For example, in 2012 *The Hunger Games* (based on a novel of same title by Suzanne Collins) was released in theaters. True to the book, which describes Rue and Thresh as having "satiny brown" skin (Collins 2008: 98), the film cast nonwhite actors in their roles. However, some filmgoers expressed disappointment on social media like Facebook and Twitter: "Why does rue have to be black not gonna lie kinda ruined the movie [*sic*]" or "Damn. . . . They would make Thresh black. Disappointed in the movie. The book is way better" (D. Scott 2012). When the film critic Vera Chan covered this racial backlash to the film in *Yahoo! Movies*, the story generated over eight thousand comments, many of which called Chan's entire story inappropriate: "The story is fake and very stupid"; "Yahoo is the biggest racist and actually promotes it to their own good"; and "I'm soooo tired of EVERYTHING being a race issue. . . . there is an obsession with it!!! And look who screams the loudest" (Chan 2012). As witnessed, when Chan simply covered the racial backlash that assumed black characters were white and that their nonwhite casting harmed the movie, many disparaged her story and *Yahoo! News* as the perpetrators of "racism." Akin to Galileo's inability to speak of heliocentrism without institutional and interpersonal backlash, today's racial discourse orbits tightly around the gravitational pull of racial neoliberalism—state and social abandonment of the pursuit of racial equality coupled with increased scapegoating of nonwhite people as the source of racial inequality and societal dysfunction. To speak of race from a perspective not including these domains can bring forth accusations that one is biased, inappropriately political, or playing the race card in heretical fashion.

For example, in one of only a couple of studies on film reviewers' appraisals of race (see also Hughey 2010), the media scholars Robert M. Entman and Andrew Rojecki's (2001) examined to what extent film reviewers would pick up on racial stereotypes in three films that had strong and varied black-white interactions and relationships: *A Time to Kill* (1996), *Independence Day* (1996), and *Jerry Maguire* (1996). They culled thirty-nine reviews of *A Time to Kill* and forty-three each of *Independence Day* and *Jerry Maguire*. They found no references to ethnic stereotypes in any of the reviews of *A Time to Kill* or *Jerry Maguire* and only three abstract references to stereotypes in *Independence Day*, but none of those three identified what those stereotypes were, and the words "race" and "racism" did not appear in any review of *Jerry Maguire*. Some reviewers picked up on the overt racial content of *A Time to Kill*, but most reviewers ignored the problematic racial themes, such as the film's overwhelming focus on the white characters' perspective to the neglect of black characters'. Summarizing their findings, Entman and Rojecki write:

> Although movie reviewers are not academic film theorists and their readers are not cinema studies majors, it is surprising how little attention reviews paid to racial images in movies that featured African American stars and commented directly on Black-White relations. . . . [R]eviewers may fail to notice these messages or believe them to be inappropriate material for commentary. Either way, the absence of more sensitivity in reviewing may be both symptom and cause of problematic movie images. (2001: 192)

Furthermore, the communications professor Alice Hall (2001) once investigated film reviewers' take on the 1998 film *The Siege*, which had been publicly criticized by activist groups before its release. Hall found that reviewers addressed racial and religious stereotypes but often muted these issues in relation to (1) the relationship of the film's plot to real-world events, (2) the intentions of the filmmakers, and (3) the constraints of the genre.

In line with these studies, I contend that film critics are not entirely unconcerned with race but often articulate racial discourse within a narrow, "commonsense" window that is framed by the dominant understandings of race today. Film, as a powerful cultural object, is intimately tied to prevailing understandings of social relations. But film is also a site of struggle, especially when engaging the topic of race. Thus, film critics who interpret and reward racialized films could contest and re-create our racialized systems of order (Gitlin 1980; Lamont and Fournier 1992).

During unsettled times (Swidler 1986), when potent and controversial racial events capture the nation's attention, the producers of film and especially film critics must contend with promoting a commonsense appraisal of film in the context of those changing times. Given that race relations are nearly a contested subject, the cultural products of film and their gatekeeping roles are even more uncertain. Thus, the normative rules, the decisions over what the public should see, what the film industry should award, and what critics deem worthy and distinguished often become apparent and explicit during these "unsettled" times. Accordingly, this chapter helps link public and dominant understandings of race relations to the variation of film reviewers' interpretations of racialized films.

These connections are complex and often paradoxical. No analysis worth its popcorn salt reveals a simple and exact correspondence between the perception of race relations and the form or quality of film reviewers' appraisals of race relations. When racial conflict or dissent erupts on the national scene, film reviews may not necessarily reflect a uniform reaction. However, when the question of where race relations stand is contested, is unsettled, or reflects a particular form of interracial struggle reviews may depict specific stereotypes or messages in order for those critics' reviews to resonate (Jackman 1994).

The past twenty-five years of the post-civil-rights era has been marked by a tendency to downplay the significance of race, even as dramatic radicalized spectacles have punctuated that period to dominate the national conversation for weeks on end. This overall reactionary stasis, coupled with the explosions of racial conflict, dissent, and watershed events, presents a crisis in the production of film reviews on movies with explicit interracial content, such as white savior films. Simply put, film reviewers—as gatekeepers determining which films the public should and should not consume—are influenced by the climate of racial conflict and the dominant discourse that purports to cover and explain that conflict.

The Relationship between Perceptions of Racial Conflict and Film Reviewers

I directly measure reviewers' appraisals of films through the publicly available published reviews on the fifty white savior films released between 1987–2011 that I analyze (see Table 2.1). The reader should refer to Appendix B for detailed description of the methodology employed in my analysis. I measure the variation of perceived racial conflict based on descriptions of events involving race as listed in the *New York Times Index*, 1987–2004. The *Index* has been used and discussed in previous analyses of ethnic and racial relations (McAdam 1982; Olzak 1992; Pescosolido, Grauerholz, and Milkie 1997). In brief, mention of race is a measure of the perceived struggle for the redistribution of social power between racial groups, particularly in a black-white context, and has become increasingly multiracial (e.g., Latinos and Asians) over the years. Drawing from the *Index*, I developed a measure of the perception of racial conflict that appears to trend downward over time (1987–2004). As Figure 3.1 shows, the frequency of mentions of racial conflict in the *New York Times* is in decline.

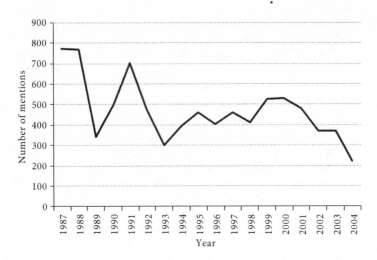

Figure 3.1: Frequency of mentions of racial conflict in the *New York Times Index*

Instead of treating any mention of race, or even mentions of subtle racial code words and racialized topics, the same as another, I separated out the three major types of racialized discourse found in the *Index* and arranged them by increasing salience: (1) group awareness, (2) group relations, and (3) group threat. Once they are separated, we can recognize the rise and fall of perceptions of varying degrees of racial conflict (see Figure 3.2). First, the awareness of racial identity heavily varies from 1988 to 2004. Second, since 1993, the measure of racial group relations has nearly disappeared. And third, the perception of racial threats has been a stable and dominant feature of national discourse (with the exception of an extreme drop-off from 1992 to 1994).

But what do these changing trends mean? With this truncated analysis, these numbers are difficult to decipher and signify very little in isolation. Given the aforementioned discussion of the continued significance of race, racism, and racial inequality, the ebb and flow of the types and frequency of racial discussions in the *Index* signify the presence of three discursive time periods: (1) 1987–1992, the (multi)cultural wars; (2) 1993–1998, the white backlash, and (3) 1999–2011, the postracial era and the redemption of whiteness.

The (Multi)Cultural Wars (1987–1992)

As the newly formed United States took institutional shape and selectively embraced certain immigrant populations, it was clear that African slaves and free persons, Native peoples, and the majority of immigrants were expected to shed their language, values, and customs and adopt U.S. holidays, civic rituals, and the English language through their institutionalization in public schooling, common law, Protestant beliefs, and social services (Omi 2001: 125–126). After the nation split and coalesced in the ideology and practice of the early Jim Crow

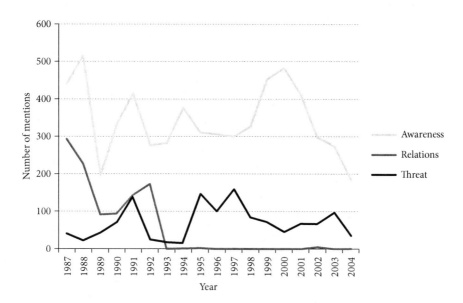

Figure 3.2: Frequency of mentions of types of racial
conflict in the *New York Times Index*

era (between 1880 and 1920), the question of what it meant to be an American
solidified in this model of what Milton Gordon (1964: 85) calls "Anglo conformity." Affecting roughly twenty-four million immigrants, many hailing from
Southern and Eastern Europe, some were immediately nationally and ethnically
"othered," while other Europeans found themselves fast-tracked to citizenship
because they were "white on arrival" (Guglielmo 2003: 6). White assimilation
was the underlying premise of the U.S. Naturalization Law of 1790, which applied only to "free white persons" (Daniels 2002: 116). The following years bore
witness to similar trends—such as the Chinese Exclusion Act of 1882 (Daniels
2002: 239), the policy of "Kill the Indian, and Save the Man" (R. Pratt [1892]
1973: 265), and the Immigration Act of 1924 (Daniels 2002: 69)—that reinforced
the primacy of select European immigration and conflated authentic Americanness with whiteness (Brodkin 1998; Ignatiev 1995; Jacobson 1999; Roediger
2005). As assimilation into whiteness was part and parcel of the national ideal,
Anglo cultural practices were increasingly normalized as indelibly nonracial;
they became neutral characteristics and behaviors to which individual citizens
should aspire and adopt rather than markers of a distinct and privileged racial
group at the center of the nation's founding (Goldberg 1993; Jacobson 1999). For
many, the white supremacist underpinnings of U.S. culture were anything but
neutral; asymmetrical race relations and the de facto status of whiteness as citizenship became, ironically, perceived as a kind of color-blind normality.

Yet a strong counterweight to the idea of WASP assimilation was the notion of "cultural pluralism" (Feuer 1991). Some gently critiqued the Anglo
conformity approach with the more utopian and egalitarian notion that the

United States was "God's Crucible, the great Melting Pot" (see Daniels 2002: 17–18). As various 1960s civil rights bills passed into law, immigration policy was revised and challenges to Eurocentric doctrines in education, family, law, and religion were mounted in diverse registers—pluralism morphed into the widely espoused ideology of multiculturalism (Higham 1975; Lieberson 1980). The sociologist Milton Vickerman writes, "Cultural pluralism's new guise, multiculturalism, is much broader and stronger than cultural pluralism ever was. . . . This ethnic and racial diversity is beyond anything ever faced by U.S. society" (2007: 150). As a consequence, ethnic and racial pride movements gained influence, and the implicit assumption that whiteness equaled Americanness suffered robust challenge.

These intertwined cultural logics of Anglo-conformity and pluralism remain at the heart of debates over the role of race and difference in the national project. This double helix of the nation's DNA—the intertwined strand of color blindness and the thread of multiculturalism—naturalizes and legitimates the racial status quo, especially with respect to whiteness and white privilege (Bell and Hartmann 2007; Gallagher 2004). This dichotomy has been anything but polite. Proponents of multiculturalism rose to question the Eurocentric and white supremacist foundations of central U.S. social structure. As Amy Gutmann writes in the introduction to *Multiculturalism: Examining the Politics of Recognition*:

> Public institutions, including government agencies, schools, and liberal arts colleges and universities, have come under severe criticism these days for failing to recognize or respect the particular cultural identities of citizens. In the United States, the controversy most often focuses upon the needs of African-Americans, Asian-Americans, Native Americans, and women. . . . [I]t is hard to find a democratic or democratizing society these days that is not the site of some significant controversy over whether and how its public institutions should better recognize the identities of cultural and disadvantages minorities. What does it mean for citizens with different cultural identities, often based on ethnicity, race, gender, or religion, to recognize ourselves as equals in the way we are treated in politics? (1994: 3)

As multiculturalism reached its peak in the late 1980s to early 1990s, others went so far as to say that the United States and the dominant cultural practice of Anglo assimilation should not relinquish its dominant place as de facto standard. For some, multiculturalism, propelled by the sometimes irreverent identity politics of the 1960s and 1970s, spelled the end of European dominance, while for others it represented the balkanization of heritage and legacy at the expense of time-honored Western traditions (Trotman 2002: ix). Indeed, the 1980s bore witness to a rise of conservative political ideology, embodied in the presidency of Ronald Reagan, whose proponents stood on a platform dedicated to their supposed defense of traditional family values and principles of Western civilization, a platform marked by the simultaneous defense of individual liberty and Christian religious thought and coupled with the censorship of art and profane knowledge thought indecent, subversive, or sacrilegious. In particular, this movement was opposed to many civil rights initiatives and policies that were hard won in the 1960s and 1970s. Hence, Arthur Schlesinger's *The Disuniting of America: Reflections on a Multicultural Society* (1991) proposed that society's unmeltable ethnics were mounting an attack on Anglo conformity and the melting-pot ideology because their rising cult of ethnicity would endanger the unity of society and the strength of the British foundations of American culture and social order.

Before we knew it, a culture war—a debate over hot-button topics such as abortion, gun politics, the separation of church and state, homosexuality, and particularly race—raged and was all the talk of pundits and media talking heads. The trope of a divisive culture war was then employed in a speech by conservative commentator Pat Buchanan at the 1992 Republican National Convention (now dubbed the "culture war speech") in which he stated, "There is a religious war going on in our country for the soul of America. It is a cultural war, as critical to the kind of nation we will one day be as was the Cold War itself" (quoted in Utter 2009: 29).

This period was marked by mainstream media conversations that fixated on racial awareness and racial group relations (see Figure 3.2). That is, mainstream discussions over race in this period were characterized by a climate in which people were highly aware of race as a meaningful category of difference and a salient aspect of identity, coupled with discourse in which various racial groups' political positioning and interest were explicitly discussed in relationship to other racial groups. Hence, much of the discussion over race was implicitly framed by celebratory discussions of intergroup cooperation (multiculturalism) or that of intergroup conflict (culture wars). However, I do not wish to overstate this era's discussion of racial conflict. Rather, the defining feature of mainstream discussion of race, as measured by the discussion in the *New York Times*, was debate over the future of these racial groups in relation to one another and a tone of polite multiculturalism. Power, inequality, and domination were certainly a part of the conversation, but they did not dominate the national media yet. We would come to see a robust discussion of racial group threat and a reactionary white backlash in the next era (1993–1998), caused in part by high-profile racial media spectacles that were prefigured in the debate over affirmative action that hit federal courts and national airwaves in 1989 (*City of Richmond v. J.A. Croson Co.* and *Wards Cove Packing Co. v. Atonio*), the 1991 Clarence Thomas–Anita Hill congressional hearing that was described as a "high-tech lynching," and probably the most explosive events that shut the door on the era of polite multiculturalism, the 1991 Rodney King beating and subsequent Los Angeles race riots of 1992.

The films reviewed in this time span (110 reviews) were *Cry Freedom* (1987), *The Principal* (1987), *Mississippi Burning* (1988), *Rambo III* (1988), *A Dry White Season* (1989), *Glory* (1989), *Indiana Jones and the Last Crusade* (1989), *Dances with Wolves* (1990), *The Long Walk Home* (1990), *Black Robe* (1991), *City of Joy* (1992), *Medicine Man* (1992), and *Thunderheart* (1992) (see Table 3.1).

TABLE 3.1. THE (MULTI)CULTURAL WARS (1987–1992)

Frame or Theme No.	Frame or Theme Title	Ratio and Percentage of Reviews Discussing Frame or Theme
Frame AI	**Celebrating Difference**	**38/110 (34.54%)**
Theme 1	Interracial Friendship	21/110 (19.09%)
Theme 2	Diversity Overpowers Prejudice	17/110 (15.45%)
Frame AII	**Essentializing Difference**	**53/110 (48.18%)**
Theme 1	Exotic Others	22/110 (20.00%)
Theme 2	Critiquing Hollywood Racism	31/110 (28.18%)
Frame AIII	**Watching Whiteness**	**53/110 (48.18%)**
Theme 1	A White Point of View	19/110 (17.27%)
Theme 2	Attacking White Saviors	18/110 (16.36%)
Theme 3	Protecting White People	16/110 (14.55%)
Frame AIV	**White Historiography**	**67/110 (60.91%)**
Theme 1	Appeasing a White Audience	27/110 (24.55%)
Theme 2	Cinematic Authenticity	40/110 (36.36%)

Celebrating Difference

The sociologists Joyce Bell and Douglas Hartmann observe:

> Everyone in America—school administrators and business leaders, political activists, marketing gurus, and Supreme Court Justices—seems to be using the language of diversity these days. It is not just *that* Americans are talking about diversity that is extraordinary; it is *how* they are talking about it: extolling the virtues of difference, celebrating diversity as a value in itself, and describing diversity as the new cornerstone of American democratic idealism. (2007: 895)

To this list, we might add film reviewers. By far, the frame with the highest frequency was critics' interpretation that these films positively celebrated diversity and cooperative interaction across the color line. In specific, reviewers repeatedly made clear that racial and ethnic cooperation was an inherent good and saw intercultural, interethnic (especially interracial) cooperation as a laudable goal and a method for achieving peace and social harmony. Reviewers parsed such multicultural celebration into two themes: (1) interracial friendships and (2) the power of diversity to overcome injustice.

Interracial Friendship

Many reviewers emphasized the potency of interracial friendship. That is, they ritually and collectively underscored the beneficial and politically progressive decisions of these films to showcase interracial friendships. Moreover, reviewers often attributed moral and value-laden attributes to the characters in the film; the camaraderie between cultural border crossers was highlighted as a prime virtue. For example, in discussing the film *Dances with Wolves* (1990), Roger Ebert writes of the central white protagonist and the Native characters:

> They meet at first in the middle of the prairie, holding themselves formally and a little awkwardly, the cavalry officer and Sioux Indians. There should be instant mistrust between them, but they take each other's measure and keep an open mind. A civilized man is a person whose curiosity outweighs his prejudices, and these are curious men. (1990a)

And again, Ebert begins a review of *Cry Freedom* (1987) with the same emphasis: "'Cry Freedom' begins with the story of a friendship between a white liberal South African editor and an idealistic young black leader who later dies at the hands of the South African police" (1987).

Returning to *Dances with Wolves* (1990), the critic Mark R. Leeper centers his analysis on the main white character's dedication to both "accept and appreciate that which is alien to him." In turn, that devotion results in friendships that are continually reforged, despite the cinematic barriers put in the character's path. Leeper writes:

> Kevin Costner directs and stars as John Dunbar, who is to have his leg amputated due to wounds in a Civil War battle. Not having the courage to face his future, he attempts suicide and in doing so accidentally makes himself a hero. This not only wins him medical care sufficient to save his leg, he is also given his choice of posting. Wishing to see the Western frontier before it is overrun by the white man, he requests a posting to an isolated and deserted fort far out on the frontier. His thoughts about facing hostile animals and more hostile Sioux are overcome by his curiosity and his willingness to accept and appreciate that which is alien to him. The film picks up his enthusiasm to meet, understand, and befriend the very alien culture of the neighboring Sioux. He must first overcome their distrust. There the storyteller somewhat unrealistically contrives circumstances in Dunbar's favor. This is a long film and each stage of his acceptance by the Sioux is shown and not overly glossed over. In particular, language problems are quite believably difficult and eventually overcome by another contrivance. Eventually Dunbar is accepted into the Sioux society and Costner can show us how Sioux lived and thought. (1990)

Reviewers consistently returned to the theme of interracial friendship as the virtue of the film, even beyond that of the animating plot that precipitated or drove their friendship in the first place. For example, in *Entertainment Weekly* the critic Owen Gleiberman writes about *The Long Walk Home* (1990), a story about the 1955 Montgomery, Alabama, bus boycott. Gleiberman focuses on neither the film's depiction of the boycott nor the ideological forces at war.

Rather, the analysis is replete with references to the emotional outpourings and mutual decency that resulted from the interracial friendship of lead characters Odessa and Miriam:

> Gradually, as the boycott progresses, the two women's lives become intertwined. We're meant to see the continuity between Odessa's fight for racial equality and Miriam's dawning feminist consciousness. Yet neither character is held up as a role model. They are both, in their different ways, blessedly ordinary. And so *The Long Walk Home*, while not a work of great depth or imagination, is able to show us how the nagging physical reality of the boycott—the overwhelming inconvenience of it, for both blacks and whites—worked its way into the texture of people's lives, changing those lives forever. . . . When Miriam finally comes over to the cause of the boycotters, it's a vibrant, soul-stirring moment. The scene is presented as an emotional choice, not an ideological one (which is why it's convincing). And Odessa, understanding the sacrifice, cries even harder than Miriam does. In the end, *The Long Walk Home* isn't simply about whites transcending their own racism. It's about how blacks, in the midst of one of the most revolutionary episodes in American history, saw that not all their oppressors meant them harm. The true liberation was in realizing that decency could come from both sides. (Gleiberman 1991)

And Roger Ebert remarks:

> "The Long Walk Home" is a powerful and affecting film, so well played by Goldberg and Spacek that we understand not just the politics of the time but the emotions as well. In a way, this movie takes up where "Driving Miss Daisy" leaves off. Both are about affluent white Southern women who pride themselves on their humanitarian impulses, but who are brought to a greater understanding of racial discrimination—gently, tactfully and firmly—by their black employees. (1991)

Whether in consideration of the U.S. civil rights movement of the 1950s, South African apartheid in the 1980s, or U.S. westward expansion in the 1800s, these reviews draw on the theme of interracial friendship as a central and valuable aspect of the film. Reviewers' patterned insistence on highlighting interracial inclusivity, closeness, and ardor certainly indicates what this community of critics values and, in turn, what they believe audiences should know.

Diversity Overpowers Prejudice

Reviewers were concerned with not only interracial friendship but also how films presented intercultural and interracial unity as a socially transformative power. In his examination of *Dances with Wolves* (1990), Chris Hicks of the *Deseret News* accentuates how the open-mindedness and commitment to intercultural sensitivity and exploration were hallmarks of the main characters and stood as the driving mechanism of the cinematic plot. To many critics, such multicultural ideals and on-screen diversity seem to automatically or easily supplant the racial and imperialist prejudices of the setting and require little to no explanation or critique. Rather, they are presented as straightforward and believable representations of historical episodes. For example, Hicks writes:

> Costner stars as Lt. John Dunbar, an inadvertent Civil War hero who can choose his own assignment. He soon finds himself in an outpost in the middle of "Indian territory," where he keeps a journal of his experiences as he rebuilds the fort, encounters a friendly wolf and eventually meets with Sioux tribal leaders. What follows is a tentative relationship that begins with fear and distrust on both sides, gradually evolving into friendship. Dunbar is expecting "savages" but instead finds a commune of people bonded together by mutual respect, tradition and family love. (1998)

And again in consideration of *Dances with Wolves*, Roger Ebert writes:

> In 1985, before he was a star, Costner played a featured role in a good Western called "Silverado" simply because he wanted to be in a Western. Now he has realized his dream again by making one of the best Westerns I've seen. The movie makes amends, of a sort, for hundreds of racist and small-minded Westerns that went before it. By allowing the Sioux to speak in their own tongue, by entering their villages and observing their ways, it sees them as people, not as whooping savages in the sights of an Army rifle. This is one of the year's best films. (1990a)

Such interracial contact nearly appears as a magical force in reviewers' assessments. In writing of a mixed-race character who is "one-quarter-Indian" but who has "never come to terms with his heritage—he's pure anglo" in *Thunderheart* (1992), one reviewer wrote approvingly of the racial transformation the lead character (played by Val Kilmer) experienced after spending time at a Native American reservation:

> And he will learn a lot, of course, including a voyage of self-discovery that will encompass his American Indian background. And he will find that life on the reservation is much more volatile than he ever imagined. Meanwhile, tribal cop Greene baits him, calling him "Little Weasel" and trying to get under his skin. But Greene recognizes that there is something inside Kilmer, and there may be a reason he's been sent there. This leads to Kilmer striking up a reluctant relationship with the tribe's medicine man (Chief Ted Thin Elk) and an activist who is also a single mother (Sheila Tousey). . . . Though [John Fusco's] script is weak in its mystery, [the film has] . . . a rich backdrop, with fascinating character development and a serious focus on the spirituality of Indian beliefs. The result is a sometimes

humorous and often thoughtful film with more depth than you might expect. (Hicks 1992)

Reviewers' collective agreement in the power of diversity was marked by
two general discursive points. First, reviewers generally contend that these
films' display of cooperation across the color line told powerful stories about
the depth of the human condition. Beneath the cultural and racial differences
displayed, these films' portrayal of struggling characters, mired in existential
and ontological angst about the meaning of life and their place in the world,
could be solved by meaningful friendships informed by the plurality of traditions and ideological viewpoints that stem from the meeting ground of different cultures. Second, and building off the first, critics argued that such
messages were a positive good that audiences should consume for their own
development. That is, critics saw these films as potent reflections of the evils
of how the world is and how the world could and should be different. Critics
hailed such on-screen diversity as a teaching and learning guide. For critics,
these films contained an inherent pedagogical value whereby their privileging
of overt diversity and intercultural contact transformed the silver screen into
a blackboard on which writers' and directors' films qua lectures could impart
valuable lessons and make a better-informed citizenry.

Essentializing Difference

An all-too-common consequence of the Westernized practices of multiculturalism is the tendency to essentialize race. Racial essentialism is an ideology and
practice that posits a permanent, natural, or fixed relationship between racial
group characteristics and traits (e.g., skin color and intelligence) that discounts
or marginalizes intragroup variation and heterogeneity. This practice often ar-
ranges the supposed natural qualities of racial groups in a hierarchy based on
lighter-skinned and European-descended superiority in terms of intelligence,
morality, and cultural values. At the same time, racial essentialist claims have
provided a foundation for marginalized groups. Given that strong internal differences and debates may exist within a particular racial group, it is sometimes politically expedient to galvanize group unity and identity under a simplified claim
to a natural and fixed collective identity. Given this interpretation of race, nonwhite "otherness" is often framed as more authentic, potent, unique, or meaningful identity compared with the invisible normality of whiteness. Indeed, the
presence of such on-screen "color capital" (Hughey 2012) was often highlighted
by critics as a special and nearly magical accoutrement to the films' stories.

Exotic Others

In attempting to draw attention to the on-screen diversity and multiculturalism of 1980s and early 1990s films, many reviewers often essentialized white
and nonwhite cinematic characters. In particular, because of the strange

intersection of multiculturalism and essentialism, reviewers often framed non-white people (their appearance, worldviews, and culture) in exotic terms. For example, Janet Maslin of the *New York Times* writes:

> The "Washington redskin" of "Thunderheart," as he is derisively called by the film's American Indian characters, is an F.B.I. agent who is sent from Washington to an Oglala Sioux reservation to investigate a crime. Raymond Levoi (Val Kilmer) does not welcome this assignment. Part Sioux himself, and too culturally assimilated to acknowledge that heritage, he resents having been selected for the job on the basis of his background. He refers contemptuously to various Indians as "Geronimo" and "Tonto" as a means of registering his unfamiliarity with their world. But during the course of the story, Ray is freed from his high-handed superiority to Indian culture, made to understand the many problems of the violence-torn Indian community (the film is set in the late 1970's) and forced to accept his own past. "The same blood that was spilled in the grass and snow at Wounded Knee runs through your heart like a buffalo," he is told by one of the story's far more spiritually aware Indian characters.... In paying its respects to that figurative family and its traditions, the film depicts a large ceremonial powwow, a sweat lodge ceremony and other authentic aspects of Indian life, including the rusted-out trailers and appalling medical facilities that are present-day features. The reservation is pointedly described by one character as "a third world right here in America." (1992b)

Here, the reviewer emphasizes the journey that Anglo-assimilated Raymond Levoi takes toward reclaiming his authentic Indian self. The reviewer does acknowledge Ray's relinquishment of anti-Indian stereotypes (calling other Indians "Geronimo" and "Tonto," the latter Spanish for "stupid"). Yet she places the remedy for this superiority in the contact with the "spiritually aware" Indians—a robust stereotype of romantic sentimentalism that views Native people as noble savages possessing a natural connection to mysticism and ethical values.

This trope repeated again in other reviewers' interpretations of films about white-Native interactions. In *Movieline*, Stephen Farber writes of *Dances with Wolves*:

> Costner the director does an impressive job with scenes of spectacle—battles, tribal rituals, an amazing buffalo hunt. The film has special value for kids who need a lesson in the darker underside of American history. It will seem less novel to older moviegoers, but even those of us who grew up with *Broken Arrow* or *Cheyenne Autumn* or *A Man Called Horse* or *Little Big Man* will be affected by Costner's heartfelt tribute to this vanished culture. (1990)

Many reviewers exoticized and essentialized nonwhite otherness relative to the supposed apolitical and boring normality of whiteness. However, not all critics engaged in such an intersubjectively shared interpretation.

Critiquing Hollywood Racism

The commitment to diversity and multiculturalism, not just in an abstract sense, but in relation to social justice and equality, was manifest in reviewers' comments. This obligation seemed to stem the tendency to racially essentialize, but its frequency waned over the era of the (multi)cultural wars (1987–1992). In critiquing the choices of *Thunderheart*'s director (Michael Apted) and John Fusco's script, the critic Mark Leeper writes:

> Twenty-five years ago this would have been a good script but it has been used, with variations, just too often. And the Indians who have been handed so many injustices deserve a better story. . . . And for one more cheap shot, the film leaves ambiguous if Indian magic might be working. I thought that went out with BILLY JACK. Native Americans don't have any magic any more than anyone else does. I wish they did. Maybe if they did, they could use it to get some justice. But Apted uses trick photography and staged scenes to imply you really can see ghost dancers who disappear in a flash or to imply that a man might have turned himself into a deer. Indians are not great magical people who live half in a spirit world. They are just a group of ethnic peoples who have been cheated and exploited and who desperately need a little bit of justice. Throwing them a bone by implying that their magic really breaks the laws of physics is just not what they need. If enough people confuse compassion for American Indians with liking this film, Tri-Star Pictures could make a bundle of money, almost none of which will go to help the Indians. (1992)

In a review of *Dances with Wolves*, Sandra J. Grossman argues:

> The whites are portrayed as such barbarians and the Sioux as such noble humans that Dunbar never has moments of doubt. Why should he? Instead of Dunbar being pulled in two directions, the medicine man is the one who has to weigh both sides and make the telling decision in the film. That is so very very wrong. (1990)

And Owen Gleiberman states:

> If you're in the mood to see a leisurely paced, three-hour hippie Western about a Union soldier who drops out of the Civil War, joins a tribe of noble and reverent Sioux, and comes to see that the Indians are In Touch With Life in a way that white men aren't, you could probably do worse than Kevin Costner's Dances With Wolves. . . . Working from a script by Michael Blake, who adapted his own novel, he comes up with a ploddingly "mythic" story that never succeeds in portraying the Indians as full-fledged human beings. . . . Essentially, *Dances With Wolves* is *Robinson Crusoe* with a tribeful of Fridays. The Indians come off as photogenic saints, which is almost as patronizing as the "we smokum peace pipe" clichés Costner is trying to undo. (1990)

In reviews such as these, the notion that Native peoples possess an essentialist connection to nature, magic, or spirituality is directly contested. Moreover, the reviewers took the stance that such films perpetuate erroneous and dangerous racial and ethnic ideologies that further marginalizes them in the off-screen, real world.

A few reviewers also connect such exoticism to the sexualizing of women of color and situate the film in question in a long ling of Occidental narratives that depict the non-Westernized world through a series of crude and essentialist caricatures that, in turn, risk rationalizing their takeover as vulgarized playthings to satisfy white cultural tourism. For example, Vincent Canby of the *New York Times* writes:

> "City of Joy" probably means well, but it exemplifies the worst kind of simple-minded Occidental literature, in which India exists to be a vast, teeming rehab center where emotionally troubled Americans can find themselves. Or, at least, those Americans who have the time and the money to fly off to India instead of taking a bus to a local clinic. (1992)

And in reviewing *Medicine Man* (1992), the *New York Times* contends:

> Shot in Mexico and featuring an extensive Brazilian Indian cast and crew, "Medicine Man" includes enough derring-do and jungle exotica to have appealed to children. Mr. McTiernan's insistence on using the near-naked Indians for cheesecake purposes (there are many playful shots of the rumps of Indian women as they perform various tribal rituals) greatly reduces the film's suitablility [*sic*] for young viewers. (Maslin 1992a)

These reviewers do not hold back their criticism of Hollywood's prostitution of exoticized racial and cultural images meant to titillate audiences. These reviews indicate a judgment in which these films' display of on-screen diversity is neither an apolitical aesthetic choice nor a neutral celebration of difference but a vehicle for the delivery of problematic ideological messages.

Watching Whiteness

When the vast majority of critics speak of race explicitly, they speak of people of color. Whiteness often goes unnamed. However, in this era of the (multi) cultural wars, the question of where whiteness fits in the equation of increasing on-screen diversity, coupled with questions of power and paternalism, is occasionally broached.

A White Point of View

A substantive percentage of reviews recognize that many films tell stories from one racial groups' position while excluding others; although many of the films center on the trials and tribulations of various nonwhite communities, they tell the story from the point of view of the white character. Critics are adamant that such a standpoint skewed the cinematic plot and conflict. For example, writing of *Cry Freedom* (1987), Roger Ebert contends:

> The problem with this movie is similar to the dilemma in South Africa: Whites occupy the foreground and establish the terms of the discussion, while the 80 percent nonwhite majority remains a shadowy, half-seen presence in the background. . . . Although Biko is played with quiet power by Denzel Washington, he is seen primarily through the eyes of Woods (Kevin Kline). There aren't many scenes in which we see Biko without Woods, and fewer still in which his friendship with Woods isn't the underlying subject of the scene. (1987)

Such dynamics are observed with frequency. Reviewers often begin their reviews by highlighting the problem of standpoint both on and off screen, as Ebert noted (e.g., "The problem with this movie is similar to the dilemma in South Africa"). Again, in a review of *Glory* (1989), Ebert writes:

> Watching "Glory," I had one recurring problem. I didn't understand why it had to be told so often from the point of view of the 54th's white commanding officer. Why did we see the black troops through his eyes—instead of seeing him through theirs? To put it another way, why does the top billing in this movie go to a white actor? I ask, not to be perverse, but because I consider this primarily a story about a black experience and do not know why it has to be seen largely through white eyes. (1990b)

Cinematic parallels with real-life racial dynamics are troubling to many a reviewer, and served to change the film from mere entertainment to that of racial propaganda. For example, Jim Emerson, writing in *Cinepad*, states of *Mississippi Burning*:

> Most of the debate surrounding the film has focused on the way it distorts key events in the history of the civil rights movement. Set in the same year that Martin Luther King received his Nobel Peace Prize, *Mississippi Burning* concentrates on the efforts of two white FBI agents—Willen [*sic*] Dafoe as agent Ward and Gene Hackman as agent Anderson—to find the Ku Klux Klan killers of James Chaney, Andrew Goodman, and Michael Schwerner, a black man and two whites. . . . In so doing, [Alan] Parker's propaganda picture implies that white liberal vigilantes in the FBI—not organized coalitions of blacks and whites dedicated to Dr. King's moral policy of nonviolence—were the ones righteously carrying the banner for civil rights in the South during the '60s, ready to fight for the cause at any cost. (1988)

As Emerson makes clear, director Alan Parker makes the civil rights movement into a kind of action film that tells the story from the point of view of white do-gooders who possess the right moral fiber to turn against the racists within their own race and bureau. Such misinformation and half-truths are also discussed as being par for the course, given the legacy of racist Hollywood filmmaking:

> Whoopi Goldberg is the dominant force in "The Long Walk Home," though Sissy Spacek is top-billed and receives equal screen time in this look at the early days of the civil rights movement. That says more about Hollywood than anything else, as movies reflecting incidents in black history continue to be told from a white point of view. (Hicks 2000)

These reviews point out that the narrative arc of any given film curves in relation to the point of view of the storyteller. Critics often illuminate how these films conflate white points of view as a neutral or omniscient worldview, thereby obfuscating the views of those on the underside of that narrative arc.

Attacking White Saviors

Many reviewers identify a lopsided point of view, but only a few recognize how a particular white character serves as a messianic savior to the characters of color. For example, Vincent Canby of the *New York Times* writes:

> "Dances With Wolves" has the makings of a great work, one that recalls a variety of literary antecedents, everything from "Robinson Crusoe" and "Walden" to "Tarzan of the Apes." Michael Blake's screenplay touches both on man alone in nature and on the 19th-century white man's assuming his burden among the less privileged. (1990)

Canby recognizes the presence of an old racial trope: the white man's burden. Such a device proposes that white people possess a moral obligation to rule over people of color given their supposed deficiencies and dysfunctions in relation to the superiority of white Western culture and government. As the film critic Frank Maloney writes of *City of Joy* (1992):

> The mere presence of a Western man in this third-world story sets off alarms; certainly, [Roland] Joffe's MISSION suffered from the white-messiah syndrome, as have most movies about apartheid in the last several years. . . . To be fair, Joffe and [Mark] Medoff seem somewhat aware of this and ensure that [Patrick] Swayze never wins a fight and that his life is saved by an Indian. Still he does tend to lecture the Indians about standing up to the Godfather who rules their lives. (1992)

Reviewers even highlight how the physical appearance of the lead white characters, coupled with characters' relationship to religious institutions and allusions, evokes the trope of the white savior. Writing of the main character of *Rambo III* (1988), Hal Hinson of the *Washington Post* concludes:

He's grown his hair longer this time out, and this, together with the sleepy, suffering eyes, makes him resemble a Caravaggio Christ—but with pecs. . . . [S]tarting with the opening scenes . . . we learn that Rambo has traveled to Thailand to become a Buddhist. Rambo's not your ordinary Eastern holy person, though. Every once in a while he journeys into Bangkok to whup the locals at stick fighting to raise money to help the monks build a monastery. Indeed, there are many paths to God. (1988)

Similarly, Janet Maslin contends that *Rambo III* possesses

a messianic streak, a pious tone and a bad tendency toward false modesty. . . . Mr. Stallone, having pumped his way to body-building perfection, has written (with Sheldon Lettich) for himself the latter-day narcissist's version of a John Wayne role, and forcefully re-invented the western to accommodate the character's munitions-mad, avenging-angel style. (1988)

Returning to *Dances with Wolves*, Stephen Farber of *Movieline* writes:

There's nothing inherently wrong with the idea of drawing us into Indian society through a white outsider, but the scenes depicting the Sioux culture are far more vivid than the personal story of Costner's John Dunbar. He emerges as a plaster saint—a 19th century flower child. With a running time of three hours, *Dances With Wolves* aspires to be a *Lawrence of Arabia* of the prairie. (1990)

Undoubtedly, these critics are not savvy sociologists able to deconstruct the nuances of white racial identity as played out in these films. However, they are quite able to call out the intrusive, paternalistic, and messianic white savior characters that stalk these cinematic landscapes.

Protecting White People

Many of the reviewers clearly identify the problematic aspects of these films: a story told from a narrow point of view that deified white heroes. Still, not all critics engage in such a reading of these films. Rather, many reviewers take the films to task for portraying whiteness in too harsh a light. Some critics bristle at films that paint white people as racially insensitive or as the recipients of racial privilege, even when those films take on subject matter as incendiary as the assassination of U.S. and international black civil rights leaders or topics as racially charged as the U.S. policy of manifest destiny against Native Americans. Numerous critics are quick to label negative representations of white people as exaggerated, misanthropic, or even racist.

The critic Mark R. Leeper writes of *Dances with Wolves* (1990), "If the film has a major weakness it is that it exaggerates the stupidity and strangeness (even if not the cruelty) of the hordes of invading white men. The positive view of the

Sioux would be more believable if the view of the White Man had more cred-ibility" (1990). Amy Dawes of *Variety* finds the depiction in *Dances with Wolves* of nineteenth-century Union Army whites as a "loutish and brutal mob" to be the "pic's weakest and most manipulative passage" (1990). Along these same lines, Jim Emerson's review of *Mississippi Burning* (1988) finds the film's depic-tion of whites entirely misguided:

> In contrast [to the film's representation of blacks], white Southerners are invariably presented in freak-show close-up as sweat-drenched, no-neck monsters—inbred gargoyles on parade. Parker brags in the film's press kit about the rogue's gallery of casting photos he kept on his wall for the film. He doesn't even seem to realize that his vision is not only racist, it's misan-thropic. Making the Klan the villains and the blacks the victims (definitely *not* the heroes in this picture) is meaningless when you treat both as if they were undifferentiated subhuman cyphers. (1988)

When Mark Leeper and Desson Howe individually reviewed *The Long Walk Home* (1990), they concluded that the film flattened out depictions of whites in 1950s Alabama as unfairly caricatured and even as racist. Leeper writes:

> With the exception of Miriam and her children, whites are uniformly por-trayed as being racist, telling racist jokes, and being hypocritical. Blacks are all honest church-going people, wonderful to each other in closely-knit families. While these stereotypes may be substantially correct, the portrayal makes it a little overly obvious where the audience's sympathies should lie. (1991)

And Howe writes:

> The social message in "Walk Home" is unmistakable. The villains (racist cops, bigoted relatives) may huff and puff for most of the movie, but the vic-tims (Goldberg, her family and the black movement) will not be blown over. Their glowing moral triumph by movie's end is a bankable certainty. (1991)

Of note is Leeper's statement that, even though the stereotype of whites as "uniformly" racist "may be substantially correct," the film goes too far in its cinematic framing. In other words, a story about the Montgomery bus boycott should not let too much truth get in the way of a good story.

In these reviews, an explicit defense of whiteness emerges. This shield man-ifests mostly in films that showcase a white defense of racist and segregation-ist structures about the black-led civil rights movement in the United States. Quite ironically, a parallel defense of people of color is nearly absent, except in reviewers' critique of films for exoticizing Native Americans or portraying nonwhite people outside the United States (e.g., India or Brazil) in a narrow and Eurocentric fashion. Accordingly, these reviews indicate that, in the midst of the declining support for multiculturalism, and in the beginning stages of the culture wars over the place and potential of racial diversity in curricula and culture, reviewers are certainly swayed by a mounting discourse that white people and white cultural traditions are unfairly represented and under attack. Indeed, reviewers support multiculturalism, but only so far. They seem to balk at films that focus on white racism or that uncover the gruesome details of white supremacy when directed at blacks in the Jim Crow United States or during South African apartheid.

White Historiography

Many of these so-called white savior films are based on a true story, a point that rarely eludes reviewers. Given that film functions as a kind of historiographer (Hayden White [1988] more properly call is it "historiophoty" to describe the representation of history in visual images and filmic discourse), film stands as one of our contemporary moment's most potent (mis)educational institutions. In specific, film defines our "collective memory" of the past and profoundly affects the ways we make sense of the present (Bodnar 2001). Visual media sustains memory through a continuous production of representations (Bodnar 2001; Monteith 2003; Morgan 2006; Griffin and Hargis 2008). In an era of widely disseminated filmmaking, wherein digitalization has dislodged cinematic consumption from theater going, more people now participate in the economy of cinematic racial history. Importantly, film does not simply interpret our racial past but makes it. Film promotes a kind of memory consensus. Given the fever pitch of debates over race and diversity in the period (1987–1992), reviewers possessed an important function—they stood as important cultural interpreters, tour guides, and authority figures who possessed the ability to either authenticate or debunk cinematic representations of racial history amid a raging battle for control over history and the present.

In two broad, and somewhat contradictory, strokes, reviewers signal two significant outcomes of these films' reliance on claims to accurate historical representation. First, some reviewers see these films as politicized forms of historical revisionism. They criticize these films for depicting controversial race relations and racial history in a way that takes pains not to confront white audiences with their legacy as beneficiaries of a racially unjust social order. Second, reviewers seem to take many of these films at their face value. That is, many hail these films as accurate and authentic depictions of triumphant encounters with racism that are solved though interracial commitments to equality and justice.

Appeasing a White Audience

Critics are often sarcastic, writing that these films are watered-down and overly sentimental depictions of turbulent racial times that leave audiences feeling good about how far they have (or have not) come in race relations. For example,

Owen Gleiberman of *Entertainment Weekly* states, "*The Long Walk Home* is a dramatization of those bitter and heroic months of struggle—in other words, it has the sort of surefire liberal-message-movie subject matter that can easily turn preachy" (1991). And in reviewing *Mississippi Burning*, the critic Jeff Meyer opines, "Watching DaFoe and Hackman ride off into the sunset, with black and white children singing together, is sugar-coating what happened in the worst way; it's almost as if Parker had never left advertising for feature films. Like, shouldn't they be holding cans of Diet Coke?" (1989). In this same vein, several critics take to task *Cry Freedom*'s diversion of the story of black South African human rights activist Steven Biko into the story of the white journalist Donald Woods. Manavendra K. Thakur argues:

> Biko's death comes almost exactly halfway through the film. In order to make the film palatable to Westerners—which is to say white audiences— the second half of the film concentrates on the Woods family as they flee South Africa and the personal turmoil Biko's death has created for them. . . . There is no denying that Mr. Woods and his family suffered greatly during their ordeal, and their story deserves to be told as well. The film, however, trivializes and cheapens their escape from South Africa by degenerating into an inane melodrama worthy of a made-for-TV movie. The film goes so out of its way to help audiences identify with the Woods family that it becomes self-apparent and almost begins to wallow in cheap sentimentality. (1987)

Janet Maslin of the *New York Times* writes, "It is most unfortunate that this film, with its potential for focusing worldwide attention on the plight of black South Africans, should concentrate its energies on a white man" (1987). And in the *Washington Post*, Desson Howe remarked:

> From here on, the movie centers on Woods—at once its major flaw. As scripted, and despite Kline's efforts, Woods pales—so to speak—against Denzel ("A Soldier's Story") Washington's Biko. When Biko dies halfway through, so does the movie. The Woods family's subsequent flight from South Africa becomes the cinematic equivalent of a Gerald Ford presidency. (1987)

Not all critics see this film as a hollow ploy to make the rather incendiary figure of Biko palatable to white audiences by concentrating on his friendship with a white journalist. Also writing for the *Washington Post*, Rita Kemply argues:

> Attenborough has been criticized for the second half, an action thriller that tags a white hero onto what some felt was a black hero's story. But that's a little like whipping Paul Simon for introducing Ladysmith BlackMambazo to American audiences. In both cases, the ends justify the means. And here that end is to expose the spiritual and physical genocide of apartheid. South

Africa hides behind a press blackout; "Cry Freedom" exposes it in the bright and persuasive light of Biko's consciousness. (1987)

While a commitment to a potent and justice-oriented multiculturalism is dominant here, some critics (as Kemply's review indicates) simply describe the film's use of a white protagonist as a device to bring audiences to the theater to achieve the end goal of illuminating injustice. Such accounts frame filmmaking as a kind of popular culture journalism to report inequality. Whether the film perpetuates its own bias is often left untouched. For example, in taking on another film about South African apartheid, *A Dry White Season*, Peter Travers of *Rolling Stone* remarks that film on this topic is burdened by having to place white actors in top-billed positions to interest white audiences:

> Brando is the reason many will see this film. [Euzhan] Palcy knows that. She also knows that once he departs early on, it will be her job to keep [whites] there. She's resoundingly up to the task. But oh, the odds. The two most recent movies about apartheid—"Cry Freedom," "A World Apart"— failed to win an audience. They were criticized for centering on white protagonists at the expense of blacks. Palcy hasn't entirely licked the problem. "A Dry White Season," a 1979 novel by South African writer Andre Brink, also concentrated on white consciousness-raising. But Palcy, who adapted the book, has made some crucial changes in focus. Du Toit, sympathetically acted by Sutherland, is still a major figure. (1989)

Still, most critics are unsympathetic to the use of white characters to tell black stories, even if they recognize that burden of selling explicitly race-based films to white audiences. For example, in reviewing *The Long Walk Home*, Roger Ebert remarks:

> Because the movie does center some of its important scenes inside the black household, it's all the more surprising that it uses the gratuitous touch of a white "narrator"—apparently to reassure white audiences the movie is "really" intended for them. The narrator is Spacek's teenage daughter, who has no role of any importance in the movie and whose narration adds nothing except an unnecessary point of view. When she talks about her memories of "my mother," we want to know why Goldberg's daughter doesn't have equal time. She probably has more interesting memories. (1991)

As Ebert's example shows, some critics still pan the device as both artistically clumsy and as unnecessary—thereby demonstrating a firm commitment to diversity and multiculturalism as a value in and of itself.

Cinematic Authenticity

When a film is based on a true story, it carries a certain cultural cachet. Juxtaposed relative to the hundreds of fictional stories made to titillate and entertain, such films possess a special legitimacy. Authenticity, as Walter Benjamin ([1936] 1968) claims, requires "uniqueness." That is, the authenticity of any given thing, that which distinguishes it from anything else, needs a "distance" from the everyday and mundane. That which is authentic approaches the sacred. The cultural anthropologist Richard Handler writes, "Contact with authentic pieces of culture . . . allows us to appropriate their authenticity, incorporating their magical proof of existence into what we call our 'personal experience'" (1986: 4). Accordingly, an audience may consume these vulgarized artifacts of history and witness them as if they were there, and with the added weight of critics legitimating their stories, they experience them as more than an ounce of truth.

When critics such as Roger Ebert write of the American Indian Movement and Indians' still-colonized and segregated status on reservations alongside the militant responses from the federal government in the 1970s, their words speak to not only the aesthetics of *Thunderheart* (1992) but also the event represented in it. In reviewing *Thunderheart*, Ebert writes:

> What's most absorbing about "Thunderheart" is its sense of place and time. [Michael] Apted makes documentaries as well as fiction films, and in such features as "Coal Miner's Daughter" and "Gorillas in the Mist" and such documentaries as "35 Up" he pays great attention to the people themselves—not just what they do, and how that pushes things along. In "Thunderheart" we get a real visual sense of the reservation, of the beauty of the rolling prairie and the way it is interrupted by deep gorges, but also of the omnipresent rusting automobiles and the subsistence level of some of the housing. We feel that we're really there, and that the people in the story really occupy land they stand on. (1992)

The long and glowing review of *Thunderheart* in the *New York Times* applauds the film's "authenticity" and the director's ability to make a "fact-filled exposition":

> Michael Apted, the remarkable documentary film maker ("35 Up") whose dramatic films often have an anthropological accuracy ("Coal Miner's Daughter," "Gorillas in the Mist"), addresses himself to life on an Indian reservation with the same curiosity and intelligence he has brought to other subjects. Mr. Apted displays too much respect for his material to overdramatize it or otherwise create a Hollywood gloss. Though "Thunderheart" is about a murder investigation and has the shape of a thriller, it also has a documentary's attentiveness to detail. . . . Filmed on the Pine Ridge Reservation in South Dakota (which is called the Bear Creek Reservation in the movie), "Thunderheart" is loosely based on violent events that took place there and elsewhere during the 1970's. The film employs many Indian actors, some of whose screen roles mirror their real lives. . . . A film this intent on authenticity might easily grow dull, but this one doesn't; Mr. Apted is a skillful storyteller. He gives "Thunderheart" a brisk, fact-filled exposition

and a dramatic structure that builds to a strong finale, one that effectively drives the film's message home. (Maslin 1992b)

Reviewers' affection for these films' commitment to telling the marginalized stories of people of color often lead them to dismiss the historical inaccuracies represented. They instructed audiences not to get bogged down in the details but to focus on the larger thesis of the films: interracial and intercultural cooperation. For example, in reviewing the film *Glory* (1989), the story of the 54th Regiment Massachusetts Volunteer Infantry (one of the first black units that saw service in the U.S. Civil War), the critic Michelle Perry urges audiences to focus not on the director's spotlight of Matthew Broderick as the white leader Colonel Robert Shaw but instead on the interracial cooperative "struggle":

> Some criticism has been directed at [Edward] Zwick because of the emphasis placed on the white characters in the story. A quick glance at *Glory* may reveal it to fit into the mold of recent anti-apartheid films, which portray blacks fighting under the guidance of white mentors. However, *Glory* is not about white officers in charge of a black regiment. It is about a group of black men who are training for combat and the interaction of white soldiers and black soldiers as they struggle towards a common goal. (1990)

Moreover, both the *Washington Post* and the *New York Times* reviews of *The Long Walk Home* hail the film's capacity to accurately capture the racism of the 1950s South alongside a struggle for civil rights that must seem, according to the reviews, a gargantuan feat because of racism's entrenched normality. The *Washington Post* review states:

> Racism is so ingrained here that it's like an aspect of natural law, as inexorable as gravity. What the civil rights movement did was nothing less than alter the physics of the South, and what "The Long Walk Home" shows is just how nearly inconceivable it was that the movement would succeed, that progress could ever have been made. (Hinson 1991)

The *New York Times* review notes:

> In attempting to present segregated Southern society matter-of-factly, it avoids shrillness and keeps its potential for preachiness more or less at bay. Its points are made best through startling understatement, as when a Thompson relative at Christmas dinner declares, "Those niggers just want too much and they're not willing to work for it." Odessa, serving dinner, overhears the remark, then blankly offers this woman a roll. The woman stares back at her without a trace of an apology. (Maslin 1990)

Reviews of film critics in the (multi)cultural wars era display strong support of multiculturalism, via their belief in the morality and progressive trend of interracial on-screen cooperation, and critique racist stereotypes (particularly those of Native Americans). They also negatively appraise select white characters' messianic and paternalistic roles in films ostensibly about people of color, their attitudes, worldviews, struggles, and stories. Yet in line with the rising culture wars that would soon break into a full-fledged white backlash (see the next section in this chapter), these reviewers vociferously defend many of the representations of whiteness. When they judge films as painting too harsh a picture of white characters, they are quick to pounce on the lack of aesthetic, historical, and social value of these films. Such a defense of people of color (with the few exceptions of critiquing the noble savage stereotype of American Indians) is largely absent. Hence, these reviewers, as an interpretive community, are largely influenced by the dominant racial discourse at play and labor to entrench and rationalize the cultural logic of race that was slowly morphing into a white backlash by the mid-1990s.

The White Backlash (1993–1998)

Until the mid-1990s, there was a clear trend across Western democracies, such as the United States, toward the increased recognition and accommodation of diversity. A variety of policies and laws that defended minority rights came to mark the slow rejection of a racially homogeneous nation-state. But by the mid-1990s, a concerted white backlash had saturated mainstream discourse. As the feminist scholar Susan Faludi writes:

> "Backlashes" . . . have always been triggered by the perception—accurate or not—that women are making great strides . . . efforts that have been interpreted time and again by men—especially men grappling with real threats to their economic and social well-being on other fronts—as spelling their own masculine doom. (1991: xix)

Although offered as an explanation to gender dynamics in the face of the modern challenge to patriarchy, Faludi's observation pertains to race in general and whiteness in specific, in that a white backlash is an attempt to retract the handful of small and hard-won victories for people of color. The sociologist Abby Ferber also writes, "Central to this backlash is a sense of confusion over the meanings of both masculinity and whiteness, triggered by the perceived loss of white, male privilege" (1999: 31). The white backlash rhetoric is marked by phrases such as "reverse racism" and the "decline of civilization." In step with the backlash and retreat from multiculturalism is the reassertion of ideas of "nation building" and "common values" and even calls for a return to "Anglo assimilation." This retreat was partly driven by white fears that the accommodation of diversity had simply gone too far and was threatening a decidedly white-dominated way of life and worldview.

This period also witnessed a rampant move toward "hyper-segregation" (Massey and Denton 1993), and mainstream news media was repeating the summation that the nation was now "racially polarized" (Tuch and Martin 1997). This racial culture war, preceded by prior civil rights gains and the banner of multiculturalism and followed by the rising white backlash, was palpable. Jennifer Fuller writes:

> In the 1990s, fears of racial fracture and desires for racial reconciliation converged. . . . Clearly the nineties was not the first era in which people feared the nation was somehow "falling apart." . . . The rediscovery of racism and a racial divide between blacks and whites threatened America's new sense of itself as a successfully integrated nation. (2006: 167, 169)

Again, mainstream news media focused much of its attention on racialized media spectacles to portray a nation bitterly divided by black and white. In 1994 O. J. Simpson was accused of a double homicide of his wife and her friend (both white), and in 1995 the courtroom finale was broadcast to an estimated 150 million people (approximately 57 percent of the U.S. population at the time[2]), complete with split-screen views of predominantly black and white audiences to capture their vastly different reactions to news of the verdict (Hunt 1999). That same year, Louis Farrakhan and the Nation of Islam held the Million Man March on the National Mall in Washington D.C. Just one week after the march, journalist Howard Fineman observed:

> In entertainment, advertising, sports and most workplaces, integration is the order of our day. In films, Denzel Washington commands millions for roles that having nothing to do with skin color. . . . But in politics, the ideal of integration is a spent force. Americans of all colors seem exhausted by the effort to come this far, and embittered by the new brand of race-based obsessions that have developed along the way. (1995: 32)

The April 3, 1995, issue of *Newsweek* ran a cover showing two black and white fists pushing against one another underneath the headline "Race and Rage." And by 1996 media was reporting an epidemic of black church arsons that led Congress to pass the Church Arson Prevention Act in 1996. Frequent news stories throughout the 1990s highlighted the supposed pathology of black-on-black crime and gang warfare, a supposition exacerbated by a moral panic over the popularity of gangsta rap and the war on drugs (Hughey 2009).

The white backlash also manifested in opposition to policies and initiatives to promote social uplift among a decidedly nonwhite lower class. On July 19, 1995, *NBC Nightly News* anchor Tom Brokaw said, "Affirmative action: two words that can start an argument just about anywhere in America. . . . We'll be hearing a lot more about this in the months leading to the 1996 election." Accordingly, in 1996 the white-led backlash against affirmative action activated

---

2. The U.S. population in mid-1995 was estimated at 263,064,000 (U.S. Census Bureau 1997).

Proposition 209 in California—a law that effectively abolished affirmative action programs.

With Democrat Bill Clinton the U.S. president, the neoconservative parties driving this challenge to multiculturalism introduced, just six weeks before the 1994 congressional election, their Contract with America, of which Newt Gingrich stated, "There is no comparable congressional document in our two-hundred-year history" (quoted in Hannity 2010: 170).[3] The chief political columnist for the *New York Times*, R. W. Apple (1986), wrote in a front-page news analysis, "Perhaps not since the start of the New Deal [in 1932], to which many of the programs now under attack can trace their origins, has Congress moved with such speed on so many fronts." A cornerstone of the contract was the Personal Responsibility and Work Opportunity Reconciliation Act of 1996, which shifted both the method of delivery and goal of federal cash assistance that the working poor received. In popular discourse, the act was often implicitly and explicitly connected to stereotypes of lazy, overweight, disheveled, sexually decadent, and endlessly fecund African American welfare recipients (recalling the "welfare queen" rhetoric of the Reagan era).

Indeed, when asked to directly compare themselves with African Americans, fully three-fourths of white respondents to a National Opinion Research Center survey rated African Americans as less likely than whites to prefer to be self-supporting. Another survey found that most of those polled, the vast majority of whom were white, thought that lack of effort was to blame for people being on welfare and that most welfare recipients did not really want to work. These beliefs were most likely to be found among the nearly half of poll respondents who believed that most people on welfare were black. Accordingly, the sociologist Charles Gallagher, writing in 1995, found that backlash-fueled anger characterized the feelings of many white college students: "Many whites see themselves as victims of the multicultural, pc, feminist onslaught . . . [and this] would be laughable if it were not for the sense of mental crisis and the reactionary backlash that underpin these beliefs" (1995: 169). The dominance of a white backlash certainly structured reviews of films during this period. The film reviews analyzed in this time span (296 reviews) were *Schindler's List* (1993), *On Deadly Ground* (1994), *Stargate* (1994), *Dangerous Minds* (1995), *Losing Isaiah* (1995), *A Time to Kill* (1996), *Ghosts of Mississippi* (1996), *The Substitute* (1996), *Sunset Park* (1996), *Amistad* (1997), and *Bulworth* (1998) (see Table 3.2).

The White Father of Morality, Revenge, and Adoration

A key feature of the white backlash era is critics' near-constant reiteration of the supposed pathologies of nonwhite people and cultures. That specter of a dysfunctional cadre of people of color hinges on a paternalistic and domineering white figure that attempts to lord over nonwhites predisposed to leaching

---

3. It was signed by all but two of the Republican members of the House and all of the party's nonincumbent Republican congressional candidates.

TABLE 3.2. THE WHITE BACKLASH (1993–1998)

Frame or Theme No.	Frame or Theme Title	Ratio and Percentage of Reviews Discussing Frame or Theme
Frame BI	**The White Father of Morality, Revenge, and Adoration**	207/296 (69.93%)
Theme 1	Father (and Mother) Knows Best: Morality Personified	68/296 (22.97%)
Theme 2	White Hot Vengeance	55/296 (22.97%)
Theme 3	Grateful "Others"	84/296 (28.38%)
Frame BII	**Dark and Dangerous Dysfunctions**	155/296 (52.36%)
Frame BIII	**Saving White Saviors**	132/296 (44.59%)

off the modern, politically correct welfare state. In turn, film reviewers speak of this white character as an upright figure that doles out a host of paternalistic morality lessons, possesses magical powers and spiritual authority, and even enacts harsh and violent revenge on those nonwhites who would dare to upend the social order.

Father (and Mother) Knows Best: Morality Personified

Under the dominant logic of the white backlash, critics seem bound to their interpretation of the savior as a virtuous hero, whose wiles, intelligence, and tenacity helped liberate and uplift nonwhite or white ethnic populations, whether in the case of Jews under the regime of the Third Reich; gang-affiliated Asians, Latinos, and blacks in South Central Los Angeles; or imprisoned African Americans in 1960s Mississippi. For instance, Todd McCarthy of *Variety* writes of *Schindler's List* (1993):

> [Steven] Spielberg and scenarist Stephen Zaillian have overcome the problem of familiarity by presenting innumerable details of this grim history that are utterly fresh and previously unexplored, at least in mainstream films. And they have triumphed over the most obvious potential pitfalls by keeping as their main focus a man whose mercenary instincts only gradually turned him into an unlikely hero and savior. (1993)

McCarthy centers the review on Schindler as a hero and, literally, a savior. In reviews such as these, the emphasis is put on the moral dedication of the white character to both serve as an example to nonwhites and to alleviate the suffering they are unable to rid on their own.

Many critics are clear that the white characters of these films, such as those in *Losing Isaiah* (1995), are the personified morality used to confront inequality and injustice. For example, Lisa Schwarzbaum of *Entertainment Weekly* notes that the white character of Margaret (played by Jessica Lange) is the "moral center" of *Losing Isaiah*:

Margaret is the motor of this movie, the moral center, too. What went into this white older mother's desire to adopt a sickly black baby could have made a great movie on another planet where children in stories aren't required to be happy before the credits roll. (1995)

Emanuel Levy and Elizabeth Guider of *Variety* state that John Quincy Adams's character (played by Anthony Hopkins) in *Amistad* (1997) is

a reluctant hero, an astute, incorruptible puritan, enamored of flowers and plants, who initially refused to help. A moralist at heart, he throws himself wholeheartedly into defending the Africans in a fervent speech that summons the Declaration of Independence and other basic tenets of the American Dream. (1997)

In a review of *Dangerous Minds* (1995), Owen Gleiberman of *Entertainment Weekly* remarks that the lead character of LouAnne Johnson (played by Michelle Pfeiffer) embodies a teacher full of moral fiber and with the righteousness and training as a former marine to overpower the "rude, taunting, rap-generation delinquents" and with a virtuous character revealed by a "gleam in [her] eye."

LouAnne, a former Marine, has never had a full-time teaching job. The only reason she's landed this one is because her students are the trouble-makers no one else wants to touch. Rude, taunting, rap-generation delinquents who don't know much about history or English or math or anything else, they think that school is a sham and that no hoity-toity teacher could possibly help them escape their impoverished, crime-addled, no-future backgrounds. Of course, the moment LouAnne stares into their hostile faces, you know she's going to disarm their cynicism and ignite the fire in their bellies. You know it because of the eager gleam in Michelle Pfeiffer's eye . . . [and because of other movies] in which soulful, dedicated teachers wander into a war zone of unruly "bad" kids, only to wake them up to the glories of knowledge. (1995)

In another review of *Dangerous Minds*, the *Tucson Weekly* frames the students in terms of their dysfunctions and inabilities. While the reviewer takes the film to task for its "oversimplification" of the white savior trope, the critic concludes that the film aptly represents the "reality of the situation."

Based on a nonfiction book by an English teacher at a Northern California high school, *Dangerous Minds* is about how a creative, caring approach to teaching turns these wolves into pussycats. You can expect oversimplification from a story like this, and the adaptation at times seems laughably naive, but the sympathetic reality of the situation wins out. This is a world where teachers, working in underfunded conditions for skimpy wages, are social martyrs. . . . With lacquered realism, the film takes these grim facts and builds a sweet little drama around them. (Woodruff 1995)

The reviewer notes that the teachers (portrayed in the film as largely, if not all, white) are "social martyrs" and the students are "wolves" and little more than "grim facts" on which the film constructs a "sweet little drama."

White Hot Vengeance

Critics often interpreted the central white characters as enacting a righteous vengeance on students of color that did not live up to the implicit moral standards associated with white mainstream behavior. In reviewing *The Substitute* (1996), a critic for the *San Francisco Chronicle* interprets the lead white character as, more than a personification of moral authority, a "killing machine" with a ".45 automatic" and "a hunting knife" set on an animalistic "pack" of nonwhite students to seek revenge for his injured girlfriend:

> Most high school films are about hope. Not this one. When the teacher is sidelined with the busted kneecap, her boyfriend, Shale (Tom Berenger), decides to pose as a substitute. Luckily, he has the appropriate educational background for teaching in the Miami school system: He's a mercenary, just back from Cuba, and is an expert at inflicting pain and death. . . . But those who appreciate the irony of a killing machine turned loose on a pack of nasty students will find "The Substitute" a source of nonstop delight. The respective teachers played by [Sydney] Poitier and Pfeiffer had moral authority. But this Shale character goes them one better. He has moral authority and a .45 automatic, a hunting knife and a briefcase full of surveillance devices. . . . "The Substitute" is a guilty pleasure, but it's not garbage. Berenger brings to the role an appealing ruggedness and world-weariness. (LaSalle 1996)

Another critic for *Variety* remarks that Shale's entrance into the black- and Latino-dominated school in *The Substitute* was a "satisfying fantasy scenario": "Fueled by a sense of righteous justice, *The Substitute* goes into action with both barrels blazing. Berenger exacts revenge much in the style of the *Man with No Name* or the hero of *Death Wish*" (Klady 1996b). A critic for *Screen It!* argues that *The Substitute* is a film based on a "hero" whose mission it is to "clean house" in a style reminiscent of the vulgar violence of Charles Bronson films:

> Harking back to the vigilante films that Charles Bronson popularized in the 1970's, this film will appeal to those who like seeing the bad guys get their comeuppance. If that's the type of film you like, this one will certainly entertain you as it does its requisite job of setting up the bad guys and then bringing in the hero whose mission is to clean house. ("The Substitute" 1996)

In the film *Bulworth* (1998), the white savior is Senator Jay Billington Bulworth (played by Warren Beatty). He is fed up with the corrupt theater of political life and decides to tell it like it really is. Reviewing this highly satiric plot, the film critic for the *Cincinnati Enquirer* concentrates on Bulworth's now uncensored rancor and spiteful rhetoric toward people of color as well as his paternalistic approach toward people of color he deems morally crooked yet redeemable:

> [Bulworth] throws out his standard stump speech and says what he thinks. He insults Jewish contributors, shocks black voters and drives his campaign manager Murphy (Oliver Platt) to despair. Then he embarks on a wild, eye-opening night in South Central Los Angeles. . . . The language grows increasingly raw as Bulworth becomes entangled with a ghetto drug dealer (Don Cheadle) and his under-age minions—a plot twist that Mr. Beatty brings to an unexpected storybook conclusion. (McGurk 1998)

And in another review of *Bulworth*, the *Boston Phoenix* pens:

> His imminent demise gives him the freedom to speak his mind: he tells the parishioners of a black South Central church to "put down their chicken wings and malt liquor"; he calls a group of Beverly Hills entertainment executives "big Jews" and brands their product "crap." (Meek 1998)

Critics of this film spend most of their word space and emphasis on the former political huckster and savior's supposed truth telling about people of color. In reviews such as these, critics rarely interrogate *Bulworth* as a blatantly racist, or even mildly paternalistic, narrative given its depiction of the supposed inherent pathologies of African Americans and Jews. Rather, they laud the film for its refreshing exposé of the fraudulent liberal platform that caters to nonwhite special interest groups who only want their handouts.

Many reviewers interpret the white savior's vengeance as a kind of in-your-face tenacity that disallows claims by people of color to victim status. In such instances, the critic underscores how the central white character drills a Horatio Alger–like ideology of self-help and no handouts into the cadre of black students, natives, or down-on-their-luck folks of color. For example, Jim Shelby of the *Palo Alto Online* writes:

> There are no victims in my classroom! the teacher puts it to the angry, disaffected students. "Your every action is a choice you make." Their eyes slowly soften as they wonder if this one could actually care. Nope, it's not "The Blackboard Jungle," "Up the Down Staircase," "To Sir With Love" or "Stand and Deliver." It's Michelle Pfeiffer, bringing a caring and savvy toughness to the role of ex-marine LouAnne Johnson in "Dangerous Minds." (1995)

Such a narrative, reproduced in the pages and screens of print and online film criticism, fit well in the climate of the white backlash in which people of color

were increasingly framed as lazy and undeserving folks who could pull themselves up by their bootstraps if they only tried hard enough. And of course, it is
the kindly white teacher-mentor who shows them this supposedly open door,
that they need only walk through with a modicum of effort.

Grateful "Others"

In addition to the framing of the white saviors as characters of virtuous vengeance and messianic morality, critics also constructed the films' nonwhite
characters as grateful recipients of the white savior's patriarchal lessons. For
example, Alan Stone of the *Boston Review* writes of *Schindler's List*:

> We experience again and again the gratitude of those who survive and the
> miracle of their survival. The children who hid in the latrine are saved. . . .
> When the war finally ends, the bankrupt Schindler delivers a marvelous
> speech convincing the guards to go home without killing his Jews. As
> though this were not enough, Spielberg gives [Liam] Neeson a final scene in
> which Schindler must have a convulsion of contrition and self-loathing as
> he berates himself for not saving more lives. His gold Nazi pin could have
> saved two lives, his automobile, five lives. He collapses in paroxysms of re-
> morse and his Jews step forward to take him in their arms and comfort him.
> (1993: 19)

In a review of *Sunset Park*, a critic for *Variety* magazine interpreted the relationship between the white coach and black players as a mentorship so powerful that it generated a deep and abiding gratitude among the players:

> The premise dictates that the plucky coach must somehow win the confi-
> dence of her players. And while her understanding of the game increases by
> leaps and bounds, she gains their trust by being there off the court. She ad-
> vises them about girls, gets them tutors for class, visits them in the hospital
> and gets them representation in court. (Klady 1996a)

The concept of nonwhite gratitude for a white benefactor is the common
strand that weaves together many of these critics' interpretations of interracial
interactions. These reviews often describe a moral economy of nonwhite gratitude toward the white benefactor. Reviewers translate on-screen interactions as
scenarios in which people of color hail the most minuscule of white actions as
monumental, antiracist endeavors. Moreover, this discursive structure of paternalistic and benign white supremacy (re)envisions whites as the valued and
active agents to which nonwhites are bound as objects. The reviews' repeated
construction of whites as the sole possessors of moral authority and education
encourages audiences' adoption of the central principle of white backlash logic
of the era: people of color are a pathological group unfairly taking resources
from hardworking and moral whites.

Dark and Dangerous Dysfunctions

Given reviewers' intense focus on the white heroes of these films, these reviewers were mutually constrained and enabled by a necessary dialectic—an emphasis on nonwhite victims. After all, a hero cannot emerge without those in
need of saving. Within this Manichaean framing, the poignancy of a racialized
savior (who just happens to be white) is heightened and rationalized as a supposedly nonracial but, rather, commonsense approach to solving on-screen social problems of folks of color in supposedly color-blind fashion. In the context
of the 1990s white backlash, reviewers centered on the problems often thought
a natural product of communities of color but also on white savior characters
who would not succumb to the learned dysfunctions of a white-dominated politically correct welfare state. In this milieu white saviors were often described
as powerful forces that transcended moral corruption on both sides of the color
line. For example, Carrie Gorringe wrote of *Dangerous Minds*:

> The film is loosely based upon LouAnne Johnson's experiences as a former
> Marine-turned-teacher-of-the-disadvantaged as recounted in the book,
> *My Posse Don't Do Homework*. As it turns out, that Marine Corps training
> comes in handy, as we witness Ms. Johnson's gradual attempts to formulate
> safe zones, beginning with her own physical safety (her karate skills are
> helpful here), and expanding to encompass her students' minds and their
> lives. She attempts to rescue them, first from their own ignorance, then
> from the ignorance of an educational bureaucracy which understands the
> concept of warehousing what it believes to be the academically inept but has
> an extreme reluctance to innovate, and finally from the alienation of the
> very hostile world of the inner cities. (1995)

Gorringe first highlights here the parallels to the book on which the film is
based—a true story based on a white teacher's attempts to save a classroom of
at-risk students of color. Interestingly, even though Johnson's skills as a marine
play a minimal role in the film, they are highlighted. Her prowess in terms of
physical control, manipulation, and violence via karate are highlighted as necessary skills that create a "safe zone" (thus protecting her own white woman-
hood) and in terms of dominating and "encompassing" the students' minds
and lives. This rather odd use of martial arts in an educational setting is presented matter-of-factly and with little explanation, exposing the assumption
that white mainstream audiences need little clarification as to why such tactics
would be employed with students of color. Forget books, pedagogical acumen,
or actual school-implemented safety concerns and practices; all you need is a
tough white woman who can dole out a martial arts beating if needed.

After highlighting the savior's potential for violence, the review seamlessly
glides into a recount of Johnson's messianic labor. The review states that Johnson attempts "to rescue them, first from their own ignorance, then from the
ignorance of an educational bureaucracy . . . and finally from the alienation of

the very hostile world of the inner cities." Here, we should not miss the drawing of distinct inter- and intraracial boundaries that distinguish the white savior character both from the rabble in their "own ignorance" and "inner cities" and from the white-dominated "ignorance of the educational bureaucracy." The pathologies for people of color are literally located in the minds and environment of their social lives—in their own cognitive failings and in their living environment. Conversely, the dysfunctions of the white world are merely a by-product of "bureaucracy"—the tried and true whipping boy of Weberian individualism that implicitly posits whites as inherently moral figures who have fallen from grace and been captured within the iron cage of inept educational absolutism and regimented autocracy.

I have elsewhere (see Hughey 2012) analyzed the creation of dual inter- and intraracial boundaries as necessary borders that surround an idealized form of whiteness, what I call "hegemonic whiteness." In this sense, the idealized white savior figure of Johnson is distinguished from both the inherent pathologies of people of color and the learned flaws of white bureaucracy. The savior thus emerges as a truly unique and special person who transcends the forces of nature and nurture. In another example, Robert Faires of the *Austin Chronicle*, reviewing the film *Losing Isaiah* (1995), notes:

> Naomi Foner's script sharply delineates the contrasts between the two sides: The birth mother is poor, single, black; the adopters are well-off, married, white. And it makes the differences—especially race—painful bones of contention on the legal battlefield. Yet it also digs beneath these figures' skins to find shared qualities. The women at odds in the suit are both strung out—one on crack, one on work—and the women playing them, Halle Berry and Jessica Lange, show the strain of their lives in their faces. They carve in tense gazes their need for this boy, the redemption he holds. Both are deeply flawed, but they are heroes, too: Berry the junkie who beats her addiction and builds a new life, Lange the social worker who gives a crack baby a home when no one else will. In fact, Foner finds heroes in everyone: in the social worker's husband who patiently supports his wife and this needful child, in the attorneys who fight the case on principle, in a boy who holds onto hope in a bleak housing project. The film is remarkable for its evenhandedness and generosity to its characters. (1995)

Fairs certainly attempts to paint an evenhanded and racially unbiased picture in his showcasing of the film's attempt to dig "beneath these figures' skins." Yet the impetus to construct a review that conforms to the white backlash logic of the 1990s undermines such an attempt. The critic tries to engage the film as a tale of two "deeply flawed" figures and their redemption: the black crack-addicted mother (played by Berry) who cannot care for her child and the white character (played by Lange). Yet strangely, the critic fails to list any "flaws" associated with Lange other than "work."

The critic then shifts tack to frame both characters as "heroes": Berry beats her addiction to drugs and Lange takes on the support for the child, assisted by a white support staff of husband and lawyers. The heroism for the black character is her mastery of her black femininity (rather than reclaiming her child from a white adoptive mother whose only crime is her devotion to work), while the white characters' gallantry is the supposed result of saving a black child from the dysfunctions of his biological mother and urban community. In both cases, the critic writes of heroic moral uplift as distance from pathological forms of blackness; even Halle Berry's character must distance herself from her drugged and dysfunctional location in the tempest of fellow black bodies that enable her addiction.

For the logic of the white backlash to hold sway, a cadre of nonwhite subjects must be continually reframed as a dangerous threat to white resources or accepted norms that supposedly rest on racially neutral moral tenets. As Chapter 2 makes clear, film plays a large role in rationalizing dominant ideology. Critics assist that ideological labor by legitimating and interpreting films. For example, in reviews of *Sunset Park* (1996), critics highlight the behavior of Brooklyn-based black basketball players as neither cinematic plot devices nor traits essential to the film's narrative but instead make explicit value judgments and matter-of-fact statements that portray such stereotypes as authentic depictions of real life. According to one:

> They aren't much interested in basketball, but they do like to impress the girls and to smoke dope in the locker room. They have no respect for authority and totally ignore Coach Saroka in the first part of the picture. Imagine a practice where the kids just dribble, shot [*sic*] as they like, . . . literally not doing anything their coach asks. They actually turn their back on her and do not listen to her at all. (Rhodes 1996)

Another says, "What raises the movie at least to the level of the mundane is the locker room and team bus banter of the ensemble, which has the sound of authenticity largely in that it is generally offensive, sexist and entertaining" (Marine 1996).

Ishmael Reed notes in "The Black Pathology Biz" that commentators in the U.S. media are the worst offenders when it comes to singling out blacks as the cause of American social problems. Such a tactic distracts from mainstream social ills and relocates them in black bodies. Reed writes, "To portray America as a pathological society would interrupt the country's cozy fetal sleep" and instead threatens "whites with a black rapist in every bedroom, an image that's been commercialized by some millionaire feminists in novels and movies for the last decade, proving that the black pathology industry is an equal opportunity gold mine" (1989).

Saving White Saviors

Given the establishment of the trope of the white savior, by the mid-1990s many critics were well versed in its deployment and positioning in cinematic plot structures. They redeemed and valorized this overdrawn trope, often marginalizing (or simply ignoring) problematic features that drew on paternalistic, racist, or xenophobic narratives. In one particularly emblematic instance, Edward Guthmann of the *San Francisco Chronicle* concluded in a review of *Dangerous Minds* (1995):

> "Dangerous Minds" doesn't drop the sentimental conventions of the good-teacher Hollywood drama but reconstitutes them with strong performances, sensitive direction by Canadian film maker John N. Smith ("The Boys of St. Vincent") and a firm belief that teachers can and will make a difference in a person's life. Smith knows how to draw the best from his actors, and Pfeiffer seems to enjoy herself in ways she hasn't onscreen before. She's playing with a bag of cliches—feisty white chick takes on dope pushers and malcontents, transforms them with wisdom, love and hip smarts—but she's so plucky and likable, you overlook the hokum and enjoy her journey. Smith shot "Dangerous Minds" at Burlingame High School, near the Carlmont campus where Johnson taught for five years. Expecting a student-teaching gig, Pfeiffer gets assigned to the "Academy," a school-within-the-school for bright, "passionate" (i.e., emotionally troubled) kids. (1995)   •

Jim Shelby writes in *Palo Alto Online* that the character of LouAnne Johnson in *Dangerous Minds* is a performance that brings the film to life in comparison to the same story of the white messianic teachers that came before:

> The idealistic new teacher/tough kids blueprint is as magnificently formulaic as the new sheriff coming into town to rustle up some law 'n' order. It's also wonderfully predictable and satisfying, and "Dangerous Minds" holds up admirably against inevitable comparisons with previous incarnations of the same story. (1995)

Even when critics are decidedly opposed to the performances, comedy, set of characters, and the setting, they seem to believe the genre itself can be the saving grace of the film. For example, in Michael J. Doyle's panning review of *Sunset Park* (1996), he writes:

> If you've seen one, you've pretty much seen them all. So what sets this movie apart from the rest? Is it the quality of the performances? No. . . . Is it the comedy? No. Is it the set of characters—those kids with the wacky personalities and the big dreams whom you come to know and love? Not really, though this is one of the stronger points of the movie. . . . Is it the setting? Well, I don't recall any students being shot or arrested in Goldie Hawn's WILDCATS or the TV show "The White Shadow." But this is hardly justification. . . . SUNSET PARK isn't the worst movie made in this genre. It's perfectly acceptable as far as these movies go. (1996)

In this same vein, Craig Marine of the *Los Angeles Examiner* also redeems *Sunset Park*:

> Considering that the premise of the movie is anything but original—white woman who knows nothing about basketball takes a job coaching black inner-city ghetto dwellers and leads them to the New York City championships—"Sunset Park" is nowhere near as bad as one might imagine. (1996)

While critics certainly seem to make strange concessions to these films (a critique counterbalanced by the inherent strength of the white savior genre), many critics advance glowing evaluations of the white savior characters and the actors playing them. For example, despite the problems of praising and deifying a Nazi in *Schindler's List* (even if he is a quasi resister of the Third Reich), critics circumvent this problem by focusing on the "presence" and "confidence" of Liam Neeson's lead character. Alan Stone of the *Boston Review* writes:

> Neeson's film presence is iconic. His carved features and size suggest some Roman statue of a god come to life. Like Schindler, Neeson was relatively unfamiliar to American film audiences and so did not carry much baggage of past roles into the part. Indeed, his physical presence in those roles was more memorable than the characters he played. We do not know yet whether he is a great actor, but it is already clear that he projects the magnetism and authority of the legendary film stars. (1993: 19)

Moreover, Janet Maslin of the *New York Times* contends that Neeson

> is unmistakably larger than life, with the panache of an old-time movie star. . . . From its first glimpse of Oskar as he dresses for a typically flamboyant evening socializing with German officers—and even from the way his hand appears, nonchalantly holding a cigarette and a bribe—the film studies him with rapt attention. Mr. Neeson, captured so glamorously by Janusz Kaminiski's richly versatile black-and-white cinematography, presents Oskar as an amalgam of canny opportunism and supreme, well-warranted confidence. (1993)

In a review of *A Time to Kill*, Lisa Schwarzbaum of *Entertainment Weekly* follows suit to focus on the film's white savior of Jake Brigance (Matthew McConaughey) as "the combative, debt-ridden counsel for the defense, [who] in fact exhibits the refined, sensual charm and stylish wire-rim glasses of a *GQ* model" (1996). Moreover, in *Rolling Stone*'s review of *A Time to Kill*, the critic maintains that the film was burdened by ineffective caricatures of white racism and hot-button social issues (e.g., the Klan and the death penalty) that took away from the "heart of the picture": the friendship "bond" between the white savior (Jake) and the black to-be-saved prisoner (Carl):

In *A Time to Kill,* way long at 148 minutes, they cram in too much, including
[John] Grisham's polemics about racism, the resurgence of the Ku Klux Klan
and the moral dilemma of the death penalty. This distracts from the heart of
the picture, which is in the bond between Carl Lee (the brilliant [Samuel L.]
Jackson is quietly devastating) and Jake, a husband and father who knows
he, too, would have shot anyone who raped his little girl. Jake's summation
to the all-white jury, instructing the members to close their eyes and imagine
their own child being brutalized, is a stirring climax. (Travers 1996)

Consequently, despite the contention that the liberal hoards of film reviewers
push an antiracist agenda, it is evident that the 1990s certainly coaxed out the
use of black dysfunction discourse as an effective mechanism for grounding
positive evaluations of the white savior genre.

The Postracial Era and the Redemption of Whiteness (1999–2011)

As the 1990s gave way to the new millennium, the dominant racial discourse
shifted from one of overt backlash politics in which whites explicitly claimed
victimhood by reverse racism to a more subtle form of postracial discourse in
which it was claimed that race no longer mattered. This refined form of color
blindness, while based at least in a small part on the notion that race should not
matter ideally, also labors to obfuscate the ways that race continues to matter
in reality. That is, if we embrace the ideology of color blindness without ad-
dressing the ways that race continues to structure our life chances, then the
acceptance of the discourse of color blindness will effectively reproduce the
racial inequities that require our attention. Moreover, this rhetoric facilitates
the demonization of those who claim experience with racial discrimination.
That is, if race no longer matters or plays a significant role in the new millennium, then those people (generally people of color) are more easily portrayed
as racial ideologues who are oversensitive or dishonestly playing the race card
for sympathy. Such logic solidified in momentous court decisions and media
pronouncements.

For example, in 2007 the Supreme Court issued a decision, written by Chief
Justice John Roberts, that signaled a complete departure from color conscious
jurisprudence on race aiming to redress racial discrimination. In *Parents
Involved in Community Schools v. Seattle School District No. 1* (551 U.S. 701
[2007]), ruling on achieving racial integration by assigning students to particular schools, Chief Justice Roberts penned a color-blind raison d'être: "Before
Brown, schoolchildren were told where they could and could not go to school
based on the color of their skin. . . . [T]he way 'to achieve a system of determining admission to the public schools on a nonracial basis' . . . is to stop assigning
students on a racial basis. The way to stop discrimination on the basis of race is
to stop discriminating on the basis of race."

A year later, on August 28, 2008—forty-five years to the day after Dr. Martin Luther King Jr. delivered his renowned "I Have a Dream" speech—Barack Obama accepted the Democratic Party's nomination for president of the United States. Exactly one hundred days later the nation awoke to headlines such as the *New York Times* "OBAMA. Racial Barrier Falls in Heavy Turnout." Seizing this watershed moment, many proclaimed the United States was postracial and that racists were no more than a few bad apples. Adam Geller of *USA Today* wrote, "The principle that all men are created equal has never been more than a remote eventuality in the quest for the presidency. . . . [T]hat ideal is no longer relegated to someday. Someday is now" (2008). Such rhetoric was reproduced in 2012 with Obama's reelection.

I contend that this postracial and color-blind rhetoric of the new millennium is intimately crocheted with the social and legal dominance of whiteness. This approach allows whites to maintain their dominant position in the racial hierarchy without directly speaking of race. The discourse of a postracial America helps alleviate the crisis of whiteness by redeeming and rebuilding white racial identity as a synonym for logic, objectivity, and the de facto normal or ideal human being. During the (multi)cultural wars (1987–1992) many argued for whites' place at the multicultural table and many others questioned the legitimacy of diversity. During the white backlash (1993–1998) many began to see whiteness as an identity under attack and thus opposed challenges to white dominance. In the era of postracial politics (1999–2011), the rhetoric of color blindness attempts to deftly avoid the issue of race altogether and in so doing tries to bring whiteness above the fray of such racial vulgarity. In the postracial climate, film critics craft their professional evaluations of white savior films in a form that redeems and rebuilds whiteness as an identity unsullied by the mudslinging of racial discourse, finger-pointing, and the playing of race cards.

The film reviews analyzed in this time span (2,393 reviews) were of *Music of the Heart* (1999), *The Matrix* (1999), *Snow Falling on Cedars* (1999), *Finding Forrester* (2001), *Monster's Ball* (2001), *Hardball* (2001), *K-Pax* (2001), *Pavilion of Women* (2001), *Tears of the Sun* (2003), *The Last Samurai* (2003), *The Matrix Reloaded* (2003), *The Matrix Revolutions* (2003), *Crash* (2004), *The Constant Gardner* (2005), *Amazing Grace* (2006), *Blood Diamond* (2006), *Children of Men* (2006), *Half Nelson* (2006), *The Last King of Scotland* (2007), *Freedom Writers* (2007), *Pathfinder* (2007), *Gran Torino* (2008), *Avatar* (2009), *The Blind Side* (2009), *The Soloist* (2009), and *The Help* (2011) (see Table 3.3).

Hagiographies of White Redemption

Film reviewers made sense of the cinema of this era of postracial politics (1999–2011) by centering their reviews on the crisis of the white protagonist qua savior. The critics often highlighted the ways that the savior encounters a flurry of assaults and insults that test his or her power, principles, and proficiency. In the end, the savior triumphs in color-blind fashion, avoiding any explicit racial attacks or backlash. The critics seem magnetized by the narrative of a white

TABLE 3.3. THE POSTRACIAL ERA AND THE REDEMPTION OF WHITENESS (1999–2011)

Frame or Theme No.	Frame or Theme Title	Ratio and Percentage of Reviews Discussing Frame or Theme
Frame CI	**Hagiographies of White Redemption**	**920/2,393 (38.49%)**
Theme 1	Salvaging Superiority	307/2,393 (12.83%)
Theme 2	Alleviating White Guilt	226/2,393 (9.44%)
Theme 3	Everyone's Racist, Not Just Whites	387/2,393 (16.17%)

character redeeming and rationalizing his or her place atop the racial hierarchy without succumbing to overt racial hostility or racism. In this sense, these reviews are racialized hagiographies: essays on the lives on cinematic saints that emphasize their natural superiority, alleviates white guilt, and overcomes prejudicial character flaws with aplomb.

Salvaging Superiority

White protagonists were often described as agents who won over the characters of color to their way of seeing things through their bootstrapping hard work and dedication to their ideals or craft. Critics often insinuated that the white savior's worldview is an appropriate and moral message. Also critics frequently wrote of saviors' ability to navigate the raw and raucous emotion of folks of color with cool and dispassionate logic. For example, in his review of *Music of the Heart* (1999), David Stratton of *Variety* remarks:

> On one level, [this] pic charts the story of a defeated woman who picks herself up from the ashes of one life and makes a resounding success of a new one. . . . But on another level, the film is a passionate plea for the continued funding of music education, seen as a vital part of a rounded teaching program. Pic also touches on race themes, with the mother of a gifted black kid pulling him from the program because "my son's got better things to do than learn dead white men's music," an attitude firmly and, in the end, successfully countered by Roberta. (1999)

The critic highlights the "race themes" of the movie by mentioning the deft ability of Roberta Guaspari (Meryl Streep) to navigate the color line through her appropriate countering of the close-minded approach of the black mother in question. For many critics, navigating "race themes" means little more than disallowing the consideration of race. Rather, it means the insistence on color blindness and the refusal to accept "racial discrimination" or "inequality" as a legitimate explanation for differential outcomes.

Many critics also highlight Guaspari's uphill battles with her own circumstances as well as with the East Harlem black parents who opposed her. In nearly every review, critics frame the interactions as a triumph of white paternalism over the myopia of black distrust. A reviewer for the *Los Angeles Times* writes:

> A movie with its heart in all the right places—music education in the schools, after all, certainly deserves such a big wet kiss—"Music of the Heart" is not what anyone would call up-tempo. Opening with Roberta being dumped by her husband (the Navy officer for whom she presumably sacrificed her musical career), the film traces her grief-driven move to East Harlem, where she finagles herself a violin program, fights entrenched attitudes and dubious parents and is vindicated by a school concert at which the pupils shine and their families are rapturous. (Anderson 1999)

In some cases, critics speak of a white savior's pedagogical paternalism as nearly magical yet paradoxically authentic; the saviors are portrayed as unexplainable yet entirely believable. Critics' evaluations thus construct these saviors as transcendent individuals who adhere to real-life situations yet accomplish superhuman feats out of thin air. Roger Ebert writes:

> "Music of the Heart" is based on the true story of a violin teacher named Roberta Guaspari, who created a high school music program more or less out of thin air in East Harlem, and eventually found herself and her students on the stage of Carnegie Hall. Most movies claiming to be based on fact pour on the melodrama, but this one basically just sticks to the real story, which has all the emotional wallop that's needed. (1999)

In review after review, the savior is upheld as a beacon of morality and knowledge who brought poor, impoverished, and ignorant people of color into the fold of Eurocentric traditions and cultural practices.

In reviewing *Finding Forrester* (2001), one critic writes that the white character of William Forrester (Sean Connery) is akin to a tough-love, paternalistic psychiatrist to Jamal Wallace (Rob Brown), who in the end will be there in Jamal's "moment of need":

> When we first meet him, 16-year-old Jamal (Rob Brown) seems like any other kid from the 'hood, hanging with his pals and shooting hoops. . . . Since he averages a no-effort C at school, it comes as a surprise when he scores through the roof on an aptitude test. Winning a full scholarship to a Manhattan prep school, he finds the administrators are as interested in his skills on the court as in the classroom. The heart of the film isn't at school, but in the dark, woody apartment of Forrester (Sean Connery), a recluse who lives in Jamal's neighborhood. On a dare, Jamal breaks into the old man's apartment, but this prank break-in leads to an unexpected friendship when Forrester, famous for the single novel he wrote decades ago, becomes the young man's muse as a writer. Theirs is a tough-love friendship. Forrester barks, "There'll be no questions about me, my family and why there was only one book." You could say Connery has the psychiatrist role played

by Robin Williams in "Good Will Hunting." . . . The movie offers a dual climax, one in the basketball court, one in the classroom. Yes, it's a little shameless, and in the film's final stretch, there's never any doubt Forrester will turn up to support Jamal in a moment of need. (Murray 2001)

And in another review of *Finding Forrester*, the critic for *Deseret News* writes that Jamal's success is less a result of his talent and intelligence and more a result of the help and whims of Forrester's guidance:

> Jamal gets a chance to explore his creative side when he's recruited to go to a prestigious prep school. But to succeed there, he's going to need help, which he gets from a most unexpected source—a mysterious neighborhood hermit (Connery) who turns out to be William Forrester, a Pulitzer Prize–winning novelist. . . . For four decades, Forrester has been content to stay in his brownstone apartment, rarely if ever talking to anyone else—at least until Jamal breaks in (on a dare). Rather than having him arrested, though, Forrester chases out the teen, who accidentally leaves his backpack in the apartment. On a whim, Forrester assesses Jamal's writing, and soon enough he's encouraging the young prodigy to write. In fact, with his help, the teen manages to impress his new teachers and fellow students. (Vice 2001)

Across the board, these reviews recount and hail the white protagonist as an active agent who, through his intelligence, rational objectivity, and hard work redeems and naturalizes the power of whiteness by taking on a poor and hapless black or brown soul as his or her charity case. The savior's achievements are highlighted, and rarely is race mentioned, unless to address the dysfunctions and close-minded prejudice of the black or brown subjects, who unknowingly await their color-blind white knight.   •

Alleviating White Guilt

Many of these film reviews, simply put, labor to alleviate white guilt. Such easing of prejudicial culpability rests on critics' ability to praise the white protagonist as a figure who turns against his tyrannical, close-minded, and racist white community and comrades. In so doing, the character stands as proof positive of whites' ability to transcend race and become truly color-blind. Such is the essence of the fantasy of white guilt alleviation. For example, in a review of *Tears of the Sun* (2003), David Edelstein of *Slate* singles out the protagonist, Lieutenant Waters (Bruce Willis), for his sudden shift from military warrior to humanitarian savior of nonwhite natives. He also bluntly underscores the film's mitigation of white, American guilt:

> When Waters discovers that among his refugees is the future leader of a democratic Nigeria, and that he's being pursued by a relentless platoon commanded by icy Col. Idriss Sadique (Malick Bowens) and his superior, a

grinning human jackal, he calls together his men and gives them a chance to sound off: He wants to know what they think of his unprecedented show of humanitarian disobedience. Then he makes an amazing declaration. He says he's saving the villagers "for all the years we've been told to stand down or stand by . . . *for our sins*." There's something about *Tears of the Sun* that rips me right down the middle. On one hand, it's an inspiring story of American valor and self-sacrifice. On the other, it seems so far removed from the real world—from any action by any soldier at any recent time— that it amounts to a sort of opium dream of heroism, a collective fantasy to make us feel better about ourselves on the eve of a controversial military action. This is how we'd *like* Americans to be seen by the rest of the world, as both great soldiers and great moral individualists—policing the planet and rescuing helpless civilians from barbarous regimes. (2003)

Such a blunt appraisal was rare among reviewers, as most were content to praise a film for accomplishing the task of making us "feel better about ourselves." For example, Kevin Crust of the *Los Angeles Times* remarked of *Freedom Writers* (2007):

As a tenacious teacher, Hilary Swank transforms "Freedom Writers." . . . As real-life teacher Erin Gruwell, Swank enters with coltish enthusiasm, dangerous naivete and a toothsome smile that suggests maybe she isn't up to the task of turning a classroom full of hardened teens, embittered by their hateful environment, into scholars. Amid the schematic setup of Gruwell attempting to win the trust of the students while overcoming the red tape of the system, something fairly amazing happens. . . . In scene after scene, it's a marvel to watch Swank determinedly making her case, shrewdly winning over the audience as Gruwell persuades her charges to give her a chance to turn them on to literature, history and the opportunity to share their own narratives. There is a raw, guileless quality to Swank that shreds any hint of condescension or exploitation. (2007)

Consider also the review of *The Last Samurai* (2003) by Lisa Schwarzbaum of *Entertainment Weekly* that centers on the white protagonist Nathan Algren (Tom Cruise):

Moved by the serenity of his new environment, not to mention by the liquid grace of Katsumoto's sister, Taka (Koyuki), Algren comes to love his enemies, and fight for them. . . . As he undergoes conversion, Algren marvels at his new friends who "devote themselves to the perfection of whatever they pursue." Cruise pursues perfection too, plying his craft as if on a celebrity mission. It's monkish work, and doesn't invite closeness, but it commands respect, in actors or in samurai. (2003)

Here the "monkish work" (a not so subtle allusion to messianic labor) is both the critic's appraisal of the film and the depiction of Algren's interactions with his newly found Japanese brethren. Critics lavished praise on these films' white saviors for abandoning their old ways and delivering on- and off-screen messages of white people as capable of healthy and cooperative interracial interactions. Such prose invites white readers to abandon their white guilt and to think of themselves as advocates of a color-blind world in which they have just as much to teach as to learn. Along these lines, Roger Ebert writes of *The Last Samurai*:

> "The Last Samurai" breaks with the convention that the Western hero is always superior to the local culture he immerses in. It has been compared to "Lawrence of Arabia" and "Dances With Wolves," films in which Westerners learn to respect Arabs and Indians, but this film goes a step further, clearly believing that Katsumoto's traditional society is superior to the modernism being unloaded by the Americans. Katsumoto is the teacher and Algren is the student, and the film wonderfully re-creates the patterns and textures of the Japanese past. (2003)

In 2008 Ebert penned a review of *Gran Torino* (2008), in which he framed the incendiary and racist character of Walt Kowalski (Clint Eastwood) as possessing two messages for mainstream audiences: one of individual growth and the other of whites' slow redemption from close-minded segregationists to those who would embrace a multicultural, humanist vision.

> "Gran Torino" isn't a liberal parable. It's more like, out of the frying pan and into the melting pot. . . . "Gran Torino" is about two things, I believe. It's about the belated flowering of a man's better nature. And it's about Americans of different races growing more open to one another in the new century. This doesn't involve some kind of grand transformation. It involves starting to see the "gooks" next door as people you love. And it helps if you live in the kind of neighborhood where they *are* next door. (2008)

Another review of *Gran Torino*, by Ty Burr, reads, "Eastwood is consciously playing with stereotypes here. . . . The real drama of "Gran Torino" lies in watching the character's black-and-white mindset melt away under a steady diet of Hmong home cooking, replaced by a starker sense of duty" (2008). Burr stabilizes the crisis of whiteness in his review. Walt is not called out as a racial-epithet-wielding product of a bygone past of white segregation but is framed as a savior of the Hmong and the exemplar of a color-blind, postmodern whiteness.

Everyone's Racist, Not Just Whites

Critics forwarded a third approach to redeeming an antiracist or color-blind whiteness: the contention that racism is not a quality exclusive to whiteness. Reviewers often remarked that everyone is subject to prejudiced and stereotypical thinking. This line of thought caresses the notion that whites need not feel too guilty, for after all they are as much the recipients of racism as they are the perpetrators of it. For example, in taking on a review of *The Help* (2011), Aubrey Ward III of *Firefox News* writes:

> Some critics might've felt that Skeeter was just another in a long line of "great white hopes" that showed the helpless Negroes how to emancipate themselves because they were far too inferior to figure out the answer by themselves. What I saw was a young Southern woman who was trying to emancipate herself from the shackles of the Jim Crow South mentality. She didn't want to be like her girlfriends and settle for being household debutantes lounging around in fancy outfits while the maids did all the work. Skeeter wanted to be a fully independent woman that didn't rely on a man to pay for her shelter, her meals and her ride. (2011)

With a straightforward tack that eschews any hint of irony, this review of *The Help* dismisses the contention that it fits in the white savior genre. Instead, while dismissing the import of class-, gender-, and race-based oppression of black women's domestic work in 1960s Mississippi, it awkwardly privileges the struggles of one white woman to "emancipate" herself from the "shackles" of a "mentality."

Along these same lines, Stephen Hunter of the *Washington Post* contends of *Crash* (2004):

> It's all here as the first-time director Paul Haggis (promoted to the Big Chair after having written "Million Dollar Baby") views a cross section of Los Angeles from God's point of view and discovers that nothing is ever simple: racism and nobility can exist in the same man, hate and love in the same woman, fear and loyalty, compromise and idealism, all the yin-yang dichotomies that make the human species so utterly confounding, yet so utterly fascinating. (2005)

The refusal to acknowledge a lopsided racial inequality (and its substitution by an idyllic postracial vision) enables critics' dual recognition and dismissal of the white savior genre. For example, in critiquing *Freedom Writers* as a film reflecting the white role model image, Tom Charity of *CNN* writes that it still portrays blacks and whites as possessing equal and parallel flaws:

> If there is something suspect about this genre's comforting images of white role models "elevating" underprivileged minority kids, it's worth noting that in the best of these films a recovered class-consciousness cuts both ways. . . . In the story's pivotal scene, Gruwell cracks down hard on a racist caricature with a stern reference to the Holocaust—until she realizes that only one of her pupils (the white kid) understands what she's talking about. Then, when she asks if anyone in the class has lost a friend or loved one to gang violence, everyone's hand goes up (except the white kid's). By making them acknowledge their shared pain, Gruwell begins to break down the racial divisions that have ghettoized the classroom. (2007)

When critics surrender to the salvific touch of characters such as Skeeter or Gruwell, their appraisals resonate with the dominant logic of color blindness. The rhetorical device of racist and oppressive commonality (in which no one group is to blame or worse off than the other) presents a one-dimensional racial landscape whereby inequality is implicitly thought the result of one's lack of hard work, intelligence, or creativity rather than the product of habitual discrimination. With the dominant depiction of a color-blind world, in which racial discrimination is the result of aberrant bad apples instead of structurally embedded inequalities, whiteness is redeemed as just another racial type awash in a newly found postracial world where color only matters to those who are intentionally racist. Such a comforting illusion then labors to reconstruct whites as neither the beneficiaries of a white supremacist world nor the defenders of Jim Crow. Rather, whites reemerge as one of many racial groups to whom nothing is owed and to whom whites owe nothing.

Conclusion

This chapter examines 2,799 film reviews of fifty films in a controversial film genre. Drawing from these reviews and in concert with three dominant ideological currents of the past quarter century, I document the strategies and frames that reviewers employ to make meaning of race. Together, the analysis of reviewers as interpretive communities illustrates the strength of these reviews as tools for mobilizing a neoliberal logic and gestures toward their function as scripts for navigating the complex terrain of the contemporary racial landscape. This analysis sheds light on how the breadth and reach of reviews reflect the anxieties and conflicts of a society that is at once both color-conscious and color-blind. At issue here is not merely another dimension of how race is understood, but rather this analysis attempts to connect the strains of commonsense thinking about race with the mechanisms of popular culture that rationalize and legitimate whiteness as paternalistic authority.

My intention is to also accentuate the ritualistic features of reviews, which in turn demonstrate the presence of an interpretive community rather than a disconnected group of critics relying on personal aesthetic judgments. In bringing attention to the collective dynamics of film reviewers, this study follows a developing trend that lies at the intersection of racial and ethnic studies, media studies, cultural sociology, and symbolic interactionism: customary practices of reviewing (racialized) films occur in concert with specific interpretive guidelines and become normalized in social space (Altheide 2000; Denzin 1992, 2001; Vannini 2004). Hence, this study integrates reviews—as meaning-making intermediaries—into the Meadian "feedback loop" (Mead 1934) between producer and consumer. Such a move adds nuance by demonstrating how the processes of cinematic interpretation are simultaneously constrained and enabled by the mediating forces between diffuse cultural logics and the cinematic racial order on one hand, and active audiences and the interactional racial order on the other.

4

Watching Whiteness

Audience Consumption and Community

It is in the interaction of viewer and film in narration that the
stereotype is granted its scope as well as its limits.
—Daniel Bernardi, *The Birth of Whiteness: Race and the Emergence
of United States Cinema*

On January 21, 2012, director Craig Zobel debuted his film *Compliance*
at the Sundance Film Festival in Park City, Utah. The film tells the
story of a robbery of a fast food eatery in which a man posing as a police officer falsely accuses an employee of theft and forces her to perform a sex
act. As the lights came up at the film's conclusion, weak applause and nervous
laughter was peppered with boos and one voice that boomed, "Sundance, you
can do better! . . . This is not the year to make violence against women entertaining" (Miller 2012). The film was based on the true story of a 2004 robbery
of a Kentucky McDonald's. A man, who identified himself as a police officer,
telephoned the eatery and coerced employees into a sexual assault. The film
aroused passionate responses. *Time* covered the film and related its content to
the Yale professor Stanley Milgram's famous experiments on authority (Corliss
2012), some reviewers questioned how a work vividly portraying violent mi-
sogyny could be entertainment (see Fear 2012), and others celebrated the film
as a feminist triumph (see K. Rich 2012).

The celebration of and controversy over *Compliance* gestures toward an in-
teresting question: Why do people care in the ways that they do? Sociologists,
and particularly those embedded in the sociology of culture, have long held interest in why and how people are attracted to various cultural products, objects,
and practices. From music to art and from comic books to toy dolls, sociologists
examine why some people find these products attractive and necessary and
others find them perfectly mundane, useless, annoying, or outright dangerous.
Objects and practices are subject to varying interpretations, whether works of
literature across the world (e.g., Griswold's [1987] study of literary interpretation in the United States, United Kingdom, and West Indies); consumption of

clothing, furniture, and leisure activities (e.g., Bourdieu's [1984] analysis of cultural distinctions and aesthetic tastes among the French elite); musical appreciation (e.g., Bryson's [1996] study of why some in the United States detest certain musical genres); a skeptical public's commemoration of an unpopular conflict (e.g., Wagner-Pacifici and Schwartz's [1991] analysis of how the controversial Vietnam War memorial came to be); or how the blues are deemed authentic (e.g., Grazian's [2005] examination of white Chicagoans' patronage of African American blues clubs). Because these topics are so varied and because people have such different interpretations, sociologists try to discover and highlight the patterns that exist amid this confusing and immense cultural landscape (Martin 2002). Accordingly, research on audience reception of cultural objects, such as film, is a central pillar in the sociology of culture (e.g., Barthes 1980; Bennett 1990; S. Hall 1997; Shively 1992).

How Does an Audience See Film?

In this chapter I labor to explain why and how people of different socioeconomic backgrounds, political persuasions, and racial and gender identities make sense of select white savior films. In specific, I examine the relationship between participants' interpretations of these films, their perceptions of race, and the effect of religious, educational, gendered, and racial interactions in small-group contexts.

There are many other factors to consider in such an exploration, and I situate my analysis in the sweet spot between structure (demographically conditioned evaluations), agency (the ability of readers to make their own atomistic meanings and evaluations), and the role of small-group interactions that might lessen or intensify structural and agency effects. I do not wish to take theoretical missteps that portray audiences as cultural dupes who remain robotically attracted to a specific film or art form because of the structural constraints (both material and symbolic) implanted in their minds. If that were accurate, people would be overdetermined as instruments of social structures and dominant ideology. Conversely, people are in complete control of neither the social world nor themselves. Such a voluntarist position thus romanticizes individuals as disconnected rational actors unfettered by socially structured (and finite) resources. While the former is overly structural, the latter is wholly antisociological and abandons the social base of human action and order as if choices are objective realities outside history and culture. Hence, I draw attention to the effects of organizational interaction, or group style (Eliasoph and Lichterman 2003), in shaping how people interpret film. While such mesolevel processes of interpersonal influence modify people's orientations toward film, the displayed debates over the meanings of a film are also certainly confined by the dominant ideologies in which these organizations and groups operate.

My setting for this exploration was composed by conversations with individuals and groups who watched at least one of the white savior films listed in Chapter 2 (see Table 2.1). I conducted in-depth interviews with individuals, conversations with purposefully constructed focus groups, and discussions with already-constructed groups and associations such as religious groups, fraternal organizations, and students in college classes (see Tables 4.1 and 4.2 for a listing of the respondents and focus groups and Appendix C for a full account of the methodology employed). By relying on such diverse sources for data, I am able to foreclose on (1) structurally conditioned patterns of taste, (2) individual readers' expression of subjective interpretations, and (3) the contributions of interpersonal influences and group dynamics to people's reception of these provocative race-based films.

TABLE 4.1. INTERVIEW PARTICIPANTS

Pseudonym	Race/ Gender	Age	Religion	Education	Father's, Mother's Education	Socio- economic Status	Group
Maureen	ME/F	38	B	C	C, C	MC	1
Brandon	B/M	22	B	SC	C, C	WC	1
Beatrice	W/F	36	B	C	C, C	MC	1
Juan	L/M	25	B	SG	HS, HS	WC	1
Sonia	L/F	24	B	SC	HS, C	WC	1
Ali	ME/M	51	B	G	G, SG	UC	1
Donald	W/M	39	B	SC	C, C	MC	1
Arlene	W/F	33	B	C	C, C	MC	1
Henry	W/M	40	B	C	C, C	MC	1
Marilyn	B/F	41	C-SB	HS	HS, C	WC	2
Douglas	B/M	44	C-SB	SC	HS, HS	WC	2
Jackson	B/M	38	C-SB	C	C, C	MC	2
Jamal	B/M	33	C-SB	C	C, C	MC	2
LaShay	B/F	25	C-SB	SC	HS, C	WC	2
Wanetta	B/F	27	C-SB	SC	HS, HS	WC	2
Nell	B/F	33	C-SB	C	C, C	MC	2
Charles	B/M	38	C-SB	C	C, C	MC	2
Maxine	B/F	44	C-SB	SG	G, G	UC	2
Valene	B/F	54	C-SB	G	G, G	UC	2
Shawn	W/M	37	C-SB	C	C, G	MC	2
Kristy	W/F	33	C-SB	C	C, C	WC	2
Clarence	W/M	19	C-ND	SC	C, G	MC	3
Van	W/M	21	J	SC	C, C	MC	3
Mark	W/M	20	C-SB	SC	C, C	UC	3
Stanley	W/M	22	C-M	SC	C, C	UC	3
Keith	W/M	21	C-L	SC	C, C	MC	3
Bruce	W/M	21	C-L	SC	C, G	MC	3
Lenny	A/M	21	C-ND	SC	G, G	UC	3
Ken	W/M	20	NR	SC	C, C	MC	3

(continued)

TABLE 4.1. (*continued*)

Pseudonym	Race/ Gender	Age	Religion	Education	Father's, Mother's Education	Socio- economic Status	Group
Rodney	W/M	21	C-M	SC	C, G	UC	3
Albert	W/M	22	C-L	SC	C, C	MC	3
Mark	W/M	20	C-L	SC	C, G	UC	3
Temeka	B/F	21	C-SB	SC	C, C	MC	4
Hannah	B/F	21	C-SB	SC	C, C	MC	4
Gina	B/F	21	C-SB	SC	HS, C	WC	4
Bridget	B/F	20	C-SB	SC	C, SG	MC	4
Caroline	B/F	21	C-M	SC	NA, C	WC	4
Clara	W/F	21	C-M	SC	C, G	WC	4
Brittany	B/F	19	NR	SC	G, G	MC	4
Cora	A/F	21	C-L	SC	C, C	MC	4
Edyth	B/F	20	C-SB	SC	C, G	MC	4
James	W/M	52	C-ND	C	C, HS	MC	5
Russell	W/M	55	C-L	C	HS, HS	WC	5
Kevin	W/M	38	NR	C	HS, HS	WC	5
Justin	W/M	47	NR	SG	HS, C	MC	5
Norman	W/M	42	C-ND	C	HS, C	WC	5
David	W/M	49	C-L	C	C, C	MC	5
Stephen	W/M	44	C-ND	SG	HS, C	WC	5
Ralph	W/M	38	C-M	G	C, C	MC	5
Tony	W/M	35	C-ND	C	C, HS	WC	5
Frank	W/M	43	C-M	C	C, C	MC	5
Tim	W/M	56	C-A	C	HS, HS	WC	5
Diana	W/F	27	NR	C	C, C	MC	6
Grace	W/F	25	NR	G	C, SG	WC	6
Kathleen	W/F	26	A	G	G, G	UC	6
Jane	W/F	29	C-ND	G	G, C	UC	6
Deanna	B/F	25	NR	C	C, C	MC	6
Laurie	W/F	28	C-ND	SG	C, C	MC	6
Jessie	W/F	30	C-ND	G	C, C	MC	6
Darius	B/M	29	A	G	C, SG	UC	6
Kai	W/M	31	J	C	C, SG	UC	6
Craig	W/M	27	S	C	C, C	MC	6
Robyn	B/F	30	S	C	C, C	MC	6
Antonio	L/M	32	C	SG	SG, SG	UC	6
Boyd	A/M	33	SH	C	C, C	MC	6
Allison	W/F	25	SH	C	C, C	MC	7
Marlon	W/M	29	B	SC	C, C	WC	7
Rose	W/M	26	C	SC	C, C	MC	7
Colleen	W/F	28	C-ND	G	C, C	MC	7

(*continued*)

Pseudonym	Race/ Gender	Age	Religion	Education	Father's, Mother's Education	Socio- economic Status	Group
Alice	W/F	30	C-M	C	C, C	MC	7
Aubrey	W/F	31	C-A	C	C, C	WC	7
Elijah	W/M	27	C-A	C	C, C	MC	7
Winston	W/M	26	C-A	SC	C, C	MC	7
Dan	W/M	26	NR	C	C, C	UC	7
Santos	L/M	23	SH	C	C, SG	WC	8
Rubin	A/M	27	A	C	C, C	MC	8
Emma	W/F	33	C	C	C, C	MC	8
Roman	W/M	36	A	G	C, C	MC	8
Joyce	A/F	25	SH	G	SC, C	WC	8
Kimberly	B/F	29	SH	SG	NA, C	WC	8
Chad	B/M	33	C-ND	SG	SC, C	WC	8
Luis	L/M	24	C	G	C, C	MC	8
Aldo	B/M	24	SH	C	C, C	MC	8

Note: Race: A = Asian; B = black; L = Latino; ME = Middle Eastern; W = white. Religion: A = Atheist; B = Bahá'í; C = Christian; C-A = Christian, Anglican; C-L = Christian, Lutheran; C-M = Christian, Methodist; C-ND = Christian, nondenominational; C-SB = Christian, Southern Baptist; J = Jewish; NR = no religion; SH = secular humanist. Education: C = college; G = graduate school; HS = high school; NA = not available; SC = some college; SG = some graduate school. Socioeconomic status: MC = middle class; UC = upper class; WC = working class.

TABLE 4.2. FOCUS GROUPS

Group Number	Type	Size	Members	Dominant Frame and Theme*
1	Bahá'í	9	Maureen, Brandon, Beatrice, Juan, Sonia, Ali, Donald, Arlene, Henry	I-1, II-1
2	Southern Baptist	12	Marilyn, Douglas, Jackson, Jamal, LaShay, Wanetta, Nell, Charles, Maxine, Valene, Shawn, Kristy	I-2, II-1
3	White fraternity	11	Clarence, Van, Mark, Stanley, Keith, Bruce, Lenny, Ken, Rodney, Albert, Mark	IV-1, IV-2
4	Black sorority	9	Temeka, Hannah, Gina, Bridget, Caroline, Clara, Brittany, Cora, Edyth	III-1, III-3
5	White Elks Lodge	11	James, Russell, Kevin, Justin, Norman, David, Stephen, Ralph, Tony, Frank, Tim	I-4, IV-1, IV-2
6	Singles group	13	Diana, Grace, Kathleen, Jane, Deanna, Laurie, Jessie, Darius, Kai, Craig, Robyn, Antonio, Boyd	II-2, III-2
7	White focus group	9	Allison, Marlon, Rose, Colleen, Alice, Aubrey, Elijah, Winston, Dan	I-2, I-3, III-3
8	Multiracial focus group	9	Santos, Rubin, Emma, Roman, Joyce, Kimberly, Chad, Luis, Aldo	II-2

* See Table 4.3.

Understanding the Audience: Structure, Agency, and Context

A vast amount of work on the reception of cultural objects such as film has been guided by perspectives that emphasize the structurally conditioned tastes and preferences of moviegoers. Conversely, another tradition has emphasized the volition of audiences to make active meanings and varied interpretations out of what they watch. A third position has, of late, attempted to strike a balance between these two approaches (Childress and Friedkin 2012; Eliasoph and Lichterman 2003; Emirbayer and Mische 1998; Hays 1994; Sewell 1992). This middle position often accentuates the role of context and locale. It affords primacy to the notion that group dynamics and style shape cinematic interpretations. Indeed, both structure and agency come to the fore, and they synthesize in any interpretive endeavor, simultaneously conditioning audience responses.

Perhaps no research paradigm in cultural sociology is as sacrosanct as the connection between cultural taste and socioeconomic status. There is consensus that social positioning drives opinions and interpretations (see Kaufman 2004) and that those opinions reflexively affect the accumulation of status (Schultz and Breiger 2010; Vaisey and Lizardo 2010). Indeed, people use and create potent symbolic boundaries to differentiate themselves from others and demarcate their social status through what they consume or display.

Cinematic audiences' varied (or homogeneous) social positions also invariably influence how they understand a particular film, and this effect is often influenced by the specific content of the film in question. For example, the already-established networks, or assumptions of networks, among people with similar demographic status (such as race or religion) will shape interpretations. When a particular film presents a story line or characters that privilege particular social categories, such as race (as is the case with white savior films), then the racial position the viewer occupies may grow more salient in moments of interpretation. In the focus group and interview data that follow, participants discussed race and religion, topics in which white savior films are intimately embedded.

But even with writers', producers', and directors' intentions clearly broadcast and highlighted in a film, individual moviegoers may evaluate the film against its intended meanings or in a multiplicity of ways previously unimagined by its creators. While early studies of audience interpretations were guided by Marxist paradigms that saw unique interpretations as evidence of false consciousness, more recent scholarship focuses on how people re-create cultural norms and values through a process of active reinterpretation. Much later, poststructural paradigms presented the view that author intention did not matter; as Roland Barthes proudly proclaimed in "The Death of the Author," "The birth of the reader must be at the cost of the death of the Author" (1977: 148).

In contrast to the preceding paradigms, other work (exemplified early on by scholars such as Wendy Griswold) contends that both author intention and audience freedom are simultaneously at play:

> Sociologists should rediscover that forgotten soul, the author, who has been deconstructed into oblivion . . . [and] there is no reason why authors, with their intentions, experiences, sociological characteristics, and "horizons" of understanding, cannot be treated in parallel fashion to readers: as agents who interact with texts, working to encode meanings. (Griswold 1993: 465)

If we consider both structure and agency, we must take seriously the interactions and contexts in which interpretations are mutually constrained and enabled. Both a priori and a posteriori networks, conventions, and group styles shape meaning-making. The effects of interpersonal influences, accountabilities, and patterns of social expectations are a central concern.

Hence, focus groups drawn from settings both naturally occurring and intentionally constructed on the basis of racial homogeneity and heterogeneity allow us some insight into how moviegoers discuss the character and content of white savior films. As the sociologist Elizabeth Long maintains, "Through this integrative process, individuals—and sometimes the group as a whole—can reach new understandings, whether about life or about the text at hand" (2003: 187). As the following data bear out, the groups in this study developed their own evaluative standards for discussing the films, some jovial and others with grave and austere expressions and with attention to their supposed consequences. While discussions in these focus groups are by no means "open" (see Hollander 2004 for discussion on "problematic silences" and "problematic speech" in focus groups), participants were interviewed before and after focus groups met to gauge their individual interpretations and how the group setting did or did not influence their interpretations.

Watching White Saviors: Dominant Frames

As outlined above, people do not simply receive messages and choose to (not) adopt them as their own. Rather, audiences select some portions of the media they encounter, while rejecting other portions of the same message, and this process often occurs in social interactions in which actors are forced to confront, debate, rationalize, and legitimate varied points of view and messages they deem more or less important given the structural and interactional exigencies of that particular context and moment. To examine how social structure, audience choice, and interactional context shape understandings of white savior films, I examined how socioeconomically varied groups made sense of at least one of three films—*Freedom Writers* (2007), *Gran Torino* (2008), and *The Blind Side* (2009)—using focus groups and interviews (see Tables 4.1 and 4.2). The participants in these focus group discussions and before- and

TABLE 4.3. OBSERVED INTERPRETATIONS

Frame or Theme No.	Frame or Theme Title	No. of Participants Expressing Frame or Theme	Focus Groups Expressing Frame or Theme Most Strongly	Frequency and Percentage of Expression of Frame or Theme
Frame I	**"Race Is Everywhere Now"**	**58**		**816 (38.15%)**
Theme 1	Diversity as an Inherent Good	34	1, 8	235 (10.99%)
Theme 2	Diversity as Danger	20	2, 5, 7	212 (9.91%)
Theme 3	White Pandering to People of Color	16	7	156 (7.29%)
Theme 4	Diversity as an Exotic Fetish	13	5	213 (9.96%)
Frame II	**"There's Really Nothing Racial about This Film"**	**21**		**629 (29.41%)**
Theme 1	A Common Spiritual Journey	17	1, 2	278 (13%)
Theme 2	White Defensiveness about Race	25	6, 8	351 (16.41%)
Frame III	**"Race Matters! Racism Exists!"**	**21**		**238 (11.13%)**
Theme 1	Cinematic Racial Stereotypes	14	4	88 (4.11%)
Theme 2	White Supremacy in Modern Film	13	6	103 (4.82%)
Theme 3	Racism Is Normal	8	4, 7	47 (2.20%)
Frame IV	**"We Need More White People Like This"**	**31**		**456 (21.02%)**
Theme 1	The White Man's Burden, 2.0	15	3, 5	205 (9.45%)
Theme 2	Ideal Whiteness	23	3, 5	251 (11.06%)
Total				**2,139/3,122 (68.51%)**

after-focus-group interviews drew on a deep reservoir of meanings to understand these films. At the same time, I found that many of their interpretations were guided and molded by common demographic characteristics that operated, to some extent, above their heads. All in all, from this data I detected four general frames and eleven second-level themes (see Table 4.3).

"Race Is Everywhere Now": Perceptions of Real-to-Reel Racial Diversity

The most dominant frame expressed by the participants was the recognition of increasing racial diversity in both real life and within televisual media products. Most saw their social world marked by amplified contact with people of different racial backgrounds, replete with cinema showcasing more and more nonwhite actors and story lines thought to resonate with nonwhite consumers. However, in watching these films, participants grounded this worldview in nuanced value judgments and interpretations of a film and its social significance.

Diversity as an Inherent Good

Many participants (thirty-four) argued that these films, far from being narratives that glorified white paternalism, represented stories about the inherent value of racial diversity and cooperation. To these viewers, *Freedom Writers* was a tale that witnessed the power of diversity to overcome inequality and misunderstandings across the color line. For example, Donald (white male, age thirty-nine) told me in an individual interview:

> I think people have become very interested in the value of diversity in recent years, in terms of racial difference and diversity, like multiculturalism and things that fight racial segregation. People see the value of having different races that come from, for the most part, different experiences and places. They see that having these different experiences in one place actually benefit[s] everyone. So, in that situation, you know, everyone learns from everyone. . . . Racial diversity is inherently beneficial to society.

This theme occurred in focus group settings. For example, Rubin (Asian male, age twenty-seven), part of focus group 8, an intentionally formed multiracial group, stated:

> When you're surrounded by people that are different, I think that changes how you think and what you say. I'm not going to try to lie to you and say I'm not more aware and cognizant of how I phrase things about race when I'm in a room like this. I mean, we all do that; we're just not as comfortable. But, I mean, that's the point, right? The more we have to confront our stereotypes or bad habits about how we might think about or, really, talk about other racial groups—so this group kind of proves the point, right? If we become more culturally aware, we become, in a way, and I don't want to be corny, but we become nice and more thoughtful people. . . . Even if we don't really mean it, if you practice it long enough, it becomes you. . . . Films like this [*Freedom Writers*] show that transformative power. Even if you critique aspects of it, I don't think you can deny the power of diversity.

Focus group discussions and individual interviews were replete with stories of the benefits of racial diversity and how films such as *Freedom Writers* or *The Blind Side* reiterate and propagate those benefits. People were adamant about the value of racial diversity to overcome social problems and they were pleased that mainstream Hollywood films with star power to attract audiences were showcasing interracial problem solving. As Darius (black male, age twenty-nine, and not in Rubin's group) told me:

Films like this, even though it's a white person at the helm, they remind me of the old *Star Trek* television shows. Captain Kirk would pilot his multicultural crew around the universe, and they worked together to figure out one bizarre thing after another. That was crazy to have a show like that back then, and the fact that this is more acceptable in Hollywood these days is just evidence, personally, that things are getting better. I mean, at least in schools, there's evidence that contact with racial diversity increased GPA scores, helps with student cocurricular involvement, it slows the dropout rate, improves self-confidence. . . . In general, the more films like this we have, the more accepted this fact will become.

A large number of participants argued that racial diversity, when connected with solving problems related to social inequality, was a boon to society. In relation to these films, they interpreted the story lines and on-screen interactions as an important and necessary step in turning entertainment such as film into a socially relevant and beneficial part of social relationships. "These films are not just something to do to relax; they help get an important message across," said Diana (white female, age twenty-seven). She continued, "It's not just a movie. For some, it's an important life lesson that some folks really need to learn."

Participants often used statistics and studies to legitimate their view of diversity as socially beneficial. "Something like more than half of white students that have cross-racial interactions have a greater sense of social responsibility than those who don't," said Maxine (black female, age forty-four). Charles (black male, age thirty-eight) responded, "I heard somewhere that the more interracial images you see in the media, the less likely, for example, whites are to have, like, an antiblack bias. . . . I don't know if that's true, but it makes sense." In general, participants were true believers in the power of diversity, in specific, in the power of these films to recuperate and mend racial wounds and divisions. As Mark (white male, age twenty) stated:

> If you look at Clint Eastwood's character [in *Gran Torino*], he's just a jerk and says some pretty racist things, but uh, by the end, all because of his friendship with the Asian kids, he's a totally different guy. He gives up his life for them. What more can you give someone than your life? . . . Now that I really think about it, it's really a strong and positive message.

Diversity as Danger

Not everyone was sold on the aforementioned glorification of these films or the contention that diversity is an inherent good. Rather, some (twenty) voiced the opinion that these movies were little more than a troubling sign, within a long-standing trend, of media propaganda in the interests of liberal politics. A number of participants explicitly stated that these films were "ideological devices" that attempted to "force" people to like "racial difference" and believe in a form of "interracial cooperation that can't ever exist." These comments and similar ones were rarely made in either individual interviews or in mixed-racial company but seemed a product of social settings of racial homogeneity—focus groups 2, 5, and 7: respectively, majority black members from a Southern Baptist church, members from an all-white Elks Lodge, and a focus group purposefully constructed as all white.

For example, the members of a white Elks Lodge (focus group 5) held the following conversation:

> MWH: So you've all said a little bit here and there about the potential effects of film. Can you speak more about the effects of a film like *Freedom Writers*? That is, what effects do you think a film like this has on society in general and race relations in specific?
>
> Russell (white male, age fifty-five): You asked, so listen, it's simple. It ain't got to be hard and made all fancy. So, just like anything, you get told something enough times, you begin to believe it. . . . I think the thing is, I've become aware of it, you see, and I don't like being forced to like racial differences. I don't. Now, I don't hate anyone else just because they're different, but I don't think everyone has the same values or does things exactly how I would like, and that's my preference, and that's okay. But I don't think it's okay that now you got some people in Hollywood pushing some liberal agenda to force us to forget about some inherent differences and just trying to make us be all happy and get along.
>
> David (white male, age forty-nine): I agree with what he's saying. *Freedom Writers*? Look, I know it said it was based on a true story and all that, but there's a lot of fiction going on in there, too.
>
> Kevin (white male, age thirty-eight): Now you got blacks and Latinos acting like they have to be the center of attention. Every other TV show or movie is about some minority and their problems and how they overcome it, and I guess that's good in terms of being a positive role model for young, uh, young blacks and Mexicans and Puerto Ricans or what have you, but that's not how things really are.
>
> Tim (white male, age fifty-six): Yeah, it's not—it's—it's not how things are at all. And, like, you're just gonna stir up trouble with the more movies like *Freedom Writers* that are made; they're just showing a way of life that isn't real. . . . It's a kind of interracial cooperation that can't ever exist. People just don't trust one another like that; it's not real, and I don't see it getting that way any time soon.
>
> Russell: We're just predisposed to be different. It is what it is. You can't make oil and water mix, no matter how hard you shake it.

As this dialogue unfolded, a uniformity of opinion coalesced around a particular set of assumptions: (1) film has messages that affect people's thoughts, (2) those messages affect us against our will, (3) those messages are politically driven attempts to socially engineer a cooperative interracial community, and

(4) that political agenda will fail because people are predisposed not to interact across the color line (akin to oil and water).

In meetings with other focus groups, this theme was reiterated, albeit with different nuance. Focus group 2 (the majority black Southern Baptist members) agreed that films such as *The Blind Side* presented more of a "liberal white fantasy" than a cogent social possibility. Nell (black female, age thirty-three) told me, "These films are just funny to me. I think they are there to either make white people comfortable with either saving us [black people] or with showing us doing things that white people like to do, like skydiving." A similar point was made in focus group 3, made up of members of a nearly all-white fraternity. Clarence (white male, age nineteen) remarked:

It's like these films are one big fairy tale about how things could be or how some liberal people consumed with race relations would like things to be. Most of the time, they have black people in coffee shops drinking lattes or wearing expensive suits so that they assimilate into mainstream, I guess "white," culture, right? Let's be real; how many times do you see black people at a nice coffee shop, and if you do, are they dressed well? I'm not trying to be harsh, but let's just be real.

As Clarence finished, Lenny, the only nonwhite (Asian male, age twenty-one) in the fraternity chapter, stated:

He's right. Look. Okay. It seems like nearly every other commercial, sitcom, and movie I see has at least one token black or Latino person in it. That's because these groups whine and complain a lot compared to other groups. They get representation for their political griping. Just look, there are hardly any Asians in mainstream films, and hardly any in these "white people go save black people in the dangerous 'hood" [*makes air quotes with his fingers*] movies. But there are hardly any Asians, I think, well, because we just—just—I guess, we just don't bitch and complain about—

Albert (white male, age twenty-two) interrupted him to say:

Well, you do see Obama or like Tiger Woods in more professional, like, clothes, but still, I agree. These films are just a part of the liberal Hollywood propaganda machine. Yeah, there are more and more minorities in the U.S., and that's fine and all, I guess, you know, because people can be who they want to be, but I don't want that. You know, I don't think we should push the issue and try to force everyone to just get along. We all have different cultures and ideas, and sometimes that's just different and will make, like, conflict, or, so, just because—so, like, like, Lenny fits in here [the fraternity chapter], and that doesn't mean all Asians will, or should. We're all different individually. . . . But it's like, if we don't take a minority as a member, then we're "racist." . . . It's all one movie like this over and over again. . . . I swear I'm going to stop watching movies.

For these fraternity members, these films were understood as little more than propaganda that forces racial cooperation, integration, and unity. Members of various focus groups were quick to point out that they had no issue with inter-racial cooperation, even as they voiced reductive and reactionary racial stereo-types about whites and their skydiving and lattes, Asians and their work ethic, or blacks and their dangerous neighborhoods. They collectively understood these films as a rose-colored display of interracial cooperation, which many interpreted as a trite and disingenuous story that others could not, and should not, be forced to emulate.

White Pandering to People of Color

A third theme was the value and place of diversity. This discursive pattern was marked by a specific interpretation of recent demographic shifts and the as-sumption that these films reflected a new form of racialized political correct-ness. In particular, some of the white respondents (seven) said that films such as *Gran Torino* reflected a widespread social expectation that whites had to pander to people of color. The following conversation about *Gran Torino*, with members of focus group 7, the all-white group, nicely demonstrates their logic.

> Marlon (white male, age twenty-nine): It just seems to me that Walt's character had to bend over backwards to accommodate the Cambo-dians. . . . Since you mentioned race, for me, the whole film is about, like, how white people have to pander to colored people, or people of color, or whatever. Like, here you have this guy, and he's old, but he's been through a lot of stuff, and so he's earned his stripes over the course of his life. Despite all he has been through, he has to kowtow to these new immigrants into the country and his neighborhood . . . and in the end, he has to sacrifice his life for them! This just seems a little bit much. . . . Hollywood just seems to be doing a lot of these types of films lately.
>
> MWH: Just to be clear, what do you mean by "these types of films"?
>
> Marlon: Like, these movies where the white guy—at least, it's usually some guy—will have to help out some problem that blacks or Latinos or Asians have, and then we're supposed to shed a tear at how heartfelt and wonderful it is. Yeah, it's wonderful for the nonwhite people in the film, but the white guy gets screwed over, and something horrible hap-pens to him because he spent all that time helping out. Just like this film—he gets killed for all he did. That's a hell of a message; that's kind of a sneaky way of portraying, like, a message for how race relations are becoming—white people are slowly turning into these kind of servants for nonwhites, especially immigrants.
>
> Colleen (white female, age twenty-eight): I don't know if it's as bad as Mar-lon makes it out to be, but I see that pattern, kind of. So when I pay attention and listen to this, it does make me realize that it's no longer acceptable to be a strong white character anymore. If you do, then that

show or movie is probably going to be called racist, so instead, Hollywood does this sacrificial white movie where the white person swoops in and helps out the down-on-their-luck black person, or whatever. Just like, in, uh, what's that—yeah, like in *Finding Forrester*. And he dies in the end, too! Right after the black kid gets to write a book that he basically wrote, or something.

Elijah (white male, age twenty-seven): Okay, so I guess I always see these types of movies as a bit far-fetched anyhow, but this all makes a lot of sense. . . . It's like central white characters have to pander to the characters of color.

Dan (white male, age twenty-six): I'm not sure it's pandering, but it's definitely like white characters have to cooperate with the nonwhites. If they don't, then that person is automatically the villain because he's racist.

Focus group 5, the Elks Lodge members, expressed a similar understanding of *Gran Torino*. David (white male, age forty-nine) stated, "Look at the award shows. Say you have two films. One has a white guy who helps starving black children. The other is a white guy that helps starving white children. The first movie wins the Oscar nine out of ten times." Kevin (white male, age thirty-five) replied:

I'm not so sure, but I agree with, I think, your larger point. Like, things are, like, I don't want to say "reverse racist" against white people, because I still think whites get a better deal in society than people of color. But at the same time, I think the movies are getting that way. . . . If you make a movie that has an interracial cast, you had better have the white guy kiss the asses of the other characters, unless you want the white guy to be the racist character on purpose.

Ralph (white male, age thirty-eight) responded:

It's reverse racism. You show me a film that does well, like [David] said, that doesn't have white people kissing black ass. You can't, at least since the sixties, 'cause they don't make those anymore. . . . Look, I hate to be all doom and gloom, but it's over. Race is everywhere now. Every time I turn on the news, it's like there's a report about more immigrants and more people of color being born than white babies, so it's becoming less white in number, and that means it's automatically going to be less prowhite. The tide is turning . . . so, of course, you're going to see these films that portray these happy white people that just *looooove* to do whatever nonwhite people want. Every year there's going to be more of it. . . . Get used to it, or just watch old movies; that's what I usually do.

Some of the white respondents recognized that, despite a demographically shifting nation, white racial identity was a substantive privilege. Yet most saw these films as potent reflections of an antiwhite world in which people of color were given undue attention and resources. For many of these white respondents, these films not only reflected these "realities" but helped usher in these changes by brainwashing others into accepting a brave new world socially engineered against white people. Expression of this view rose in direct correlation with a group's white homogeneity. Spaces of white homophily seemed to exacerbate (akin to an echo chamber) white fears of a growing nonwhite cadre that demands resources and erodes white privileges.

These dynamics, coupled with the whites' internalization of these white savior films' depictions of dysfunctional people of color that require salvation at the hands of a moral white benefactor, help explain how "subjective meanings become objective" facts (Berger and Luckmann 1966: 18). Watching film collectively helps legitimate and rationalize these participants' expressed worldview; these films then function as a crude measuring stick by which a powerful, yet seemingly vulnerable, group of whites gain an understanding of not just cinema but also themselves in which tilted social relations are reinterpreted as a cumulative disadvantage.

Diversity as an Exotic Fetish

The last theme concerns the interpretation of nonwhite racial diversity as a form of entertainment for white audiences uninformed as to the styles, traditions, and patterns thought essential and unchanging traits of blacks, Latinos, or Asians. For some of these participants (thirteen), but especially the members of a nearly all-white fraternity chapter, focus group 5, the on-screen interactions in *Freedom Writers*, *Gran Torino*, and *The Blind Side* were interpreted as informative and entertaining insights into the soul of nonwhite cultures. Through this supposed cinematic lens, these participants saw a world in which nonwhite racial differences were essentially distinct from their own and often interpreted these variations as dysfunctions that were dangerous yet entertaining on-screen spectacles.

In discussing the film *Gran Torino*, Mark and Stanley repeatedly discussed the Cambodian family as an "exotic" group with a host of characteristics they found exciting yet simultaneously disturbing.

> Mark (white male, age twenty): That family, I mean, they didn't speak any English and were expected to just be accepted, so I can see why Walt didn't like them in his neighborhood. But to me, that's how the country is; like, it's becoming more diverse with immigration, and so, I guess they were just, like—I guess what I mean is that family, because they were Cambodian, they were like the comedy in the film. Walt was the straight guy, so you need some crazy ethnic characters to liven things up a bit. . . . They have bright clothes and the witch doctor guy, and the daughter had to explain all their traditions and things to Walt, so in a way, they were like the real entertainment, aside from Walt being a bit old school.

Stanley (white male, age twenty-two): Honestly, I mean, I saw them as entertainment too, but they were really the educational part of the film for me. I had no idea that Cambodian people were migrating to the U.S. or that they were "hill people," like they said. So, it's really cool. . . . I mean, it's kind of like with *Freedom Writers*. I'm not from the 'hood, so I don't know a lot about what people who are—I mean, statistically, they are from those places that are lower socioeconomically, like different people of color who come from those places—I just don't really identify with what they go through, so these kind of films that show what they have to go through is valuable for white people like me that can't identify with those races.

Lenny (Asian male, age twenty-one), then remarked:

I'm just happy that it's another kind of different view of Asian people. We're not all the model minorities that are great at math or computer technology. I mean, we're different; we have different languages and cultures and come from different nations with different histories. . . . Your average person doesn't seem to know the difference between Japanese and Pacific Islander people, so any—I mean, *any*—more diversity about Asian people is good in my book.

Bruce (white male, age twenty-one) responded:

Yeah, but for me, as a white guy, I love films like this, because, well, it might sound funny, but like [Stanley] said, I can't identify with blacks or whatever, so it's really cool that I get to learn so much about them in these films. That's the real value, I think, of these films for society. I mean, especially when you see how funny black people are, or like how the religions are with the Cambodians, you can't possibly be racist if you keep an open mind to how cool they all are. It's like this. Every race, I think, has its strength, and I can really be entertained and appreciate that diversity when it's a big part of the movies, like these are.

In individual interviews many other participants told me of their fascination with racial "otherness" in the films. For example, Ken (white male, age twenty) told me:

I wouldn't have said this in the [focus] group, but I absolutely love watching films like these. It's like they kind of give me a optimistic feeling about the world, like the race problems will be solved one day, and on top of that, like, I feel like I get kind of a, like, secret view of stuff that most white people don't know. Like, I don't think most white people watch movies like *The Blind Side*. It's kind of made for black people. So, because I'm more open-minded to films like these, I get all kinds of knowledge about blacks that others don't get.

In a private interview, Laurie (white female, age twenty-eight) told me:

> Honestly, I don't get racism. Black people are so cool, so how—I mean, why would you hate them? . . . If you just watch—I mean like *really* watch— movies like *Freedom Writers*, you can see how, like, naturally poetic and, like, good at dancing they are.

And in a one-on-one discussion with Kristy (white female, age thirty-three), she remarked:

> If you look carefully at *Freedom Writers*, you can see that it's one of the most progressive films out there, because they actually let black people and Lati- nos and Asians be themselves. You know, in a lot of films they try to make the people of color be like white people, like really stiff and unnatural, in suits and ties and prim and proper, but that's not who they are. . . . I think it's difficult for some people to admit or say, but I think we all know that black people and, well, Latino people too, they are just cooler than most white people, like in terms of dance and music, and just their overall culture is more laid-back and not as uptight. . . . Black folks know how to party, and you can see that in *Freedom Writers* or another one of those older films like *Dangerous Minds*.

Many across the United States today associate racism with active hate or negative appraisal of one racial group by someone of another group. Such at- titudes of racial superiority are quite noticeable, but they have also declined or moved to private, backstage areas in recent years—a trend that led many to claim society is now postracial. Many of these supposedly postracial pontifica- tors might also read the cinematic interpretations of focus group 5 as racially benign or even as socially progressive. These participants not only refrain from negative judgments of people of color but also heap praise on them, celebrat- ing what they believe to be their natural and essentially different qualities that make them special and significant participants in a diverse society.

Yet this supposed praise is guided by a kind of racial objectification that is historically embedded in the North American context. As the racial category of whiteness emerged as a superior yet normal, neutral, and cultureless identity in the 1600s, nonwhites were marked as inferior, yet prized as reflecting vari- ous kinds of primordial and exotic ethnicities that possessed cultures rich in potent, carnal, and raw expressions and meanings. This correlation of people of color with music, dance, folk wisdom, spirituality, and raw human emo- tions untainted by the cultivation of Eurocentric dispositions, manners, and cognitive discipline became accepted as a commonsense truism. Throughout the centuries, whiteness was seen as somehow deficient in these more base and crass expressions that were thought the proper domain of people of color. In turn, whites approached these cultural expressions with a mixture of fascina- tion and fear, whether blackface minstrel shows in the 1800s, early 1900s white attendance in Chicago's black-and-tan jazz cabarets promising release from the constraints of Victorian prudishness, the naming of professional sport teams after indigenous clans and tribes, and white fascination with West Indian religions and foods associated with Rastafarianism and Obeah. Against this backdrop, the cultural critic bell hooks finds that many whites often see non-whites as

> a new delight, more intense, more satisfying than normal ways of doing and feeling. Within commodity culture, ethnicity becomes spice, season-ing that can liven up the dull dish that is mainstream white culture. . . . [F]antasies about the Other can be continually exploited, and that . . . exploitation will occur in a manner that reinscribes and maintains the *status quo.* (1992: 21–22)

Hence, white interpretations of ethnic and racial otherness as a kind of spice—within the context of a commodity-driven cultural industry, such as that of Hollywood film—work to remarginalize the status of nonwhites as objects for white consumption and entertainment. The value of nonwhites in an ever-diversifying world remains chained to the pedestal of entertainment adoration. Given that this meaning-making strategy depends on the belief that nonwhite culture and ethnicity has a kind of authentic and virile culture, it is reminiscent of the words of the postcolonial writer Frantz Fanon: "To us, the man who adores the Negro is as 'sick' as the man who abominates him" ([1952] 1967: 8). Fanon's words drive home the point that, regardless of the best or worst of intentions, the objectification of people of color as objects for the purpose of white entertainment can be a kind of sickness—a racism embedded in white supremacist desires for contact with, and control over, darker "others."

"There's Really Nothing Racial about This Film": Color-Blind Interpretations

Unlike the attention to racial diversity presented in the previous section, some individuals and focus groups did not see these films as directly related to race or racism. Many interpreted them as nothing more than a human interest story or a buddy film that tells tales of cooperation and collective problem solving that supposedly transcend the parochial topic of race.

A Common Spiritual Journey

Especially for focus groups 1 and 2 (religiously affiliated assemblies), the par-ticipants often spoke of these films as positive stories that glorified the univer-sal virtues of friendship and mutual aid. When I introduced the topic of race, my questions were politely rebuffed, as if inquires about race, whiteness, and paternalism were entirely off base. For instance, members of focus group 1 said:

Maureen (Middle Eastern female, age thirty-eight): No, I don't think *The Blind Side* is about race. I mean, I guess you could see it that way, but to me, it's about cooperation, parenting, charity. These are, at least, I think, more universal qualities about what it means to be spiritually connected to others. I really liked the movie because it's a tale everyone can relate to rather than just about race, which is only relevant to certain people.

Brandon (black male, age twenty-two): I could see it being about race; I could. But I think that's a bit parochial. I think a better way of describing the film is to concentrate on the common spiritual journey that it portrays. Here you have common denominators of the human condition, like [Maureen] said about parenting. That's a basic thing that everyone can relate to, and about needing someone to care for you and needing something to care for. It just doesn't get more basic than that.

Arlene (white female, age thirty-three): Honestly, not everything is about race, so in that sense, you could have this same movie with the football player being white, and it would be just as good. I don't think you need race to be a part of it, unless maybe you're overly concerned with that to begin with. . . . If anything, it's a religious message.

Members of focus group 2, a largely black Southern Baptist association, were also adamant that these films were more about religion and spirituality than race. In discussing *Gran Torino* and *Freedom Writers* the members concluded the following:

Douglas (black male, age forty-four): If anything, I could see why people want to make films like this about race, but really, it's arbitrary. Any type of difference, whether gender, class, age, religion—it really doesn't matter—but any type of difference would work because tales like this are about people helping others across social lines of division. Both people have to be different somehow, and that's the point, because it shows that this is a universal tale of despair, help, and redemption. In the end, *both* people get something from the other, so there's a spiritual message to be taken away.

Wanetta (black female, age twenty-seven): I can see how some white people might love a movie like *Freedom Writers* because it makes the white teacher look like the hero, but that's just one way to look at it. Instead, I look at these films as spiritually driven. Any time you have kids turning toward education and morals instead of drugs and street life, then that's a message of hope and salvation that everyone can relate to.

These religion-affiliated groups were certainly influenced by their common bond in faith and belief. While many of these same members spoke about the role of race in these films when in private communication with me, they were substantially less likely to do so in the context of the group interaction—a particular milieu in which a focus on the qualities of acceptance and cooperation, thought universal, spiritual, and inherent to the human condition, took precedence.

White Defensiveness about Race

Not all participants' color-blind interpretations were guided by religious or spiritual paradigms. For some (twenty-five) their racial identity paradoxically structured their belief that race was not a central issue, neither in these films nor society writ large. In focus groups, white participants often claimed that race was not an inherent part of these films; rather, people of color were too sensitive about race, and whites were incorrectly characterized as racist. In specific, these points manifested as polite, yet somber, discussions between participants in the racially heterogeneous focus groups 6 and 8.

In discussing the role of race in *Freedom Writers*, Diana (white female, age twenty-seven) said in a matter-of-fact tone, "I'm tired of discussions like this being all about race. It's not. It's about education. It's just—okay, I'm just going to say it. White people are made out to be bad because some—not all, but some—people who are not white are too sensitive about race." This comment opened the floodgates for the discussion. Darius (black male, age twenty-nine) immediately responded, "Who's saying that the movie's all about race? I didn't. But just because it's a movie about a school doesn't mean that it's not *also* about race, too." Others chimed in:

> Craig (white male, age twenty-seven): Look, I think, that, uh, what she's saying is that, uh, it's not really about race. So, um, yeah, there are a lot of people of color in the movie, so some people might think it's automatically about race because so many movies are so, you know, overwhelmingly white, and this one is so different from that. But, uh, just because there are lots of black or Latino people in the film doesn't mean that it's, like, automatically a movie about race.   •
>
> Darius (black male, age twenty-nine): No one's saying that it's automatically about race because there are more African Americans or Latinos or Asians in it than whites. I think some are suggesting that it's a film that *is* about race because of the dynamics between the white teacher and the students. I mean, when's the last time you saw a film with some black teacher that comes and teaches a bunch of little rug-rat white kids how to get their stuff together? That movie doesn't exist, and that's *my* point. That's what makes it racial. It's the same old white-hero-to-the-dumb-kids-of-color rescue movie.
>
> Jane (white female, age twenty-nine): See, I feel like you're saying that white people are racist just because they want to help. If she were going into the classroom and burning a cross, then she'd be racist, and she's basically doing the opposite, and she's still a racist. So, white people, no matter what they do, I mean, they can't be good. That's ridiculous; I'm sorry, but that's just crazy.

Deanna (black female, age twenty-five): Hold up. No one's saying that the teacher is racist or all white people are racist, but I mean, it's kind of obvious that these same old movies, like he said, are made over and over again. This is like that *Dangerous Minds* movie with what's-her-name, uhhhh, Michelle Pfeiffer. And—

Kathleen (white female, age twenty-six): It is the same old film, one about education and helping out students. It doesn't matter what color the people are. The teacher could be black. So what if she's not; it's all random anyhow. Do you think there's some conspiracy out there to make all the good teachers white or something?

Grace (white female, age twenty-five): Yeah, the race thing just doesn't matter. There are more black people in the film than white characters anyway, and you don't hear people complaining about that. It's just not about race, no matter how much you talk about it, and honestly, I mean, it's only becoming a thing because we're talking about it. If we just ignored the topic [race], then it wouldn't be an issue. . . . Talking about race is what makes race an issue.

This interaction was tense and I made a point to follow up with the participants in the individual debriefing interviews after the focus group session. Each of the white members in the group (Craig, Diana, Grace, Jane, Jessie, Kai, Kathleen, and Laurie) expressed a belief that the nonwhite participants (Antonio, Boyd, Darius, Deanna, and Robyn) took race too seriously and seemed "ready to call white people racist" or that they were too "angry" or "bitter." Many expressed a vigorous defensiveness over their interpretations of the film. Jessie (white female, age thirty) told me in a post-focus-group interview, "It's just a movie. A movie! I don't see why they [people of color] get so caught up in things like our interpretations of it. It's just a movie. . . . Race isn't a big part of things anymore. . . . It's just in their minds. They should let it go." Kai (white male, age thirty-one) told me:

That discussion made me really uncomfortable, but not because of their opinions about the film. . . . What I didn't like was their [people of color] insinuations that white people are racist or close-minded. It's like, I hate to say it, but they just talk too much about race, and they blame anything they don't like on white people. That's just an excuse. If you don't like the movie, then fine, but don't blame your own inability to really articulate why you don't like it on the teacher in the film, who's the star of the show, just because she's white.

Jane (white female, age twenty-nine) stated, "*Freedom Writers*? It's based on a true story, remember. That teacher was white, and she did a good thing, so if you have a problem about race over that, then you're really the racist. . . . I think black people are more racist than white people these days."

Color-blind interpretations of these films were evidenced in patterned responses by whites in heterogeneous settings and among different racial groups
when emphasizing other meanings seen in the film—for example, spiritual
messages of virtuous behaviors such as cooperation, sacrifice, and redemption.
When the topic of race was broached, varied responses were used to marginalize, discount, or deny the significance of race, such as disclaimers, mitigation,
euphemisms, excuses, reversals, blaming the victim, and other face-keeping
presentations of self. Teun A. van Dijk, a scholar of racial discourse, makes
clear:

> The denial of racism is one of the moves that is part of the . . . strategy
> of positive ingroup presentation. General norms and values, if not the law,
> prohibit (blatant) forms of ethnic prejudice and discrimination, and many
> if not most white group members are both aware of such social constraints
> and, up to a point, even share and acknowledge them. . . . [E]ven the most
> blatantly racist discourse . . . routinely features denials or at least mitiga-
> tions of racism. Interestingly, we have found that precisely the more racist
> discourse tends to have disclaimers and other denials. (1992: 89)

It is important to note that despite the differences in discourse for these
different social groups, this kind of talk can be found in a variety of contexts.
Regardless of the source, the strategic denials and dismissals of race labor to
protect and manage the self-images of those who engage in that discourse. Such
identity work is an important aspect of social life in an increasingly diversi-
fying United States. Significantly, these interpretations can rationalize and legitimate the racial order, in which the criminalizing of people of color as race
obsessed or overly sensitive remain essential building blocks of society. Even
though overt attitudes and ideologies are blatantly inconsistent with dominant
norms and ideals of egalitarianism, these subtle interpretations protect the social order against damaging claims of racism.

"Race Matters! Racism Exists!" Frustrations
with Film and Fellow Filmgoers

Nuanced and race-conscious analyses of *Freedom Writers*, *Gran Torino*, and
The Blind Side surround the color-blind interpretations of these films. Many of
the participants of color took exception with these films and with any contention that racial meanings were absent or insignificant.

Cinematic Racial Stereotypes

Some participants (fourteen) were clear that these films displayed offensive and
dishonest racial stereotypes. For many of these participants, the presence of
these negative representations were understood as not just evidence of a racist

film but a reflection of larger social norms about race and strategies for appeasing white filmgoers. Especially for the members of focus group 4, nine members of a historically African American sorority chapter, these films were understood as racially problematic, in terms of the intentions of the writers and producers and the effects of watching it. Caroline (black female, age twenty-one) stated of *Freedom Writers*:

> So really, let's get this straight. A woman comes into a classroom and tries to do her job. She's really bad at it and then works hard to get better. She finally learns how to do her job at the end, and we're supposed to think she's some kind of amazing hero? That's not a very thrilling movie; it's just not. That's too basic and everyday. . . . But let's throw in a whole lot of crazy racial stereotypes about black and Hispanic gangsters, drug dealers, abusive families, et cetera. It's like white people have those problems too, but you can't tell from the film. But so anyway, the whole reason you have those stereotypes is so that the movie entertains white people. They see that woman as some amazing hero that goes into this horrible place and turns them all around with her charm. That's ridiculous. The movie isn't about the white "savior" or whatever; it's about perpetuating a stereotype about people of color that white people think is true and even a bit funny. They can go to that movie and laugh at us and then feel better about saving us at the same time. And this is 2011?

Another member of group 4, an Asian member of the predominantly black sorority named Cora (female, age twenty-one) later explained, regarding *Gran Torino*, how negative stereotypes of black men help audiences identify with the lead white character.

> So the Walt guy is a complete racist jerk, but they have that scene with the three black men that are intimidating that Cambodian girl, so in storms the white man to the rescue? Come on! Without those three jerks in the film, Walt is just a racist ass—excuse me, but he is. And so as far as I can tell, the only reason those three black men—who are acting as stereotypical as you can: talking slang and cursing, disrespecting the girl, being violent, wearing baggy jeans, being rude, and smoking. I mean, smoking? When's the last time you saw someone smoke in a recent film? Only bad and, you know, evil characters smoke in modern movies.

Bridget (black female, age twenty) then remarked of *The Blind Side*:

> Yep, it's the same with all of these films. So, I guess they want us to take away that Sandra Bullock's family is so loving and nice and caring, because they make the football player a little slow and show how he comes from some single-parent household in a poor black neighborhood, with this weird, like, uncaring mother and these gangster-like characters outside, prowling

the streets. It's just—give me a second, okay? [*Long pause as she collects herself*] Black people are made to look like animals. That football player is like some stray dog they take in, and the rest of those gangster characters are made out like a pack of prowling wolves or something. I mean, come on! I get so sick of this. [*Long pause*] I mean, I'm black, and I come from a single-parent household, and my experiences were nothing—and I mean *nothing*—like that. But white people don't know all that, 'cause they just go to the movies and see those scenes over and over again and think that's the black experience, and then they look at me and think, "Oh, she's like that too." I'm not. I'm not.

Many other members of focus group 4 felt that the constant reiteration of black pathologies in these films would have a negative effect on not only white perceptions of nonwhites but black self-perceptions. Many were quite adamant that these films harm black self-esteem and cause some people of color to believe racial myths about themselves. Toward this end, Hannah (black female, age twenty-one) stated:

I'm not going to sit here and say that I haven't watched films like this before, 'cause I have, and I've enjoyed them, too. But a few years ago I swore off these types of movies, 'cause I just think they're harmful psychologically. I don't have any concrete evidence, but it just felt like—even me as a black woman—like I started to believe these things about black men, like they were all bad or messed up, and I know that kind of thinking doesn't fall out of the air, and I've never really had any bad experiences with black men, so it doesn't make sense that I would feel that way. But I really do think that the media, and especially films like this that are really glorified and have a big effect in pop culture, and get these stars and get rewarded and so forth, like, they are part of the problem in that the more of this you watch, the more you believe it. . . . Like any type of propaganda system, they first have to convince you that you are less than you actually are. . . . So now that Jim Crow is gone, now we have white saviors.

For these black women, the three films had three basic functions. First, the movies reproduced racial stereotypes about people of color. Second, white savior films were understood as less about the white characters than about entertaining white audiences with tales of black and brown misery and pathology. Third, these movies were thought akin to propaganda that poisons black self-esteem.

White Supremacy in Modern Film

Unlike most of the comments from focus group 4, a few comments from participants (thirteen) in focus group 6 were adamant that these films were about white characters, and many were explicit in their argument that these characters were subtle and nuanced reflections of white supremacist messages and meanings made for a time when it is not politically correct to espouse overt white supremacist ideology. Robyn (black female, age thirty) told me in a private interview before the focus group discussion:

> These films, boy! I mean, you really want us to get talking about these movies, huh? You picked some good ones. I mean, not "good" as in I think they're "good," but "good" in terms of there's a lot to say about them. I'll tell you what I think, now. . . . Really, here you have the white character, almost like a superhero for the 'hood, but the character is always white. That's important. Because if the character is not white, then the film just doesn't make sense, and no one would come watch it. . . . White people don't care about black people fixing their own problems. . . . They need to see one of their own roll into town with guns blazing and then clean up the bad little Negroes and save the good ones and then hug and kiss and ride off into the sunset together at the end. It's a complete white narcissistic fantasy. . . . The underlying message is a racist one: white people know better than black folks, and black folks need white folks to come and fix them. But it's all done in this covert, like, multicultural, happy song and dance.

During the discussion in focus group 6, she—and many others—were just as explicit about their view of the film as a "delivery system" for white supremacist ideology. Antonio (Latino male, age thirty-two) commented:

> So, what would you do if you wanted to get black, Latino, or Asian kids to really look up to white people and still, like, deify them in a time when that's not politically correct? I mean, you've still got white leadership and authority and political power in white hands, so you need to convince people of that even in their entertainment and media. It's why blaxploitation and racial revenge movies in the 1970s are no longer acceptable; they were stories of people of color fixing their own communities that were being attacked by white people. Now, you've got the opposite; you've got these lily-white teachers and parents and football coaches or whatever coming into the deepest, darkest ghettos and magically fixing the problems of these soon-to-be grateful black kids or Latino kids or anybody not white. . . . In the end, it's a message about white superiority because the white character always has the knowledge and the morals, and it's never the other way around.

Discussing *Gran Torino* in the same discussion and focus group, Boyd (Asian male, age thirty-three) stated:

> I guess in some ways, these films are like an acceptable delivery system for white supremacy in a time in which we're constantly told to be multicultural and diverse. . . . You can't have a movie about a neo-Nazi that, like, goes into some Asian neighborhood and makes fun of them. But you can have some

old white guy that's really racist in what he says, who then lives next to some crazy Cambodian family and their gangster cousins who drive around in souped-up Hondas, and because he's supposed to be all old-school smart and been around the block, he teaches the poor, stupid, little Cambodians how to be better people. The message is the same: white people are better, but Clint Eastwood has to be used instead of some idiot with a swastika.

A few others outside focus group 6, mainly people of color, picked up on the savior device as a clear message of white superiority. However, a few white participants in focus group 6 agreed that the films possessed subtle messages of white superiority and black inferiority. For example, Craig (white male, age twenty-seven) said:

> I guess now that people mention it, it does seem a little strange that the person that sets things straight, like the problem solver, in the film is always white. There are some lessons that the white protagonist learns, too, but those are often about the subtleties of the other culture in question. Like, Walt [in *Gran Torino*] learns that he likes Cambodian food, but big whoop; like, so what? . . . In the end of these movies, the white person who's the teacher, and I mean "teacher" as in the formal or informal sense—like in *The Blind Side*, Bullock is clearly the teacher there. But anyhow, what I was saying is that, you know, if you keep having this pattern of bad and kind of immoral people of color, with these kind-hearted white people, who might have issues too but get over it all on their own, then that's going to send a clear message to kids watching these films about who is better than who, and that's not right.

Shawn (white male, age thirty-seven) also remarked:

> I still think that this type of film is more about human cooperation, but I do see the racist element, but in totality, you know? Like, if this were just one or two films, I could say that we're making too much a deal about race in this context, but the more folks bring up films like *Amazing Grace* and *Avatar* and *Amistad*, and I mean, those were really popular movies, and I'm not even that into movies, and I've seen 'em, so I know others have. . . . That's kind of sad to think about—that we keep getting this message about whites being in control of things, even African Americans' lives.

Some of the participants in this study were easily able to recognize the white savior motif, with little to no prompting on my part. In the context of the discussion group, some expressed surprise at the white supremacist trope once it was made explicit but were readily convinced of its presence and legitimacy.

Racism Is Normal

While some participants were entirely unmoved and dubious of such a cinematic message (see the earlier discussion with focus group 5), a small few (eight) were willing to accept that contemporary film could be or is a potent vehicle for the dissemination of racist messages, even if there is no bad intention on the part of the writers or producers. As Emma (white female, age thirty-three) from focus group 8 said:

> I totally see how messed up these films are in terms of the racial message it sends: white people have intelligence, morals, integrity, hard work ethics, and blacks have bad qualities and need that white person to come save them. But I do want to say I don't think that is any plot or intention on the part of Hollywood. They just want to sell movies, . . . and that's a larger and disturbing realization for me, because that means that racism is really a normal part of everyday life.

These moments of realization came frequently for some white participants but were offered in a mundane style by the participants of color. Some nonwhite participants were much less shaken by the conversation and were confident that racial dynamics in film and other aspects of life were quite normal. For example, Antonio (Latino male, age thirty-three) told me:

> I'm always told that race doesn't matter by white people. I'm sure they think it doesn't matter for them. They're the ones who benefit the most from their race and don't have to think about it every day they wake up. I think about race when I see the police, when I go into a store, when I think about applying for a loan, or when I decide what clothes to put on, because I know some people might think I'm some gangster if I wear plaid, like I'm some Vato. White people don't think about race until they are surrounded by black or Latino people. . . . I bet the first time any of them thought about race, at least for a long time, was probably in that focus group discussion.

Robyn (black female, age thirty) stated, "How can you honestly say race doesn't matter? Well, you can if you're white because you don't have to deal with race on an everyday basis. . . . I just—sometimes I feel like screaming, like, 'Race matters! Racism exists!' How can anyone that's got their eyes open say any different? It's right in front of you!"

In addition, Kimberly (black female, age twenty-nine) remarked:

> I don't want to sound like I have an apathetic attitude, but I mean, racism is a normal part of this country. Sorry to be a downer, but I'd rather be real about it than sugarcoat the fact that there are huge gaps in wealth, pay, discrimination, and lots of other things that run along racial lines. . . . Part of the problem is that we can't have discussions about these issues, but we can have these white hero movies.

Such an attitude may not be properly categorized as "apathetic." The social formation of the United States has been historically racialized, thus its normal dynamics include a racial component. Indeed, the cultural production of movies will reflect, reproduce, and resonate with the already-established logic and habits of the society in which it is embedded. Hence, it should be no surprise that many who have to contend with the double standards or oppression of the racialized system (those marked as nonwhite) are more conscious of its operation and conclude that such procedures are normative. The sociologist Eduardo Bonilla-Silva writes:

> Racialized social systems are societies that allocate differential economic, political, social, and even psychological rewards to groups along racial lines; lines that are socially constructed. After a society becomes racialized, a set of social relations and practices based on racial distinctions develops at all societal levels. I designate the aggregate of those relations and practices as the racial structure of a society. . . . [O]n the basis of this structure, there develops a racial ideology (what analysts have coded as racism). . . . Racial phenomena are regarded as the "normal" outcome of the racial structure of a society. . . . Instead of explaining racial phenomena as deriving from other structures or from racism (conceived of as a free-floating ideology), we can trace cultural, political, economic, social, and even psychological racial phenomena to the racial organization of that society. (1997: 474–475)

Many participants expressed frustration and exasperated incredulity at the other participants who did not see the racism that was "right in front of [them]." Many of the participants of color (thirty-six) approached the discussion from an entirely different starting point in which racism and racial inequality in modern society was a given and uncontested fact. For many whites (forty-seven), they were unconvinced of that fact or believed that the world was slowly becoming antiwhite.

"We Need More White People like This": Embracing White Paternalism

While a number of the participants recognized the white savior trope and were quite critical of it as a mechanism for the reproduction of white supremacist ideology and rhetoric, a substantial number were not as skeptical of the films. For many, the films' lead characters, whether Erin Gruwell of *Freedom Writers*, Walt Kowalski of *Gran Torino*, or Leigh Anne Tuohy of *The Blind Side*, represented a wonderful and progressive kind of white person who fits hand in glove into a society increasingly attentive to diversity and "multicultural imperatives" (Hunter and Hughey 2013).

The White Man's Burden, 2.0

Many of the participants in this study understood the white savior character as weighed down by, and laden with, the moral responsibility to assist and save those people of color with whom the savior comes in contact. Accordingly, many white participants (fifteen) said they wished they could more resemble these characters. Moreover, they often remarked how the movies were "based on true stories" and thus a distinct probability for emulation in their own lives. Participants in focus groups 3 and 5 were most likely to voice this nouveau narrative. That discourse held two main characteristics: (1) white savior films were understood as a progressive art form that breaks substantially from Hollywood's prior history of overt, racist filmmaking, and (2) these films were thought to shine a harsh, but necessary, light on the dysfunctions and pathologies of people of color that are swept under the rug in a politically correct culture.

In a discussion that bounced among Bruce, Rodney, and Keith (in focus group 3), the three friends and fraternity brothers made clear the contention that *Freedom Writers* and *The Blind Side* are progressive movies that portray race relations and nonwhite characters in a much better light than movies of years past:

> Bruce (white male, age twenty-one): I took this film class last year, and we spent a lot of time examining the history of Hollywood and its really racist movies. Like, these movies, we watched clips, you know? Well, they were insane! I mean, they were filled with these horrible stereotypes about blacks and Asians and Indians, and it was just, I mean, it was really bad. . . . But these films [*Freedom Writers* and *The Blind Side*] are a thousand times better in comparison. I mean, I didn't really notice anything bad, you know, racially, with them . . . especially in comparison to the films that used to be so normal.
>
> Rodney (white male, age twenty-one): I think so, too. Because after all, if you, you know, just look at what kind of changes Hollywood has made, and because of society and the civil rights movement, that it's so much better today because of those, like, political and social changes; like, it's—it's just not okay to be racist anymore, at least not like it used to be, you know?
>
> Keith (white male, age twenty-one): If you approach film like art, like an art product, then I think you can see how the standards for evaluating it have changed over the years. What was once, let's say, a fairly racist film, like *Gone with the Wind* and the black maid in it, well, that film would be panned today, because it just doesn't fit in our world. . . . We've moved on past racism. . . . Sure, you've got crazies out there that will do and say racist things, but Hollywood invests too much money in its products to be racist.
>
> Bruce (white male, age twenty-one): Exactly, or like *Birth of a Nation* that was about the Klan and Reconstruction. That's a racist film because it's, like, you know, purposeful propaganda. There's no comparison today.

As the discussion makes clear, these participants felt that time had marched past the nadir of race relations and that Hollywood had, because of aesthetic and economic incentives, relinquished its prior use of racist images and story lines. In this line of reasoning, racism no longer made sense and would generate neither critical acclaim nor ticket sales.

Other participants disagreed that racism was long-gone from theaters but made a sharp distinction between racist moves and *Freedom Writers, Gran Torino,* or *The Blind Side*:

> Clarence (white male, age nineteen): I don't know; racist films are still out there, but when you have a story about different racial groups cooperating and learning from one another and trying to overcome some difficulty together, then that kind of plot and conflict resolution, when it's so interracial and cooperative, I mean, I find that hard to put in the same group as, like, I don't know, another prejudiced movie out there.
>
> Stanley (white male, age twenty-two): I agree. But also, you just wouldn't have the types of movies like *The Blind Side* fifty years ago. You wouldn't. So, I mean, race still matters in some ways, to a lot of people, but so, we're not postracial so much as we're kind of beyond racism, like we're almost postracism, you know? Because, like, some white family in Mississippi taking in some black kid to help him out—that would have been crazy fifty years ago, like before civil rights, so yeah, like, these films, I think, indicate how far we've come.

The narrative that race relations had improved over the past fifty years was a staple in these conversations. With this assumption firmly embedded and intersubjectively shared, many participants could find little wrong in the white paternalism of these films. Indeed, if the measuring stick for racial progress is *Birth of a Nation* or *Gone with the Wind,* there is little found wanting in *Freedom Writers, Gran Torino,* or *The Blind Side*.

The white man's burden, 2.0, was supported by another trope: that of the culture of poverty. The anthropologist Oscar Lewis used the term to explain why nonwhite communities, particularly Mexican and Puerto Rican (in *The Children of Sanchez* [1961] and *La Vida* [1965], respectively), held negative attributes such as frequent violence, a poor work ethic, the inability to delay gratification, a disregard for education, and so forth. Lewis extrapolated his findings to suggest a universal culture of poverty among these racial and ethnic groups. A half century later, many believe this research a valuable truism: that people of color lack important values, keeping them in a perpetual state of servitude and poverty. This assumption is a necessary component in interpreting the white savior film as progressive. The cinematic messiah in question must interact with a nonwhite culture in need of moral instruction. Otherwise, there is no plot, no rising action, and no climax whereby the nonwhite characters abandon their bad values and adopt the right (read, white) ways.

Some participants believed these films to properly illuminate the pathologies inherent to nonwhites. In a world thought overly politically correct and dominated by cordial niceties, a saving grace of these films lay in their ability to expose the problems inherent to black, Latino, and select Asian cultures. The following comments from some members of focus group 3 express this.

> Clarence (white male, age nineteen): I think that maybe these movies, like, show a bit of the less-than-popular side of how things are for some minorities. Like, in *The Blind Side* when Bullock's character goes to Michael's neighborhood and audiences get to see how things, like, really are. That's valuable because we don't really talk about the darker side of things.
>
> Keith (white male, age twenty-one): It's true. We don't discuss how bad things are for folks, and in some ways, it's a really wonderful story. I mean, it is true, anyway, about how people who care can change lives with enough hard work and planning.

After the discussion, Keith told me in an interview, "This might be a little controversial, but if a film like *The Blind Side* can show how bad people's values are in the 'hood, then maybe it will be a wake-up call."

This line of reasoning was echoed by many members of focus group 5. For example, Justin told me in a pre-focus-group meeting, "It's unpopular to say, but immigrants and black people have some issues with hard work. I think they just want handouts, and liberal white folks are more than happy to give it to them.... At least this movie [*Freedom Writers*] shows how bad it really is in those black schools." In the discussion itself, the following conversation took place:

> David (white male, age forty-nine): They don't sugarcoat the problems in those schools, that's for sure. And if we can at least expose the problems with the history of forcing people to interact, then maybe our schools would be better. I think things were better for everyone before busing tried to force races to interact; now both whites and blacks are getting a bad education.
>
> James (white male, age fifty-two): I agree wholeheartedly. I do. I really do. That's the one thing that film got right, I tell you what. At least it wasn't this fiction of a school where everyone was holding hands and getting along. I mean, that doesn't exist, and I don't think it can.
>
> Justin (white male, age forty-seven): At least that part of being "based on true story" was true. . . . If we could only have more honest conversations about the bad values with some people that just want handouts and are always complaining about discrimination. . . . How can you honestly complain about racism when all you're getting are handouts?

As these comments demonstrate, many interpreted the films as showing an often-hidden aspect of the bad values of the racial underclass. Such depictions were redeeming qualities of these films and satisfied their already-held beliefs about the supposed superiority of white culture, in terms of habits, values, and dispositions toward work and education.

Ideal Whiteness

A number of participants (twenty-three) argued that these films pulled back
the curtain on a culture of poverty run amok in communities of color and also
provided a readily available and easy-to-follow blueprint for how white people
should live racially progressive and interracially cooperative lives. These films
were valuable assets in an increasingly antiwhite world in which the criticism of
white people was a constant fixture of modern social structures. This was most
pronounced among focus groups 3 and 5). The following exchange between
Tony (white male, age thirty-five) and me in a post-focus-group interview is an
example.

> Tony: I think what one of the best things about these movies is that, you
>   know, they kind of like teach young white people how to be better in
>   terms of maybe, like, their own prejudices, or racial fears, or um, so
>   like, they present—I don't want to say, like, a role model, but in a way,
>   they show how you can be a white person that gets race right.
> MWH: What do you mean "gets race right"?
> Tony: Like, it's—okay, give me a second. So you know how in the beginning
>   of the films, like, there's this common pattern where the white person
>   is kind of, not stupid, but she just doesn't quite get how to interact with
>   black people or other, like, people of color?
> MWH: Okay.
> Tony: So, by the time the film ends, that character has learned how to mean-
>   ingfully interact, and I mean, she's a real friend to the other minorities,
>   you know. Like even Walt in *Gran Torino*, like he's pretty prejudiced
>   and mean-spirited, but like, he gets it. . . . I think these movies could
>   be instructive, especially for young white kids to learn how to talk with
>   minorities.

Members of focus group 5, an all-white Elks chapter, also remarked that
these films held the potential to teach white people how to interact with people
of color, but mainly to avoid the pitfalls of racialized political correctness.

> Russell (white male, age fifty-five): I suppose one good thing about films
>   like this is that white people can learn how to navigate the minefield
>   that is race. . . . Liberals love this type of white person that bends over
>   backwards for people of color. . . . It's the politically correct thing to do,
>   and if you're white and don't learn that, then you're in for it.
> Tim: Being white and having to deal with minorities is something that,
>   well, it's just not fair, at least for folks of my generation, because the
>   world has changed so much, and it's just pitfall after pitfall if you're not
>   careful. . . . At least these types of movies might teach white people how
>   to talk to folks of color.

After this discussion I met with Tim (white male, age fifty-six) for a one-on-
one interview:

Tim: I meant what I said. It's just hard to be white today, because you've got all these rules on how to talk and what to say and what not to say, and before you know it, someone is calling you a racist. That's a real burden that I live with every day, and I'd venture to say that I'm not alone. . . . At least with these films, some people—you know, white people who feel like I do—could take this liberal claptrap and turn it against itself.

MWH: I'm not sure I follow.

Tim: If you approach a film like this as a chance to learn the racial script . . .

MWH: I'm sorry, "racial script"?

Tim: The racial script. The racial script is that way we're all expected to act, like, you know, it's a scripted play. We all have our parts and lines and, well, like Shakespeare said, right? So anyway, if you're interested in avoiding that whole trap of being called a racist, then you can watch these do-gooder films and learn how to talk with minorities. . . . It might even help some of them out, too.

Such members' pessimism was not widespread, but it was pronounced among members of focus groups 3 and 5. For these participants, the white savior characters were anything but paternalistic figures; they were instructors for white pupils to learn the perils of modern race relations.

For many participants, these white savior heroes embodied a kind of white racial identity that I and other scholars have called "hegemonic whiteness" (Hughey 2010, 2012; Lewis 2004). Across these different focus groups and discussions, many, regardless of their critical or sympathetic view, saw the white savior character as an ideal way of being white that stands alongside other ways of being white that become complicit, subordinate, or marginalized in relation to that ideal. The sociologist Amanda Lewis unpacks this dynamic:

Whiteness works in distinct ways for and is embodied quite differently by homeless white men, golf-club-membership-owning executives, suburban soccer moms, urban hillbillies, antiracist skinheads, and/or union-card-carrying factory workers. . . . In any particular historical moment, however, certain forms of whiteness become dominant. (2004: 634)

These white savior characters resonated with an array of participants because they were able to navigate the tempest of modern race relations and emerge as the hero. Whether giving his life in the process (e.g., Walt in *Gran Torino*) or reflecting the real-life story of a Long Beach, California, high school teacher who then hit the big leagues as a Distinguished Teacher in Residence at California State University, Long Beach (e.g., Erin Gruwell's story in *Freedom Writers*), these characters were often perceived as the ideal way to perform whiteness among racially charged contexts and interactions. In this sense, the character is particularly hegemonic—it garners people's consent to the image because of a belief in its inherent moral legitimacy and social authenticity.

Conclusion

The data and my analysis reveal four important patterns regarding audience interpretation of *Freedom Writers* (2007), *Gran Torino* (2008), and *The Blind Side* (2009). As shown, participants often made meaning of these films in contradictory ways and, at times, via each individual worldview. However, these interpretations were also guided by the primacy of a particular social category to which they belong (e.g., racial identity or religious ideology) as well as shaped by the particular film being discussed and the direction of the conversation at any particular moment. Such a statement should not be (mis)understood as my contention that these audience members' interpretations were idiosyncratic. Rather, individual agency and structural and situational effects were quite pronounced in guiding how these participants made critical meaning of these movies. But such a general overview is insufficient; several specific conclusions are discernable.

First, pre-focus-group interviews indicate the importance of one's master status identity—or the specific characteristic that holds a significant meaning—on interpreting these films. That is, participants' understandings were conditioned by the interplay of important sociodemographic characteristics (such as their racial, gender, and religious identity) with the films' dominant meanings. While I make no claims to know the authorial intentions of writers, producers, and directors, it is evident from the marketing and promotion of these films (see the discussions in Chapters 1 and 2) that themes of cooperation and salvation across cultural and racial divides figure prominently. Accordingly, many participants who had a strong religious background were substantively more likely to view these films less as having to do with race and more as stories that spoke to universal qualities of human existence, such as suffering, cooperation, and redemption through virtuous behavior. For these participants, the religious allegories of these films were paramount in import, and issues related to race were a distraction from the religiously guided moral and ethical position they promoted. Yet African Americans, particularly females, were much more likely to admit that race and racism are still significant in contemporary society. Moreover, many of the black women in this study were adamant that these films held the likely possibility of rationalizing and legitimating negative views toward people of color and claimed that the films should thus be seen as both a significant form of propaganda and a threat to pursuing a racially just and equal society. The observed homogeneity of this finding may be explained, at least in part, by the salience of the master status of these participants; race and religion are substantive antecedent variables in the relationship between cinematic content and individual interpretive evaluations.

Second, my analysis of focus group conversations and post-focus-group interviews indicates that the localized process of social influence experienced in the focus groups changed views previously espoused in pre-focus-group interviews. The ephemeral group styles and temporary associations of focus groups influenced how people evaluated and made sense of film. Participants' encounters with these differing viewpoints and varied interpretations adjusted their individual appraisals of these films. The informal and relaxed nature of these group meetings seemed to moderate, rather than entirely disrupt, the power of one's sociodemographic master status. For example, it is clear that white participants—especially when in the context of focus groups marked by white racial homogeneity—were much more likely than others to embrace messages of white paternalism in these films, and the focus groups often intensified these members' pre-focus-group evaluations. Repeatedly, many white male participants interpreted these films as evidence of the new white man's burden to save people of color from their supposed cultural dysfunctions. This demographic also embraced the white savior protagonist as an appropriate role model for young whites to emulate in order to properly navigate the dictates of a culture more attuned to racial differences and social inequality. But for some others, the focus group discussion altered their views against their original, pre-focus-group interpretations. Some of the white participants in focus group 8 became defensive about the veracity of the film being discussed, believing it was little more than a dramatic retelling of a "true story" and that the topic of race was not relevant to its story line. For example, whereas Jessie (white female, age thirty) told me in a pre-focus-group interview, "I felt like some of the scenes made people of color look a bit helpless," she told me after the focus group was conducted, "It's just a movie! . . . Race isn't a big part of things anymore. . . . It's just in their [people of color's] minds. They should let it go." In sum, the influence of these groups intensified some pre-discussion viewpoints and altered others. In either case, the social discussion of these films had an effect and shows the power of the social context on the interpretive process.

Third, taken separately, these aforementioned two findings are unsurprising. However, what is most significant about this discourse is that the pre- and post-focus-group interviews show an unfolding temporal process by which private interpretations of the films were partially conditioned by their master status identities (i.e., race, gender, or religion) and by the content of the films, but that neither overdetermine participants' understandings. Audience members' interpretations are weakly constrained by the stated intentions of the writers and producers of these films. While I do not go so far as to say that the cinematic text does not matter, it is clear how rarely these films generated a singular and cohesive response. Also, one's master status and sociodemographic position, thought to cement one's standpoint, were redirected or significantly deepened on the basis of conversations anchored to differing social contexts. The power of symbolic interactions is both highlighted and specified: the structure of meso-level networks and associations matter to cultural reception. The role of interpersonal influence is paramount. The context may systematically construct a general consensus where there previously was none, generate contentious argumentation, or facilitate an even deeper and more devoted belief in the meaning of a cultural object than before.

5

The Significance of White Saviors in a "Postracial" World

The depoliticizing of politics is evident, in part, in the ways in which the new conservative formations use the electronic technologies of image, sound, and text not only to alter traditional systems of time, space, and history, but also to displace serious political issues to the realm of the aesthetic and the personal. In this context, discourses of style, form, and authenticity are employed to replace questions concerning how power is mobilized by diverse dominant groups to oppress, marginalize, and exploit.

—Henry A. Giroux, "Reclaiming the Social: Pedagogy, Resistance, and Politics in Celluloid Culture"

In late 2012 and early 2013—a century and a half since Abraham Lincoln's Emancipation Proclamation and the beginning of the slow demise of de jure chattel slavery—Steven Spielberg's *Lincoln* (2012) and Quentin Tarantino's *Django Unchained* (2013) were released. *Lincoln* grossed over $182 million (over $20 million outside the United States), played at over two thousand theaters in the United States alone, and received ninety-two award nominations, twelve of which were Oscars. The controversial *Django Unchained* raked in over $162 million in the United States (an astounding $117 million in foreign markets) and garnered five Oscar nominations ("Box Office/Business for Lincoln" 2013; "Box Office/Business for Django Unchained" 2013). To top it off, the two films were pitted against one another for two Oscar categories: Best Performance by an Actor in a Supporting Role and the prestigious Best Motion Picture of the Year.

Both of these films' plots focused on a powerful and skilled white man who supposedly despised slavery and who used his power and gave his life by film's end to secure black emancipation. In the case of Spielberg's *Lincoln*, the actions of the titular character (played by Daniel Day-Lewis) led to millions of ex-slaves being able to live out their life's dreams unencumbered by shackles, set to the auditory backdrop of tear-jerking, orchestrated violins. In stark contrast, Tarantino's *Django Unchained* highlighted one slave (played by Jamie Foxx) who, once liberated by a German bounty hunter, goes on a white-killing rampage to liberate his enslaved wife, all to the tune of James Brown's "The Payback" remixed with the lyrics of rapper Tupac Shakur.

Both films also demonstrate a persistent and stable presentation of a bifurcated whiteness. On the one hand are a mass of overtly and virulently racist whites who represent a harsh and unyielding cadre of evil incarnate. On the other stands the sole white savior. He or she is the enlightened and progressive soul who possesses the right combination of work ethic, intelligence, bravery, and holy virtue to bring people of color out of their lowly social station into the promised land of freedom.

The preceding description speaks not to these two films in isolation but to a growing genre of white savior films that captured the attention of a global audiences and critics. I draw attention to the labor these films commit as part of a larger, and increasingly global, narrative. The story these films tell is quite robust and predictable. It portrays a righteous white racial persona that rescues a nonwhite counterpart and in so doing redeems or reconciles an ideal or "hegemonic whiteness" (Hughey 2012) as the answer to injustice. This ideal is not reducible to specific white bodies and does not signify a one-dimensional white culture. Rather, the idealized white savior purports to embody and deliver a modern and objective rationality and cost-benefit analysis to those in need— what the sociologist Pierre Bourdieu called an "anthropological monster" (2005: 209). In films that focus on U.S. or U.K. slavery, South African apartheid, or Nazi Germany, such as *Cry Freedom* (1987), *A Dry White Season* (1989), *Glory* (1989), *Schindler's List* (1993), *Amistad* (1997), *Amazing Grace* (2006), *Lincoln* (2012), and *Django Unchained* (2013), the white savior—the idealized species of *Homo economicus*—is a penetrating figure who engages in a civilizing or redeeming project whose place makes sense in an increasingly shared global imaginary populated with nonwhite noble savages with cultural dysfunctions alongside whites who own and wield principles of logic, science, objectivity, and an unconquerable work ethic. The assumption of such essential racial differences, and these films' focus on the dysfunctions of nonwhite groups and the superiority of key white individuals, obfuscates the banality of the racism in these historical events. And given these films' increasing popularity in global markets, their fame and overall acceptance together signal white supremacy's saturation of the fabric of the mundane and everyday in diverse places across the planet.

The Global Seduction of White Saviors

In 1977 Jeremy Tunstall declared, "The media are American." And while he has revised that thesis to admit the recent growth and success of some non-American media, Hollywood's dominance remains. In the mid-1980s, 41 percent of movie tickets sold in Europe were for films made in the United States. By the mid-1990s, that number was 75 percent (Olson 1999). Over the first decade of the 2000s, total box-office spending on Hollywood films rose about one-third in North America while more than doubling outside the United States and Canada ("Bigger Abroad" 2011). By 2000 the gross domestic box office receipts for motion pictures in the United States was $7.66 billion, an increase

TABLE 5.1. U.S. AND GLOBAL MARKETS

Year and Films	U.S. Gross	Worldwide Gross (including U.S.)	No. of Films Produced	Gross Hollywood Global Average (per film)
2003		**$9.35 billion**	**455**	**$2,053,945**
Tears of the Sun	$43,426,961	$86,468,162		
The Last Samurai	$111,110,575	$456,758,981		
The Matrix Reloaded	$281,492,479	$742,128,461		
The Matrix Revolutions	$139,259,759	$412,000,000		
2005		**$8.95 billion**	**507**	**$1,765,286**
Crash	$54,580,300	$98,410,061		
The Constant Gardener	$33,579,797	$81,079,798		
2006		**$9.25 billion**	**594**	**$1,557,239**
Amazing Grace	$21,208,358	$27,213,386		
Children of Men	$35,286,428	$68,327,768		
2007		**$9.63 billion**	**611**	**$1,576,104**
Freedom Writers	$36,605,602	$43,090,741		
2009		**$10.65 billion**	**557**	**$190,860**
Avatar	$760,507,625	$2,782,275,172		

(in constant dollar terms) of 28 percent, from $5.97 billion in 1986. Following this increase, the exportation of Hollywood films grew even more rapidly than domestic markets, especially in European countries such as the United Kingdom, Germany, and the Netherlands (which alone accounts for 35 percent of all rental exports from the United States) (A. Scott 2002).

Moreover, Hollywood films that succeed in U.S. markets tend to do well in foreign markets (A. Scott 2002), such as the eight white savior films listed above. While data is limited, it is obvious that the last decade of white savior films have far outpaced other Hollywood films in global market performance. The Motion Picture Association of America reports that the recent average gross from Hollywood films has hovered around $1.5 million. Recent white savior films' gross, however, has ranged from $27 million to $2.7 billion (see Table 5.1). Their success, especially in consideration of blockbusters such as Avatar, is nearly unmatched. The success of Hollywood film has three explanations.

First, Hollywood possesses a nearly unmatched competitive advantage in terms of production, distribution, and marketing of firms compared to film industry outside the United States. The U.S. government has labored to create trade relationships in concert with pushing open foreign doors (especially to Western European nations with strong filmgoing trends) to allow the importation of Hollywood film. This push has been facilitated by a global embrace of neoliberal deregulation (e.g., the North America Free Trade Agreement or programs espoused by the World Trade Organization) of (mostly United States–based) media conglomerates that has cleared the ground for investment and sales in global markets. A centralized global system, dominated by the Big Six media conglomerates (controlling 85 percent of the cinematic market; see Chapter 2), reduces competitive risk; it enhances profits by studying what kinds of products sell and replicating those products. These trends add to the materialist explanation: largely because of economic hegemony, U.S. media subverts and replaces the development of other countries' domestic film production and other foreign competition (see Herman and McChesney 1997; McChesney 2003). Hollywood's global expansion continued in 2012. Hollywood's box office sales reached $34.7 billion (up 6 percent from 2011), in large part because of the increase in international box office sales ($23.9 billion), and Hollywood's returns went up 32 percent from 2008–2012, driven by growth in China, Russia, and Brazil (Motion Picture Association of America 2012).[1]

We must also consider the developmental explanation. In this approach, media communication is understood as a powerful influence on developing nations and domestic locales. Following from Daniel Lerner's theory of "dynamic equilibrium" or "want/get ratio" (Lerner 1958; quoted in Jahandary 1977), people in underdeveloped areas require assistance in learning how to balance what they want with what they can reasonably get, with media as the guiding force. Media educate people and create desire to emulate the lifestyle presented in films; U.S. film thus functions "as a watchman . . . a horizon-widener; as an attention focuser; as an aspiration raiser; and as a creator of a development climate" (Olson 1989: 69). In this view, U.S. media popularity is seen as either a tool or a crutch that creates either development or dependency.

A third approach considers Hollywood cinema a propaganda system that engages in mass persuasion. Discussing radio, Hadley Cantril and Gordon Allport (1935) argued that the rhetorical conventions of mass media oversimplified complex issues. Many began to worry that radio commentators were controlling their listeners by instructing them on "what to eat, what to read, what to buy, what exercise to take, what to think of the music we hear, and how we treat our colds" (Cantril and Allport 1935: 23). With Woodrow Wilson's creation of the Committee on Public Information to influence U.S. support for World War I and the rise in use of cinematic propaganda by both the Axis and Allied powers in World War II, many thought that certain media messages could act as "magic bullets" or "hypodermic needles" to directly capture attention and influence audiences (Hovland, Lumsdaine, and Sheffield 1949: 9–10).

---

1. Hollywood's dominance should not be oversimplified as a one-way flow of Western cultural or economic influence; it should be considered in relation to Hollywood's increasing involvement with the production and distribution of locally produced films (e.g., in select Asian markets) and its increasing dependence on selling films with content relevant to international markets.

While much of that research was discredited, films are still commonly blamed for having direct effects on audiences: from inciting violence and teaching immorality to manufacturing commercial desires and generating unthinking obedience (see Sullivan 2013). Today, research on media's limited effects and on how film can cultivate audiences' conceptions of reality remains en vogue. And as Chapter 4 demonstrates, individual agency and group context certainly moderate the dominant messages of the media product.

While these three paradigms do not sum up the diversity of explanations for why Hollywood media is globally diffuse and popular, they do reflect a common theme of anxiety over media effects. That is, many are preoccupied with what Hollywood media is supposedly doing to both American and foreign cultures. This concern is often marked by a fear of cultural homogenization. In this light, American film is akin to a Trojan horse. It is believed to covertly sneak in a host of commercial, elitist, and Western cultural forces that will overpower both U.S. locales and foreign indigenous beliefs to install a global monoculture in which people will embrace a narrow set of values, folkways, and normative behaviors.

But with no clear and definitive answer as to how Hollywood film generates its own popularity, these debates rage on. I resist engaging in a coup de main whereby I pronounce one paradigm as the correct and definitive approach. Rather, I shift tack. Instead of asking, "What effect do Hollywood films in general and white savior films in specific have?" I ask, "Why do these white savior films resonate with audiences?" While the three explanations (materialist, developmental, and propaganda) each afford important insights to explain Hollywood dominance, we must take into account the intersection and alignment of the properties of the text (the common denominators of these films' narrative) and the political, social, and interpretive context into which they enter. Film success is a function of their desirability, and their appeal is a function of the qualities an audience believes those films to have. As Scott Olson writes in *Hollywood Planet*, "The American media form a fairly unique bond between text and audience, and this bond accounts, to a significant degree, for the dominance the U.S. media enjoy at this historical juncture" (1999: xi).

I view Hollywood film as more than a materialist commodity and see its popularity as more than the result of political economy. Cinema is a symbolic system. White savior films' popularity partially resides in the synthesis between textual and interpretative resources. In consideration of the text, I do not place the onus for such popularity in the magic of Hollywood stories but rather (in synthesizing insights from the aforementioned three approaches) understand that generalized cultural matters such as race constitute established references "in conjunction with aesthetically oriented discussions of texts . . . which permit transnational circulation, ready comprehension and attractiveness" (O'Regan 1990: 306). Hollywood's domestic and international circulation is an outcome of the synthesis of shared audience interpretations and dominant ideological currents.

An Iron Fist in a Velvet Glove:
The White Savior in a Postracial World

The story lines of white savior films fit with many Western democratic nations' tendency to embrace a supposed postracial approach to race in terms of law, policy, and the promotion of popular culture consumption. This postracial or color-blind moment in which white savior films are produced, reviewed, and consumed is marked by five distinguishing and incredibly contradictory characteristics: (1) a prevalent hope and desire for a societal change to an authentically egalitarian society absent racial prejudice and discrimination, (2) a collective embrace of individualist explanations and solutions to achieve the aforementioned racial inequality, (3) a widely shared belief in the cultural or moral dysfunctions of people of color, (4) intersubjectively shared racial fatigue whereby many are largely impatient with or entirely disinterested in race-based discussions and policy, and (5) the downplay and minimization of racial inequality.

Hope and Change: Toward a Racial Utopia

First, many people within the Westernized nations, where these movies carry the most resonance (and garner the most ticket sales), claim that they are ready to move beyond the old racial and ethnic lines of division. Many within the United States express racially egalitarian views on many attitudinal measures— from interracial marriage to integrated neighborhoods. Many now reject overt practices of racial discrimination and hierarchy that mark their nations' past. In so doing, many claim that these societies have reached, or are nearly within, a postracial era. The sociologist Larry Bobo writes that the term "postracial" can "signal a hopeful trajectory for events and social trends, not an accomplished fact of social life. It is something toward which we as a nation still strive and remain guardedly hopeful about fully achieving" (2011: 13). Simply put, many desire a world where each one's fate and character will not be generalizable to the supposed traits of a racial or ethnic group.

In 2012 film critic James Hoberman of the *New York Review of Books* wrote, "I've been wondering for a while now when we were going to see an Obama-inflected Hollywood cinema." While Hoberman wrote that he expected such cinema to circulate around color-blind themes of community organizers and messengers of abstract qualities such as hope and change, I take a different tack. Coinciding with Obama's reelection, such inflected films might be better understood as stories that highlight the racist past to make our racial present seem hopeful and progressive simply by comparison. For example, 2012–2013 bears witness to the release of at least nine films on the question of slavery: *12 Years a Slave* (2013, directed by Steven McQueen), *Belle* (2013, directed by Amma Asante), *The Keeping Room* (2013, directed by Daniel Barber), *The North Star* (2013, directed by Thomas K. Phillips), *Something Whispered* (2013, directed by Peter Cousens), *Tula* (2013, directed by Jeroen Leinders), *Savannah* (2012, directed by Annette Haywood-Carter), and the aforementioned *Lincoln* (2012) and *Django Unchained* (2013). Never before has Hollywood embraced this theme, and at the sesquicentennial of the emancipation proclamation (and Obama's embrace of the image of Lincoln[2]), these films trade on belief in the racial and national mythology of linear progress.

Moreover, *Lincoln* and *Django Unchained* fall within the genre of white savior cinema. In *Lincoln*, both Abraham Lincoln and Thaddeus Stevens (Tommy Lee Jones) are enlightened individuals whose morality, attitudes, and psychological dispositions guide them through the sea of white hate to legislate equality. Blacks are neither equal contributors nor even subservient helpmates but passive background things to be rescued. For Stevens, his arrival home after the passage of the Thirteenth Amendment is framed by his bed sharing with his black housemaid (and rumored lover) Lydia Hamilton Smith (S. Epatha Merkerso) who then sets out to read the amendment aloud. As for Lincoln, his messianic moment is foreshadowed by the audience's knowledge that he will die for his country's sins at Ford's Theatre. His impending death only cements his status as the shepherd of his temporarily wayward flock. And while *Django* has been billed as a "black revenge fantasy" (Baker 2012), it fits comfortably within the white savior genre. Django is no antebellum Shaft. The white German King Schultz (Christoph Waltz) buys Django's freedom; trains him in the art of bounty hunting; finds Django's stolen wife, Broomhilda (Kerry Washington); kills his wife's master, Calvin Candie (Leonardo DiCaprio); and ends up sacrificing his life for Django and Broomhilda's freedom. Django's rampage arises not from a love for his people or the principle of freedom but out of affection for a single person. Django is not a cause of black liberation but an effect of a white paternal redeemer. In either case, white control and domination is marked by a time long gone, an era of slaves and Klan-style white supremacy that died long before Obama swore his oath to the presidency on Lincoln's Bible.

Individualism: Bad Apples and Racial Saviors

Second, the discourse of a postracial society is now marked by individualist explanations for the causes of, and solutions to, racial inequality. The focus on individual people thus shifts focus from historical and contemporary structural inequality to that of individual bad apples. In *The Political Mind*, George Lakoff remarks that we often employ this meaning-making strategy: "All you have to do is find the bad apples in the organization and get rid of them. The organization is redeemed. There was never anything wrong with it. The problem was the bad apples" (2008: 163–164). The focus on the individual bad white

---

2. Obama-Lincoln comparisons might have begun when in 2007 at Old State Capitol in Springfield, Illinois, Obama announced his presidential run. Comparisons have solidified with Obama's statements that Lincoln is his favorite president and mainstream media's continued comparison of the two figures (e.g., Hirschkorn 2009).

person as the root cause of racism allows audiences to ignore the deep systems, institutions, and resources that resulted in and now reproduce contemporary structures of inequality. By blaming "bad white people," rather than a system of symbolic and material violence, we can easily ignore the damage of systemic racist laws and organizations.

For example, rather than address the logic and legacy of slavery, *Glory* (1989) makes one Union colonel, James M. Montgomery (Cliff De Young), an evil man bent on inflicting pain on the innocent. Rather than reflect on the economic, political, and social institutional collaboration that underpinned the transatlantic slave trade, *Amistad* (1997) makes Secretary John Forsyth (David Paymer) the evil mastermind behind the racist attempt to keep Cinque and the rest of the Africans enslaved. And instead of drawing attention to the systemic labor discrimination and violently unsafe working conditions of black female domestic servants in Jackson, Mississippi, that serves as the backdrop for *The Help* (2011), the film makes Hilly Holbrook (Bryce Dallas Howard) an evil, white segregationist who conceived the "Home Help Sanitation Initiative," requiring all Mississippi homes to have separate bathrooms for their black employees under the racist assumption that black people carry diseases, passed by toilet seats, that are especially harmful to white people.

This individualist logic also works in the converse; if there are bad apples, there must be good ones, too. Despite many critics' evaluation of these films as liberal or progressive stories, the films concentrate on the processes by which the sole white savior brings about a contented obedience and acquiescence to his or her moral and intellectual authority. In this sense, people of color in these films are often minor characters or background figures who play the role of disciplined and docile bodies, who come to completely trust—and even to love—the panoptic gaze of their white savior. Such asymmetrical social relations, reframed through the implicit logic of a necessary white paternalism, are a form of cinematic torture. We are forced to endure the few cross-racial friendships that do grace films as representations of the best of progressive and liberal Hollywood.

The villain versus the good guy is certainly not a new invention. For example, it was a staple of the spaghetti Western in the 1960s. However, when applied to race relations, the constant deification of an atomistic white actor who has the right qualities to magically liberate oppressed people from their conditions does provide the right ideological lubricant to the machinery of hegemonic, neoliberal white supremacy on a global stage. The white savior is an individual not bound by laws or political correctness. He or she is the small-government hero of a neoliberal age; a libertarian Dirty Harry of our era—simply witness Clint Eastwood as Walt Kowalski in *Gran Torino*.

People of Color: Dark Dysfunctions

The third aspect of the postracial worldview is the belief in cultural dysfunctions of people of color. This widely held belief is the white savior's raison d'être. Film critic James Snead writes, "American films do not merely feature this or that debased black image or this or that glorified white hero in isolation, but rather they correlate these images in a larger scheme of semiotic valuation" (1994: 4). This tenet contradicts the aforementioned tenet of individualism, which itself gestures toward an important point. The very concept of Western *individualism*, itself, is racialized. And white savior films play on this social fact. For the white savior to materialize, he or she must do so not for the reason of saving a sole person of color. Rather, the chosen person or classroom of a darker hue must be contextualized within an overall culture of nonwhite poverty, dysfunction, and pathology from which there is no self-salvation.

In this sense, Leigh Anne Tuohy cannot save Michael Oher unless he comes from a black Memphis ghetto full of neighborhood violence and family turmoil in *The Blind Side* (2009), Walt Kowalski cannot rescue Thao and Sue without their placement in an immigrant community threatened by Cambodian gangsters driving souped-up Hondas in *Gran Torino* (2008), and Erin Gruwell cannot deliver her multicultural classroom from the gun violence, sexual abuse, and lure of quick drug money unless her pedagogical grace is set against the sins of East Lost Angeles.

The key people of color to be saved from their darker communities (generally the few with a speaking role, or the folks who say more than a few stereotypical and racialized lines in a diction associated with their group) are exceptions to the rule. The individuals in the film are of only two types: the white savior and the aforesaid villain who acts as an unsuccessful spoil and plot device, making the white savior character seem all the more triumphant. These films thus trade on, and in so doing reproduce, many of the already-held beliefs in black and brown dysfunction. As the sociologist Eduardo Bonilla-Silva (2010) has written, such "cultural racism" assumes that people of color are not individuals per se but a collective mass who share a worldview marked by bad values such as a lack of work ethic or the inability to delay gratification.

Racial Fatigue

I contend that these films also resonate globally because they implicitly deal with interracial cooperation without being too focused on race. Especially regarding white savior films made after 1998 (the time in which the postracial film era begins), the story lines showcase interracial cooperation without ever becoming a modern race film.[3] In a time in which many white populations in Western nations feel that their attitudes have positively changed and that as a

3. I refer to the "race film" as a specific film genre in the United States from approximately 1915 to 1947. These films, approximately five hundred or so, were produced for a black audience and featured all, or almost all, black casts. Modern race films were produced in a brief moment in the 1990s and increasingly addressed race, racism, and racial conflict as a theme or major subplot (e.g., *Jungle Fever* [1991], *Malcolm X* [1992], *A Bronx Tale* [1993], *Higher Learning* [1995], *Rosewood* [1997], *Beloved* [1998], and *The Hurricane* [1999]).

result racial inequality should have declined along with it, many now express exasperation with overt talk of race. In this sense, such white savior films provide a tale that makes them feel good about whiteness (*à la* the savior and in counteropposition to the bad white apples) while also freeing them from any responsibility to address lingering or structural inequalities. If at the end of each film the select people of color escaped their dangerous and dark communities and classrooms with little more than their hard work and white cheerleader, then the film labors to subvert the evidence of systemic and organized racial discrimination that has been empirically verified in study after study (see Barton and Coley 2010; Bertrand and Mullainathan 2004; Entman and Rojecki 2001; Oliver and Shapiro 1997; Pager and Shepherd 2008; Reskin 2012). Such a sincere fiction represents a significant retreat from empirical and grounded views on race and, hence, the actual pursuit of racial equality.

The Minimization of Racial Inequality

White savior films nearly always present history as linear; as a relatively upward arrow in which the evils of the past are constantly dispelled and in which we inch closer and closer to a future racial utopia, without backsliding or repeating prior mistakes. In nearly every white savior film, life is better off than in the beginning, in large part because of the recognition that racism is a moral wrong and socially wasteful. The effect is a view of society as inching farther and farther away from racism—itself conceptualized as something long dead and located in the past, whose lingering effects only manifest here and there. Such minimization allows those in the dominant racial group to ignore or downplay claims of racial inequality from individuals and communities of color who experience it and thus provides license to disregard racial disparities as little more than liberal propaganda, race baiting, and the playing of the race card. Hence, the minimization of racism suggests that discrimination is no longer a central factor in social life (Bonilla-Silva 2010).

Together, these five characteristics of our contemporary cinematic moment rationalize a disturbing worldview that takes the shape of a particularly seductive and attractive global commodity. That cinematic vision and film product is marked by a singular message—the continued significance and necessity of white racial paternalism. And with the advent of electronic distribution, the worldwide consumption of Hollywood film is all the more easy. Consumers' choices and desires are not just limited but shaped and manufactured by the global reach of Hollywood in the context of a white-dominated Western audience that simultaneously desires a view of interracial cooperation and equality but refuses to acknowledge the racial conflict and inequality within society. As Mary Jackman argued in *The Velvet Glove* (1994), the ideology of paternalism coerces subordinates through a discourse grounded in love rather than hate. In this scenario, whites who pronounce authoritatively on the welfare of all and then profess to provide for those needs are seen as postracial heroes—those who care about racial "others" without making "racism" an issue. Hence, these films provide a view of white saviors delivering love, affection, and praise to nonwhites as long as the ones in need of saving comply with the terms of their unequal relationship. Such interracial "cooperation" subtly redefines discriminatory actions as benevolence while making affection contingent on compliance.

From Color-Blind Ideology to an Ideal White Identity

These five characteristics make up a postracial racial ideology: a system of meanings that manifests in a range of discourses to reinforce and reproduce beliefs and assumptions about individuals based on their affiliation with a particular racial group without seeming conventionally racist. These racial ideologies are mediated by film and are "meaning in the service of power" (Bonilla-Silva 2001: 63). Given white savior films' popularity, we can theorize that members of various racial and cultural groups across the globe select these media on the basis of their availability and perceived material and symbolic utility. Given Hollywood's increasing dependence on the global market, it is perhaps surprising that the neocolonialist dynamic of white saviors and nonwhites-in-need resonates so well. Since Hollywood film companies will go to extraordinary lengths not to alienate a global audience, we might consider that these films are commonly understood as nonracial narratives of individual success and triumph in the face of adversity, tales of redemption and salvation, and battles of good versus evil. An equally plausible notion is that whiteness is a global signifier for these supposedly nonracial ideals that are, in turn, now largely accepted as normal and natural. White savior films are received not just as a representation of how things are but as a depiction of how things should be. The paternalistic protagonists of these films may particularly resonate with an increasingly homogeneous global taste culture (Fu and Govindaraju 2010) and with white audience members regardless of location. As film scholar Oscar Gandy Jr. writes:

> What we understand about the nature of identity formation leads us to believe that the mass media performs a critical symbolic function in providing role models that we use in self-evaluation. We make adjustments on the basis of comparisons between who we think we are at present and who we think we would like to be in the future. That projection, or *ideal self*, is often informed by reference to *role models*, and those role models are, more often than not, accessible to us primarily through the mass media. (1998: 86)

White savior films share a perspective that associates that ideal white self with order, rationality, self-reliant individualism, courage, fortitude, and the ability to overcome personal deficiencies. This character is demarcated and constructed through two symbolic boundaries: inter- and intraracial distinctions. In the former, the ideal white self is made in counterdistinction to nonwhite communities stereotyped by disorder, carnality, violence, unbridled emotion, and moral depravity. In the latter, the ideal white self emerges in relation to evil, ignorant, and overtly racist whites.

The ideal white self, or what I have elsewhere called "hegemonic whiteness" (Hughey 2010, 2012), is a flexible and malleable example that retains white dominance through subtle forms of color-blind racial paternalism while castigating overt and ugly forms of white supremacy. Along these lines, Richard Dyer writes in his landmark essay "White":

> The strength of white representation . . . is the apparent absence altogether of the typical, the sense that being white is coterminous with the endless plentitude of human diversity. If we are to see the historical, cultural, and political limitations (to put it mildly) of white world domination, it is important to see similarities, typicalities, within the seemingly infinite variety of white representation. (2011: 826)

Across the diversity of cinematic settings in the United States as well as global locales (e.g., *Cry Freedom, Rambo III, A Dry White Season, Indiana Jones and the Last Crusade, Black Robe, City of Joy, Medicine Man, Schindler's List, Tears of the Sun, The Last Samurai, The Constant Gardener, Amazing Grace, Blood Diamond, Children of Men,* or *The Last King of Scotland*), these films showcase a wide variety of white representations. Out of this host of white characters, a savior emerges as the ideal type of whiteness. The deification of this now stock character obfuscates the mechanisms of white supremacy through a cinematic conflation of coercive power with kindness. The supposed care and grace of white saviors are never revealed as a means of establishing or reinforcing a vulgar white supremacist social order. Quite the contrary, these films show images of nonwhite happiness after white intervention, even as those nonwhite faces act as little more than impotent puppets of white paternalism and gentile instruction. Any raw power exerted by the white savior does not come across as naked force but as a natural extension of his or her job as teacher, military leader, neighbor, or football coach. On the rare occasion that we see a display of force by the white savior it is against either those atypical and caricatured white racists or against the lone person of color who dares resist the sage advice of the savior. Without question, the white racists are shown the folly of their ignorant ways, and the autonomous person of color who refuses to submit to white paternalistic authority suffers a severe or even mortal fate.

White Saviors beyond the Silver Screen

In "The Cinematic Racial Order" Norman Denzin writes, "Each decade since 1900 has articulated its version of the white man's burden" (2002: 38). Indeed, the white man's burden is not simply a product of Rudyard Kipling's time. Racial paternalism is alive and well today in these films and in many people's imagination. In our postracial, and now post-Obama, moment, these films are increasingly popular with Western-located whites (in both the United States and Europe), as they are marketed as plausible and moral narratives in which whites are invited to idealize and identify with these white saviors and role models and to take up a racial crusade. Thus, Hollywood continually searches for real-life examples of white heroes to represent or simply insists on their fabrication and insertion. For example, the film *Machine Gun Preacher* (2011) is based on the alleged true story of a Christian nationalist biker gang member and former drug dealer named Sam Childers who journeyed to Africa to build homes and then picked up arms to fight local militias as a kind of white, Tarzanesque hero (not surprisingly, the veracity of the story is being questioned) (Gilson 2011). Also, after the monumental success of the 2007 publication of *Three Cups of Tea* (a book by white Americans Greg Mortenson and David Oliver Relin) that details their years of building schools for impoverished girls in Pakistan and Afghanistan, there was talk of a Hollywood film detailing their heroic travels. However, after a 2011 *60 Minutes* investigative report alleged that many events depicted in the text did not take place (e.g., some of the schools were either not built or were abandoned) and that chartable donations were misused (e.g., used to pay for the authors' travel expenses on speaking tours), talk of a film evaporated. Relin committed suicide in November 2012 ("Questions" 2011).

When Melvin and Mario Van Peebles sought funds to produce the film *Panther* (1995), based on the formation of the Black Panther Party in Oakland, California, in 1966, they were urged repeatedly to create a white savior out of thin air to make the film more palatable to mainstream audiences. Mario Van Peebles stated:

> We went around to Hollywood studios and we kept on getting the same message: "You really need to make this more mainstream." But when pressed to explain what they meant, it turned out that they meant that there had to be a white person as one of the main heroes of the movie. "People knew about the destruction of the Indians for years," we were told, "but no one really cared about it until they got Kevin Kostner [*sic*] to star in *Dances With Wolves*. The civil-rights movement might have been led by Stokely Carmichael and Martin Luther King, Jr. but Americans didn't care to see a movie on that till *Mississippi Burning* tells the story from the standpoint of white FBI agents. So you've got to write this story in a way that gives focus to some big white stars, and then you can do your thing." One of the studio heads suggested that we make one of the leading Panthers a white man. Others suggested focusing on a Berkeley white person who would meet five young black guys, teaches them to read and stand up for themselves, and then they become the Panthers! (Tikkun 1999)

In 2008 African American actor Danny Glover attempted to produce a Hollywood film on Haitian independence and the military hero Toussaint-Louverture. To back the project, he approached a host of financiers and hopeful coproducers, but few were interested. Glover stated, "Producers said, 'It's a nice project, a great project . . . [but] where are the white heroes?' . . . I couldn't get the money here, I couldn't get the money in Britain. I went to everybody. You wouldn't believe the number of producers based in Europe, and in the States, that I went to" ("Danny Glover's Slavery Film" 2008).

As these examples show, if one can abide by the white savior script and convince others of the story's legitimacy, these tales will find production and resonance with the mainstream. Moreover, as the popularity of these films attest, they may also serve as potent blueprints for both constructing and legitimating neocolonial relationships between whites and nonwhites in off-screen settings. For example, the political scientists Andy Baker and Jennifer Fitzgerald (2012) found that even when the need of Africans and Europeans is objectively equivalent, whites who possess prejudicial racial attitudes are more supportive of aid to Africans than to Anglo-Europeans. Baker and Fitzgerald thus contend that racial prejudice may manifest as a seemingly generous paternalism, rather than as a form of uncharitable resentment we would expect from traditional racists.

As with white savior films, audiences may find a host of other popular culture examples for white paternalism laced with strange performances that blur the line between mimicry and mockery, as well as the division between real and reel life. For example, supermodel Kate Moss donned blackface to grace the cover of the September 21, 2006, issue of the *Independent* (which was temporarily renamed "The Africa Issue"), whose sales proceeds would "help fight AIDS in Africa." In another strange blackface performance, white celebrities such as Richard Gere, Sarah Jessica Parker, Liv Tyler, and Gwyneth Paltrow donned face paint and beaded jewelry over captions of "I Am African" in a 2010–2011 fundraising campaign for antiretroviral drugs for African nations. A civilizing and paternalistic ideal white identity appears in the interracial and transnational adoptions by Madonna, Angelina Jolie, Brad Pitt, and Sandra Bullock. And such white paternalism dangerously and violently manifested in 2010 when ten white Christian missionaries from Idaho traveled to Haiti and attempted to take several Haitian children back with them. When questioned as to why they had neither passports nor adoption paperwork, one of the children reportedly broke free and yelled, "I am not an orphan! I do have my parents!" ("Detained Americans" 2010).

While some might wish to serve as apologists for these performances and actions, I single them out as neither essentially good nor evil. Rather, I point to such episodes of real-life white saviorhood as spectacles that are hailed and idealized in Hollywood cinema and in the tabloids that hound Hollywood celebrities. In this light, I draw attention to the trend of media illumination of whites who swoop to the rescue of supposedly feeble folks of color rather than whites who would confront white supremacist ideology, practices, or laws. Such a trend is by no means new, as the historian George Lipsitz points out in *The Possessive Investment in Whiteness*:

> Our history and our fiction contain all too many accounts of whites acting with unctuous paternalism to protect "helpless" people of color, but very few stories about white people opposing white supremacy on their own. Members of aggrieved racialized groups appear most often as threatening strangers or

servile sidekicks in the stories we tell about our past and present, and only rarely as self-active agents operating in their own behalf. (1998: xiv)

Whereas the contemporary versions of white supremacy and colonialism explicitly disavow white desire for domination, a subordinate dark "other" is required for the production (and glorification through consumption) of a heroic white self. Daniel Bernardi in *The Birth of Whiteness* thus writes:

> In film, arguably the most popular and profitable form of culture in the last one hundred years, racist practices dominate the industrial, representational, and narrational history of the medium. . . . U.S. cinema has consistently constructed whiteness, the representational and narrative form of Eurocentrism, as the norm by which all "Others" fail by comparison. (1996: 4–5)

Such popular cultural iconography normalizes a hierarchical relationship in which Westernized nations and ideal and elite white identities in the Northern Hemisphere regularly exploit the people and resources of the Global South as well as standardizes the unequal relations between lighter- and darker-skinned people within Western nation-states. This relationship is glossed over by the image of well-meaning white celebrities fixing the problems of Africans by appropriating token objects that supposedly represent aspects of an African culture (read, beads, face paint, and dark skin) while paradoxically claiming a kind of membership in a downtrodden group ("I am African") to rationalize their care for a group in which they temporarily stake claim. The exploitative, hierarchical, and unequal racial relationship is both mystified and reproduced when dark-skinned people of peripheral nations and areas become symbolic objects and one-dimensional caricatures to be saved by supposedly color-blind white role models and benefactors. The popularity of this relationship—as both a media device and a model to emulate—demonstrates the continued power of whiteness to cast a long and wide shadow across the globe.

Appendix A:
Data and Methodology for Content Analysis of Film

To discover more consistent and illuminating aspects about the white savior film in modern cinema, I adopted a research design that incorporated the strengths of traditional content analysis and mitigated its weaknesses. While conventional quantitative-based content analysis has its merits, including the ease of reporting numerical correlations as findings, its Achilles' heel is that numerical categories do not necessarily capture the meanings encoded in a given image or narrative. As a consequence, this work incorporates a qualitative approach in place of a purely quantitative examination.

The choice of subject for this study was prompted by observations of popular Hollywood feature films that qualified as white savior films made between 1987 and 2011. "Feature film" is a term the film industry uses to refer to a film made for initial distribution in theaters. The Academy of Motion Picture Arts and Sciences, the American Film Institute, and the British Film Institute all define a feature as a film with a running time of 40 minutes or longer. The Centre National de la Cinématographie in France defines it as a 35-mm film that is longer than 1,600 meters, or 58 minutes and 29 seconds for sound films, and the Screen Actors Guild defines it as a film with a minimum running time of 80 minutes. Generally, a feature film is between 90 and 210 minutes.

To structure the methodology, I developed a study population ($n = 50$) drawn from the extant social sciences and humanities literature on white savior films. I first searched for the terms "white savior," "white messiah," and "great white hope" in conjunction with "film," "movie," and "cinema" in the following databases: Academic Search Premier (EBSCO), Ethnic NewsWatch, Google Scholar, Humanities International Complete (EBSCO), ICPSR (Inter-university Consortium for Political and Social Research), JSTOR, LexisNexis Academic, Project MUSE, SocIndex with Full Text (EBSCO), and WorldCat (OCLC FirstSearch). This search yielded hundreds of returns. When I limited the search to peer-reviewed social scientific and humanities journals that labeled a film as a "white savior" (or related term—e.g., "white messiah"), I was left with a population of 127 films. When I limited that result to films that were released during the study time frame (1987–

2011), the population was reduced to 83 films. I then reduced that number by selecting the 50 most frequently mentioned films (see Table 2.1 and the list at the end of this appendix).

Once I had selected the study population, I analyzed the films' plot and character synopses (using scripts when synopses were not available) to determine whether a film could be classified as a white savior film. Synopses and scripts for feature films are from the Internet Movie Database (http://www.imdb.com), the Internet Movie Script Database (http://www.imsdb.com), and the Moving Image Archive (http://www.archive.org/details /movies). The analysis did not disqualify any films from the population. I then analyzed the films and scripts through a rigorous coding process. This step had three substages. First, I watched the films and read the scripts (January–August 2011) in their entirety to obtain deeper insights into the plot, character development, and racial meanings of each. I made note of patterned frames and themes to develop "sensitizing concepts" (Blumer 1954: 7). Well-entrenched traditions of social inquiry view sensitizing concepts as invaluable starting points for the development of interpretive devices (see Charmaz 2003; Morse and Field 1995; Padgett 2008; Patton 2002). Kathy Charmaz clarifies:

> Sensitizing concepts offer ways of seeing, organizing, and understanding experi-
> ence; they are embedded in our disciplinary emphases and perspectival proclivi-
> ties. Although sensitizing concepts may deepen perception, they provide starting
> points for building analysis, not ending points for evading it. We may use sensitiz-
> ing concepts *only* as points of departure from which to study the data. (2003: 259;
> emphasis in original)

Second, I watched the films again and reread the scripts in a deductively guided search for common themes related to white savior films (e.g., race, racism, inequality, power, education, authority, and bureaucracy [see Bernardi 2007; Chennault 1996; Giroux 1997; Moore and Pierce 2007; C. Rodríguez 1997; Stoddard and Marcus 2006; Vera and Gordon 2003]). This secondary viewing refined the inductive coding process. This inductive and deductive process generated seven frames, one or more of which was the focus of a film. I found that at least one of seven frames cut across all of the fifty films in question. These frames were (1) crossing the color and culture line, (2) his saving grace, (3) white suffering, (4) the savior, the bad white, and the natives, (5) the color of meritocracy, (6) white civility, black savagery, and (7) "based on a true story": racialized historiography.

Third, I watched the films again and coded them (August–December 2011). Thirty-second intervals of film served as the unit of analysis. The fifty films totaled 6,207 minutes (mean = 124), or 12,414 thirty-second units of analysis. I began the formal coding process to determine exact frame and theme frequency and form. During this stage, I coded judi-ciously, identifying a frame only when it was clear that the thirty-second unit of analysis had one or more frames. Some frames were intimately linked, and when the unit of analysis referred to more than one frame or theme at a time, each unit of analysis scored a 1 to create overlapping categories (0 = frame or theme not present, 1 = frame or theme present) (see Table 2.3 for the numbers of frames, their ratios per film and per year, and percentages of frames per film and per year).

While this form of nonprobability population construction disallows inferences from the study population to the entire general population of white savior films originally iden-tified by the extant literature (*n* = 127), the work aims to delineate transferable, rather than generalizable, conclusions. This form of qualitative content analysis consists of reflexive movement between concept development, sampling, data collection, data coding, data analysis, and interpretation. The aim is to be systematic and analytic but not rigid. Al-though categories derived from the extant literature on white savior films initially guided the study, others emerged throughout the study. Thus, such content analysis is embedded in constant discovery and constant comparison of relevant situations, settings, styles, images, meanings, and nuances. The empirical results reflect a deeper cultural code about mythologies concerning whiteness and adopts the contention that analysis of racial media representation is one of the most fruitful areas of study for discreetly measuring social life and also a rich repository of ideological meaning and cultural significance.

Cry Freedom (1987; 157 min.)

Director: Richard Attenborough
Writers: John Briley (screenplay) and Donald Woods (book)
Stars: Denzel Washington, Kevin Kline, and Josette Simon
South African journalist Donald Woods is forced to flee the country after attempting to investigate the death in custody of his friend the black activist Steve Biko.

The Principal (1987; 109 min.)

Director: Christopher Cain
Writer: Frank Deese
Stars: James Belushi, Louis Gossett Jr., and Rae Dawn Chong
A teacher is assigned to be the principal of a violence- and crime-ridden high school.

Mississippi Burning (1988; 128 min.)

Director: Alan Parker
Writer: Chris Gerolmo
Stars: Gene Hackman, Willem Dafoe, and Frances McDormand
Two FBI agents with wildly different styles arrive in Mississippi to investigate the disappearance of some civil rights activists.

Rambo III (1988; 102 min.)

Director: Peter MacDonald
Writers: David Morrell (characters), Sylvester Stallone (screenplay), and Sheldon Lettich (screenplay)
Stars: Sylvester Stallone, Richard Crenna, and Marc de Jonge
Rambo's Vietnam commanding officer, Colonel Trautman, is held hostage in Afghanistan, and it is up to Rambo to rescue him.

A Dry White Season (1989; 97 min.)

Director: Euzhan Palcy
Writers: Andre Brink (novel), Colin Welland (screenplay), and Euzhan Palcy (screenplay)
Stars: Donald Sutherland, Janet Suzman, and Zakes Mokae
Ben du Toit is a schoolteacher who always has considered himself a man of caring and justice, at least on the individual level. When his gardener's son is brutally beaten up by the police at a demonstration by black schoolchildren, he gradually begins to realize his own society is built on a pillar of injustice and exploitation.

Glory (1989; 122 min.)

Director: Edward Zwick
Writers: Kevin Jarre (screenplay), Lincoln Kirstein (book), Peter Burchard (book "One Gallant Rush"), and Robert Gould Shaw (letters)
Stars: Matthew Broderick, Denzel Washington, and Cary Elwes
Robert Gould Shaw leads the U.S. Civil War's first all-black volunteer company, fighting prejudices of both his own Union army and the Confederates.

Indiana Jones and the Last Crusade (1989; 127 min.)
Director: Steven Spielberg
Writers: Jeffrey Boam (screenplay), George Lucas (story), Menno Meyjes (story), George Lucas (characters), and Philip Kaufman (characters)
Stars: Harrison Ford, Sean Connery, and Alison Doody
> When Dr. Henry Jones Sr. suddenly goes missing while pursuing the Holy Grail, eminent archaeologist Indiana Jones must follow in his father's footsteps and stop the Nazis.

Dances with Wolves (1990; 181 min.)
Director: Kevin Costner
Writers: Michael Blake (screenplay) and Michael Blake (novel)
Stars: Kevin Costner, Mary McDonnell, and Graham Greene
> Lt. John Dunbar, exiled to a remote western Civil War outpost, befriends wolves and Indians, making him an intolerable aberration in the military.

The Long Walk Home (1990; 97 min.)
Director: Richard Pearce
Writer: John Cork
Stars: Sissy Spacek, Whoopi Goldberg, and Dwight Schultz
> Two women, one black and one white, in 1955 Montgomery, Alabama, must decide what they are going to do in response to the famous bus boycott led by Martin Luther King.

Black Robe (1991; 101 min.)
Director: Bruce Beresford
Writers: Brian Moore (screenplay), Brian Moore (novel)
Stars: Lothaire Bluteau, Aden Young, and Sandrine Holt
> In the seventeenth century a Jesuit priest and a young companion are escorted through the wilderness of Quebec by Algonquin Indians to find a distant mission in the dead of winter. The Jesuit experiences a spiritual journey while his young companion falls in love with the Algonquin chief's beautiful daughter under the imposing and magnificent mountains. Dread and death follow them upriver.

City of Joy (1992; 132 min.)
Director: Roland Joffé
Writers: Dominique Lapierre (book), Mark Medoff (screenplay)
Stars: Patrick Swayze, Pauline Collins, and Om Puri
> Hazari Pal lives in a small village in India and becomes homeless. Upon saving an American man, Dr. Max Lowe, they strike up a friendship and join forces to overthrow a greedy landlord.

Medicine Man (1992; 106 min.)
Director: John McTiernan
Writers: Tom Schulman (story), Tom Schulman (screenplay), Sally Robinson (screenplay)
Stars: Sean Connery, Lorraine Bracco, and José Wilker
> An eccentric scientist working for a large drug company is working on a research project in the Amazon jungle. He sends for a research assistant and a gas chromatograph because he is close to a cure for cancer. When the assistant turns out to be a "mere woman," he rejects her help. Meanwhile the bulldozers get closer to the area in which

they are conducting research, and they eventually learn to work together and begin falling in love.

Thunderheart (1992; 119 min.)
Director: Michael Apted
Writer: John Fusco
Stars: Val Kilmer, Sam Shepard, and Graham Greene
> *A young mixed-blood FBI agent is assigned to work with a cynical veteran investigator on a murder on a poverty-stricken Sioux reservation.*

Schindler's List (1993; 195 min.)
Director: Steven Spielberg
Writers: Thomas Keneally (book), Steven Zaillian (screenplay)
Stars: Liam Neeson, Ralph Fiennes, and Ben Kingsley
> *In Poland during World War II, Oskar Schindler gradually becomes concerned for his Jewish workforce after witnessing their persecution by the Nazis.*

On Deadly Ground (1994; 101 min.)
Director: Steven Seagal
Writers: Ed Horowitz, Robin U. Russin
Stars: Steven Seagal, Michael Caine, and Joan Chen
> *Mystical martial artist/environmental agent takes on a ruthless oil corporation.*

Stargate (1994; 121 min.)
Director: Roland Emmerich
Writers: Dean Devlin, Roland Emmerich
Stars: Kurt Russell, James Spader, and Alexis Cruz
> *An interstellar teleportation device, found in Egypt, leads to a planet with humans resembling ancient Egyptians who worship the god Ra.*

Dangerous Minds (1995; 99 min.)
Director: John N. Smith
Writers: LouAnne Johnson (book), Ronald Bass (screenplay)
Stars: Michelle Pfeiffer, George Dzundza, and Courtney B. Vance
> *An ex-marine teacher struggles to connect with her students in an inner-city school.*

Losing Isaiah (1995; 111 min.)
Director: Stephen Gyllenhaal
Writers: Seth Margolis (novel), Naomi Foner (screenplay)
Stars: Jessica Lange, Halle Berry, and David Strathairn
> *The natural and adoptive mothers of a young boy are involved in a bitter, controversial custody battle.*

A Time to Kill (1996; 149 min.)
Director: Joel Schumacher
Writers: John Grisham (novel), Akiva Goldsman (screenplay)
Stars: Matthew McConaughey, Sandra Bullock, and Samuel L. Jackson
> *A young lawyer defends a black man accused of murdering two men who raped his ten-year-old daughter, sparking a rebirth of the KKK.*

Ghosts of Mississippi (1996; 130 min.)
Director: Rob Reiner
Writer: Lewis Colick
Stars: Alec Baldwin, James Woods, and Whoopi Goldberg
> *The widow of murdered civil rights leader Medgar Evers and a district attorney struggle to finally bring the murderer to justice.*

The Substitute (1996; 114 min.)
Director: Robert Mandel
Writers: Roy Frumkes, Rocco Simonelli, and Alan Ormsby
Stars: Tom Berenger, Raymond Cruz, and William Forsythe
> *Having completed some jobs for the CIA, ex-marine John Shale is visiting his high school love, Jane. She is now a teacher at Columbus High School in Miami. Soon after his arriving, Jane has her knee cap broken while jogging. After that, John decides to go undercover as her substitute in the high school. Very soon he finds out that a gang named Kings of Destruction is terrorizing the school. Shale is going to give everything to stop them, even his own life.*

Sunset Park (1996; 99 min.)
Director: Steve Gomer
Writers: Seth Zvi Rosenfeld, Kathleen McGhee-Anderson
Stars: Rhea Perlman, Fredro Starr, and Carol Kane
> *A white schoolteacher takes over a talented but undisciplined black high school basketball team and turns it into a winning team.*

Amistad (1997; 155 min.)
Director: Steven Spielberg
Writer: David Franzoni
Stars: Djimon Hounsou, Matthew McConaughey, and Anthony Hopkins
> *The film tells the story of an 1839 mutiny aboard a slave ship that is traveling toward the northeastern coast of America. Much of the story involves a courtroom drama about the free man who led the revolt.*

Bulworth (1998; 108 min.)
Director: Warren Beatty
Writers: Warren Beatty (story), Warren Beatty (screenplay), Jeremy Pikser (screenplay)
Stars: Warren Beatty, Halle Berry, and Kimberly Deauna Adams
> *A suicidally disillusioned liberal politician puts a contract out on himself and takes the opportunity to be bluntly honest with his voters by affecting the rhythms and speech of hip-hop music and culture.*

Music of the Heart (1999; 124 min.)
Director: Wes Craven
Writer: Pamela Gray
Stars: Meryl Streep, Cloris Leachman, and Henry Dinhofer
> *A schoolteacher struggles to teach violin to inner-city Harlem kids.*

The Matrix (1999; 136 min.)
Directors: Andy Wachowski, Lana Wachowski

Writers: Andy Wachowski, Lana Wachowski
Stars: Keanu Reeves, Laurence Fishburne, and Carrie-Anne Moss
> *A computer hacker learns from mysterious rebels about the true nature of his reality and his role in the war against its controllers.*

Snow Falling on Cedars (1999; 127 min.)
Director: Scott Hicks
Writers: David Guterson (novel), Ronald Bass (screenplay), Scott Hicks (screenplay)
Stars: Ethan Hawke, Max von Sydow, and Youki Kudoh
> *A Japanese American fisherman might have killed his neighbor Carl at sea. In the 1950s, race figures in the trial. So does reporter Ishmael.*

Finding Forrester (2000; 136 min.)
Director: Gus Van Sant
Writer: Mike Rich
Stars: Sean Connery, Rob Brown, and F. Murray Abraham
> *An Afro-American teen writing prodigy finds a mentor in a reclusive author.*

Monster's Ball (2001; 111 min.)
Director: Marc Forster
Writers: Milo Addica, Will Rokos
Stars: Billy Bob Thornton, Halle Berry, and Taylor Simpson
> *After a family tragedy, a racist prison guard reexamines his attitudes while falling in love with the African American wife of the last prisoner he executed.*

Hard Ball (2001; 106 min.)
Director: Brian Robbins
Writers: Daniel Coyle (book), John Gatins (screenplay)
Stars: Keanu Reeves, Diane Lane, and John Hawkes
> *An aimless young man who is scalping tickets, gambling, and drinking agrees to coach a Little League team from the Cabrini Green housing project in Chicago as a condition for getting a loan from a friend.*

K-Pax (2001; 120 min.)
Director: Iain Softley
Writers: Gene Brewer (novel), Charles Leavitt (screenplay)
Stars: Kevin Spacey, Jeff Bridges, and Mary McCormack
> *Prot is a patient at a mental hospital who claims to be from a faraway planet. His psychiatrist tries to help him, only to begin to doubt his own explanations.*

Pavilion of Women (2001; 116 min.)
Director: Ho Yim
Writers: Pearl S. Buck (novel), Yan Luo (screenplay), Paul Collins (screenplay)
Stars: Willem Dafoe, Yan Luo, and Sau Sek
> *With World War II looming, a prominent family in China must confront the contrasting ideas of traditionalism, communism, and Western thinking, while dealing with the most important ideal of all: love and its meaning in society.*

Tears of the Sun (2003; 121 min.)
Director: Antoine Fuqua

Writers: Alex Lasker, Patrick Cirillo
Stars: Bruce Willis, Cole Hauser, and Monica Bellucci
Bruce Willis plays a Special Ops commander who leads his team into the jungle of Nigeria to rescue a doctor played by Monica Bellucci, who will only go with them if they agree to rescue seventy refugees too.

The Last Samurai (2003; 154 min.)
Director: Edward Zwick
Writers: John Logan (story), John Logan (screenplay), Edward Zwick (screenplay), and Marshall Herskovitz (screenplay)
Stars: Tom Cruise, Ken Watanabe, and Billy Connolly
An American military advisor embraces the samurai culture he was hired to destroy after he is captured in battle.

The Matrix Reloaded (2003; 138 min.)
Directors: Andy Wachowski, Lana Wachowski
Writers: Andy Wachowski, Lana Wachowski
Stars: Keanu Reeves, Laurence Fishburne, and Carrie-Anne Moss
Neo and the rebel leaders estimate that they have seventy-two hours until 250,000 probes discover Zion and destroy it and its inhabitants. During this, Neo must decide how he can save Trinity from a dark fate in his dreams.

The Matrix Revolutions (2003; 129 min.)
Directors: Andy Wachowski, Lana Wachowski
Writers: Andy Wachowski, Lana Wachowski
Stars: Keanu Reeves, Laurence Fishburne, and Carrie-Anne Moss
The human city of Zion defends itself against the massive invasion of the machines as Neo fights to end the war at another front while also opposing the rogue Agent Smith.

Crash (2004; 112 min.)
Director: Paul Haggis
Writers: Paul Haggis (story), Paul Haggis (screenplay), Robert Moresco (screenplay)
Stars: Don Cheadle, Sandra Bullock, and Thandie Newton
Los Angeles citizens with vastly separate lives collide in interweaving stories of race, loss, and redemption.

The Constant Gardener (2005; 129 min.)
Director: Fernando Meirelles
Writers: Jeffrey Caine (screenplay), John le Carré (novel)
Stars: Ralph Fiennes, Rachel Weisz, and Hubert Koundé
A widower is determined to get to the bottom of a potentially explosive secret involving his wife's murder, big business, and corporate corruption.

Amazing Grace (2006; 117 min.)
Director: Michael Apted
Writer: Steven Knight
Stars: Ioan Gruffudd, Albert Finney, and Michael Gambon
The idealist William Wilberforce maneuvers his way through Parliament, endeavoring to end the British transatlantic slave trade.

Blood Diamond (2006; 143 min.)
Director: Edward Zwick
Writers: Charles Leavitt (screenplay), Charles Leavitt (story), C. Gaby Mitchell (story)
Stars: Leonardo DiCaprio, Djimon Hounsou, and Jennifer Connelly
> *A fisherman, a smuggler, and a syndicate of businessmen match wits over the possession of a priceless diamond.*

Children of Men (2006; 109 min.)
Director: Alfonso Cuarón
Writers: Alfonso Cuarón (screenplay), Timothy J. Sexton (screenplay), David Arata (screenplay), Mark Fergus (screenplay), and Hawk Ostby (screenplay)
Stars: Julianne Moore, Clive Owen, and Chiwetel Ejiofor
> *In 2027, in a chaotic world in which humans can no longer procreate, a former activist agrees to help transport a miraculously pregnant woman to a sanctuary at sea, where her child's birth may help scientists save the future of humankind.*

Half Nelson (2006; 106 min.)
Director: Ryan Fleck
Writers: Ryan Fleck, Anna Boden
Stars: Ryan Gosling, Anthony Mackie, and Shareeka Epps
> *An inner-city junior high school teacher with a drug habit forms an unlikely friendship with one of his students after she discovers his secret.*

The Last King of Scotland (2006; 121 min.)
Director: Kevin Macdonald
Writers: Peter Morgan (screenplay), Jeremy Brock (screenplay), Giles Foden (novel)
Stars: James McAvoy, Forest Whitaker, and Gillian Anderson
> *The story is based on the events of the brutal Ugandan dictator Idi Amin's regime, as seen by his personal physician during the 1970s.*

Freedom Writers (2007; 123 min.)
Director: Richard LaGravenese
Writers: Richard LaGravenese (screenplay), Freedom Writers (book), Erin Gruwell (book *The Freedom Writers Diary: How a Teacher and 150 Teens Used Writing to Change Themselves and the World around Them*)
Stars: Hilary Swank, Imelda Staunton, and Patrick Dempsey
> *A young teacher inspires her class of at-risk students to learn tolerance, apply themselves, and pursue education beyond high school.*

Pathfinder (2007; 99 min.)
Director: Marcus Nispel
Writers: Laeta Kalogridis (screenplay), Nils Gaup (1987 screenplay *Veiviseren*)
Stars: Karl Urban, Clancy Brown, and Moon Bloodgood
> *A Viking boy is left behind after his clan battles a Native American tribe. Raised within the tribe, he ultimately becomes their savior in a fight against the Norsemen.*

Gran Torino (2008; 116 min.)
Director: Clint Eastwood
Writers: Nick Schenk (screenplay), Dave Johannson (story), Nick Schenk (story)
Stars: Clint Eastwood, Bee Vang, and Christopher Carley

Disgruntled Korean War vet Walt Kowalski sets out to reform his neighbor, a •
young Hmong teenager, who tried to steal Kowalski's prized possession: his 1972
Gran Torino.

Avatar (2009; 162 min.)
Director: James Cameron
Writer: James Cameron
Stars: Sam Worthington, Zoe Saldana, and Sigourney Weaver
   A paraplegic marine dispatched to the moon Pandora on a unique mission becomes
   torn between following his orders and protecting the world he feels is his home.

The Blind Side (2009; 129 min.)
Director: John Lee Hancock
Writers: John Lee Hancock, Michael Lewis (book)
Stars: Quinton Aaron, Sandra Bullock, and Tim McGraw
   Michael Oher, a homeless and traumatized boy, becomes an All-American
   football player and first-round NFL draft pick with the help of a caring woman
   and her family.

The Soloist (2009; 117 min.)
Director: Joe Wright
Writers: Susannah Grant (screenplay), Steve Lopez (book)
Stars: Jamie Foxx, Robert Downey Jr., and Catherine Keener
   A Los Angeles journalist befriends a homeless Juilliard-trained musician while looking
   for a new article for the paper.

The Help (2011; 146 min.)
Director: Tate Taylor
Writers: Tate Taylor (screenplay), Kathryn Stockett (novel)
Stars: Emma Stone, Viola Davis, and Octavia Spencer
   An aspiring author during the civil rights movement of the 1960s decides to write a
   book detailing the African American maids' point of view on the white families for
   which they work and the hardships they go through on a daily basis.

Appendix B:
Data and Methodology for Film Reviews

Data analyzed in Chapter 3 come from two main sources and measure two distinct social
phenomena. First, the measure of mainstream perceptions of racial conflict was drawn
from the descriptions of events involving race as listed in the *New York Times Index*, 1987–
2004. The *Index* has been used and discussed in previous analyses of ethnic and racial relations and is a source for measuring the diffusion of a particular idea in the public sphere
(Charles, Shore, and Todd 1979; McAdam 1982; Olzak 1992; Pescosolido, Grauerholz, and
Milkie 1997; Van Belle 2000; Winter and Eyal 1981). Second, the film reviews were gathered
from *The Movie Review Query Engine* (MRQE, http://www.mrqe.com/), an online database
providing general film information and a clearinghouse of online and print film reviews.
The MRQE has been used in previous scholarship on film reviews, cinematic gatekeeping,

and pedagogy (Aridor et al. 2000; Finn and Kushmerick 2006; Laskowski 2004; Son 2008). I detail here the data collection, steps of analysis, and theoretical rationale.

Perceptions of Racial Conflict and the *New York Times Index*

While objective measures of racial conflict are available, I was not so much interested in actual racial conflict as I was in the dissemination and reception of news about racial conflict—namely, the perception of racial conflict. To tap this amorphous concept, I turned to the *New York Times* as the largest local metropolitan newspaper in the United States and its reputation in the journalism industry as a national newspaper of record.

In 1990 the *Times* circulation was approximately 1.1 million, 1.15 million by 1995, 1.1 million by 2000, and 1.13 million by 2005, but it had declined to under a million by 2010. Still, because of the *Times* adaptation to the digital age, the paper's growth kept pace with its past trend and even grew in circulation when considering digital subscriptions; the *Times* had an increase of more than 40 percent in total circulation from 2011 to 2012 (from 1,150,589 to 1,613,865). The *Times* circulation even jumped 73 percent in the six-month period between October 2011 and March 2012, fueled by the growth of the online subscription business it started in 2011. Its average digital circulation for Monday–Friday papers totaled just over 896,000 in 2012 (an increase of 136 percent from 2011). And of all papers in the United States, the *Times* had the third-highest total daily circulation in 2012 (after the *Wall Street Journal* and *USA Today*) (Alliance for Audited Media 2012). According to Kevin Stoker, "The success of the *Times*, combined with its position as a trendsetter for the U.S. press, helped validate objective reporting" (1995: 7), and Foad Izadi and Hakimeh Saghaye-Biria contend that the *Times* is a leading newspaper "with regard to the coverage of international news and views, drawing readers from every state and around the world" (2007: 148). All in all, the *Times* both reflects and reproduces a certain view of the world, and in turn, emerges as a historically dominant outlet to which many turn to understand and gauge our social climate.

To foreclose on the dominant perceptions of racial conflict, I turned to the *Index* to measure the frequency of racial conflict. I operationalized this concept by capturing every mention of the following forty-eight categories in the *Index* (1987–2004): affirmative action (in story abstracts); affirmative action, blacks; affirmative action, civil rights; affirmative action, colleges and universities; affirmative action, education and schools; affirmative action, housing; affirmative action, labor; affirmative action, minorities; affirmative action, news and news media; affirmative action, police; Asian Americans (in story abstracts); Asian Americans, assaults; Asian Americans, crime and criminals; Asian Americans, education and schools; Asian Americans, housing; Asian Americans, labor; Asian Americans, police; blacks (abstracts); blacks, assaults; blacks, crime and criminals; blacks, education and schools; blacks, housing; blacks, labor; blacks, police; hate groups, Ku Klux Klan; Latinos/Hispanics (in story abstracts); Latinos/Hispanics, assaults; Latinos/Hispanics, crime and criminals; Latinos/Hispanics, education and schools; Latinos/Hispanics, housing; Latinos/Hispanics, labor; Latinos/Hispanics, police; racial groups; racial relations (in story abstracts); racial relations, assaults; racial relations, colleges and universities; racial relations, crime and criminals; racial relations, education and schools; racial relations, housing; racial relations, organizations, societies, and clubs; racial relations, police; whites/Caucasians (in story abstracts); whites/Caucasians, assaults; whites/Caucasians, crime and criminals; whites/Caucasians, education and schools; whites/Caucasians, housing; whites/Caucasians, labor; and whites/Caucasians, police. I then tallied each mention of every category in each year (see Table B.1), which resulted in a total of 8,495 mentions.

TABLE B.1. FREQUENCY OF
MENTIONS OF RACIAL CONFLICT
IN *NEW YORK TIMES INDEX*

Year	No. of Mentions of Racial Conflict
1987	774
1988	767
1989	343
1990	499
1991	703
1992	475
1993	300
1994	395
1995	461
1996	405
1997	460
1998	411
1999	526
2000	531
2001	481
2002	370
2003	372
2004	222
Total	8,495

On this measure, it would appear that the frequency of perceived racial conflict has been on a steady decline from 1987 to 2004 (see Figure 3.1). While this data trend certainly aligns with theory on the rising tide of postracial and color-blind belief and discourse, I am not satisfied it is proof, given that this trend holds only if one assumes that all discourse is the same. As Catherine Cassell and Gillian Symon suggest, one should maintain

> a focus on interpretation rather than quantification; an emphasis on subjectivity rather than objectivity; flexibility in the process of conducting research; an orientation towards process rather than outcome; a concern with context—regarding behaviour and situation as inextricably linked in forming experience; and finally, an explicit recognition of the impact of the research process on the research situation. (1994: 7)

Treating one mention of race, or even the mentions of subtle racial code words and racialized topics, the same as another not only washes out the nuanced variation and multiple connotations of the data but can lead to a superficial analysis without respecting the contexts in which the text appears and within which it should be interpreted and analyzed (Altheide 1996; Mostlyn 1985; Ritsert 1972; Rust 1980; Wittkowski 1994).

Hence, I arranged the three major types of racialized discourse I found in the *Index* by increasing salience: (1) group awareness (n = 6,194), (2) group relations (n = 1,033), and (3) group threat (n = 1,257). The first type, group awareness, measures instances in

TABLE B.2. FREQUENCY OF MENTIONS OF TYPES OF RACIAL
CONFLICT IN *NEW YORK TIMES INDEX*

Year	Awareness	Relations	Threat
1987	442	292	40
1988	517	228	22
1989	196	93	44
1990	334	94	71
1991	417	144	142
1992	276	174	25
1993	281	0	18
1994	379	0	16
1995	312	2	147
1996	307	0	98
1997	300	0	160
1998	325	0	86
1999	453	0	73
2000	485	1	45
2001	413	0	68
2002	298	5	67
2003	273	0	99
2004	186	0	36
Total	6,194	1,033	1,257

which black Americans, Latino Americans, Asian Americans, or white Americans were mentioned, thus serving as a reflection of how much the mere awareness and mention of racial identity was expected to resonate with a reading public. The second type, group relations, moved past that of recognition of identity to that of racial group interests and relations between racial groups. This type captured mentions of race relations in concert with crime, assaults, and police; organizations and clubs; and political organization and identity politics. The third type, group threat, is the most salient of the three in that it moves beyond both the recognition of racial identity and past awareness of racial group interests and relations to that of overt racial conflict. This type was constructed from mentions of direct competition or struggle over resources, such as debates over affirmative action or the mention of racial hate groups such as the Ku Klux Klan.

After having allowed for variation in the types of racial discourse, we are immediately struck by the rise and fall of perceptions of racial conflict (see Table B.2 and Figure 3.2). First, the measure of the awareness of racial identity fluctuates greatly over the time period, from a high point of 517 mentions in 1988 to a low of 186 in 2004. Second, the indicator for racial group relations nearly vanished in 1993, with but a few mentions of racial group relationships. And third, the measure for the perception of racial threats—as defined by mentions of overt contestation between racial groups—experienced a great deal of change over the time period but was still a dominant feature of national discourse (with the exception of a sharp drop from 1992 to 1994).

Film Reviews and the MRQE

To examine how reviewers make meaning of the past twenty-five years of white savior films, I created a collection of film reviews via the MRQE. When I accessed the clearing-house in January 2012, it held 901,002 reviews on 99,523 films. The preliminary search for reviews of the fifty films identified in Chapter 1 yielded a total of 2,916 film reviews. However, selecting only English-language reviews from either the United States or Canada, reduced the final number of reviews I analyzed (n = 2,799). The reviews ran the gamut from the most mainstream and originally print-based sources (e.g., the *Atlanta Journal-Constitution*, the *Boston Globe*, the *Los Angeles Times*, the *New York Times*, *Rolling Stone*, *USA Today*, and the *Washington Post*) to the more arcane and solely web-based (e.g., *Reeling Reviews* and *The Flick Filosopher*) and from more well-known web-based reviews (e.g., *PopMatters* and the *Onion*'s *A.V. Room*) to race- or gender-specific sites (e.g. *Black Flix* and *The Movie Chicks*). All the reviews were published between November 6, 1987 (with several reviews of *Cry Freedom* published on that day), and August 9, 2011 (corresponding with the July 12 release date of *The Help*).

Each review was coded in three stages that mirror the approach I took in the content analysis in Chapter 2. First, a single review served as the unit of analysis. I read reviews read in their entirety and took notes to inductively obtain an overview of the review's thrust. I made note of patterns in frames and themes to develop "sensitizing concepts" (Blumer 1954: 7), which served as the genesis for the development of these coding catego-ries (see Charmaz 2003; Morse and Field 1995; Padgett 2008; Patton 2002).

Second, I again analyzed the reviews with a deductively guided search for common themes related to white savior films (e.g., race, racism, inequality, power, education, author-ity, and bureaucracy [see Bernardi 2007; Chennault 1996; Giroux 1997; Moore and Pierce 2007; C. Rodríguez 1997; Stoddard and Marcus 2006; Vera and Gordon 2003]) in order to refine the first inductive coding pass. This step was guided by the search for first-level frames and second-level themes. "Frames focus on what will be discussed and how it will be discussed," whereas themes are the "recurring typical theses that run through a lot of the reports" (Altheide 1996: 31) and are the dominant ideas that take shape within the material.

Third, I determined exact frame and theme frequency and form through the final coding stage, whereby I denoted frames and themes only when it was clear that the review reflected those different codes. As most were intimately linked, when reviews referred to more than one at a time, each scored a 1 to create overlapping categories (0 = not present, 1 = present). This third stage of coding took place from January to May 2012. In sum, the first and second pass in the data resulted in the following (see Tables 3.1, 3.2, and 3.3): Time period A, the (multi)cultural wars (1987–1992), resulted in four frames and nine themes out of 110 reviews. Time period B, the white backlash (1993–1998), resulted in three frames and three themes out of 296 reviews. Time period C, the postracial era and the redemption of whiteness (1999–2011), resulted in one frame and three themes out of 2,393 reviews (for a sum of 2,799 reviews).

This approach—a type of frame analysis—spans disparate approaches (D'Angelo 2002; Hallahan 1999; Maher 2001). While framing finds applicability in management-organizational and social movement studies, I am concerned with its relation to meaning-making and interpretive communities. The work of Shanto Iyengar (1991), Robert Entman (1993), and Stephen Reese (2001) is emblematic of this convention. Reese writes, "Frames are organizing principles that are socially shared and persistent over time, that work sym-bolically to meaningfully structure the social world" (2001: 11). Such a definition avoids rooting frames in a static feature of the media text or in the black box of the individual mind. Hence, I identified what codes cohered and supported larger, prominent, and over-arching themes, which the film reviewer may assume readers understand a priori.

As sociological constructs, the various levels of frames are defined as both competing and cooperative social structures that organize symbolic material so that certain perspectives are understood as logical, sensible, and normal (Gamson 1992; Kosicki and McLeod 1990). Frame analysis has been useful in examining the methods by which media frames are constructed (Entman and Rojecki 1993; Morreale 1991), how frames are influenced by political advocacy groups (Hertsgaard 1988), and how framing directly affects media consumption (Gamson 1992; Livingstone 1990). Media researchers commonly employ frame analysis as an extension of the agenda setting model. However, I employ framing to venture beyond the agenda setting approach to examine how frames both (re)produce and contest the aforementioned logic of racial neoliberalism grounded in the three discursive eras of the multicultural wars (1987–1992), white backlash (1993–1998), and postracialism (1999–2011).

Appendix C:
Data and Methodology for Film Audiences

Analyzing audience reception of a media text affords attention to the variability and heterogeneity of responsive decodings as they align with categories of social difference (e.g., race, class, and gender), the dominant messages of the texts themselves, and the patterns of interpretation that cut across conventional social distinctions and are situated within group contexts. As Michael Schudson writes:

> The relevance of a cultural object to its audience, its utility, if you will, is a property not only of the object's content or nature and the audience's interest in it but of the position of the object in the cultural tradition of the society the audience is a part of. That is, the uses to which an audience puts a cultural object are not necessarily personal or idiosyncratic; the needs or interests of an audience are socially and culturally constituted. What is "resonant" is not a matter of how "culture" connects to individual "interests" but a matter of how culture connects to interests that are themselves constituted in a cultural frame. (2002: 145)

To empirically home in on the resonance of this genre for different individuals and groups, I conducted focus group discussion studies and in-depth interviews in Charlottesville and Richmond, Virginia, and Washington, DC, over a four-month (May to August) period in both 2010 and 2011. Interviews and discussions were held in reserved and public rooms at the university and collegiate libraries of the University of Virginia, the University of Richmond, George Washington University, Georgetown University, and Howard University. A total of eighty-three subjects agreed to participate and were drawn from local religious, civic, and fraternal groups and from recruitment posters and snowball sampling.[1]

Focus Groups

Focus groups are used to obtain specific information from a clearly identified and purposefully selected set of individuals. That is, a focus group is not a haphazard discussion or brainstorming session of people who were conveniently sampled; it is a well-planned

---

1. Sometimes called chain sampling or referral sampling, "snowball sampling" is a nonprobability technique in which existing study subjects recruit other subjects from among their acquaintances. Thus, the sample group appears to grow as a rolling snowball does. This sampling technique is often used to study hidden populations, which are difficult for researchers to access, or taboo or controversial subjects, such as the intersection of race, racism, and film.

research endeavor. Focus groups were originally developed to quickly gather individual information in a group context and were first employed by survey and marketing researchers but later adjusted for sociological use to study the effects of wartime propaganda (Merton, Fiske, and Kendall [1956] 1990). While many still use focus groups to obtain individual-level data (see Morgan 1988; Ward, Bertrand, and Brown 1991), others value the approach as an efficacious way to gain access to interactional processes among groups and study the processes of interactive meaning construction (see Kitzinger 1994a, 1994b; Lunt and Livingstone 1996). Several recent studies on race in the media demonstrate the utility of focus groups to delineate audiences' responses (see Bird 2003; Bobo 1989; Bobo et al. 1995; Hunt 1997; Jhally and Lewis 1992).

This study used eight focus groups (ranging from eight to thirteen members each), of which six were purposefully culled from existing organizations and two created for the purposes of this study: (1) a multiracial group of eight people drawn from the greater DC and northern Virginia area who all belong to the Bahá'í Faith and who were already familiar with one another, (2) a mostly black group of twelve Southern Baptists from a church in the Charlottesville, Virginia, area, (3) eleven members of a mostly white fraternity chapter at the University of Virginia, (4) nine members of a mostly black sorority chapter at Howard University, (5) an all-white group of eleven members of an Elks Lodge from the greater Washington, DC, area, (6) a multiracial group of thirteen members of a singles group from the greater Richmond, Virginia, area, and (7 and 8) two focus groups of nine members each (one all white, one multiracial) drawn from the Charlottesville, Virginia, area that were constructed via recruitment posters and snowball sampling or two-step ties (e.g., friend-of-friend or friend-of-family tie).

Recruitment posters approved by the institutional review board (IRB) were hung at college and university campuses; hung at bus stops and community centers; and distributed to local religious, civic, and educational- and cocurricular-related organizations. Individuals were not coerced with any reward or payment. The recruitment posters yielded thirty-four responses, but out of that original population only eleven respondents agreed to participate in the final study. Those eleven individuals helped me locate an additional thirty-one participants through snowball sampling. The remaining forty-one participants were generated from the aforementioned extant social groups. I moderated all focus group discussion. Tables 4.1 and 4.2, respectively, list individual participants and the precise makeup of focus groups.

Upon agreeing to be a part of the focus group, the subjects were given an IRB-approved informed consent agreement, which provided extensive details on their rights as research participants. Before and after each focus group discussion, I interviewed a sample of the participants (see below on interview techniques and methodology). Also, after the initial interview, I gave each member a DVD of *Gran Torino* (2008) and *The Blind Side* (2009). I asked each participant to watch either or both films before the focus group met. An overwhelming number (fifty-nine of eighty-three, or 71 percent) reported that they watched both films, while nearly 90 percent watched at least one of the films (seventy-three of eighty-three; 88 percent). I asked each participant to take notes on the film and bring those notes to the focus group. I gave participants a movie guide to read before watching the films that posed several questions and would focus their note taking.

When it came time for each focus group to meet, nearly two-thirds (fifty-five of eighty-three, or 66 percent) brought their notes with them. Each focus group watched the same film together: *Freedom Writers* (2007). I selected this film because of its recent release; its star power (lead roles were played by Hilary Swank, Imelda Staunton, and Patrick Dempsey); its being based on a true story, which I hoped would give focus groups treating the film as art a reflection of real social dynamics; and its not receiving any of the major five film awards and thus having less media discussion, which might influence focus group members.

As moderator I facilitated an audio-recorded discussion about their views on the movie, including questions about their opinions on the plot, the characters, and intended and unintended messages of the film; whether they would recommend it and why or why not; whether they thought the film contained any stereotypes; and what they felt the point of the film was. Throughout, I remained conscious of keeping the discussions guided yet relaxed so data would emerge from the natural flow of conversation. When I did redirect the conversation, I did so by asking additional and leading questions or by probing participants to further explain their rationale or logic behind a statement. Discussions lasted from 72 minutes (the shortest discussion) to 130 minutes (the longest discussion). These discussions were later transcribed and all potentially identifying information—per IRB stipulations—was removed or replaced with pseudonyms to protect participants' guaranteed confidentiality.

Pre- and Post-Focus-Group Interviews

Upon agreeing to a pre- and post-focus-group interview, subjects were given an IRB-approved informed consent agreement, which provided extensive details on their rights as subjects. The semistructured, in-depth interviews provided a deep understanding of how participants made sense of these movies, specifically in relation to precisely which ideologies and logics played a role in their interpretations. By employing a semistructured interview approach I engaged in a relatively free-flowing discussion, making sure to cover certain topics. This approach allowed for a realistic discussion with questions embedded naturalistically, thereby increasing the likelihood of candid and representative responses.

Eighty-three participants took part in focus group discussions; nearly two-thirds agreed to a pre-focus-group interview (sixty-five of eighty-three, or 78 percent), but fewer agreed to a post-focus-group interview (twenty-five of eighty-three, or 30 percent). All twenty-five who agreed to a post-focus-group interview also agreed to and carried out a pre-focus-group interview.

I combined two modes of interviewing inquiry. The first was the traditional hermeneutic method that aims to understand how specific comments and situations countervail or complicate abstract generalizations. Such a technique allows examinations of how subjects make sense of situations, which then provides a glimpse of the forces that shape both the places they inhabit and the criteria that reflect people's perceptions of the meanings of those social forces. The second is what Hans-George Gadamer characterizes as the "hermeneutics of suspicion," whereby the researcher is geared toward revealing the meaningfulness of statements in an unexpected sense and "against the meaning of the author" in ways that challenge the validity of ideologies (1984: 54). Thus, in the former I simply tried to listen and encourage more explanations so that I could obtain as much rich, detailed information as possible. In the latter, I challenged the validity of statements so that respondents had to expose the rationales, logics, and ideologies that underpinned and gave valid sense to their statements.

Each of the in-depth interviews was audio recorded (and transcribed later for analysis) while I simultaneously took extensive notes. The initial pass at data analysis took place during the interview period, when I used my notes to record initial thoughts regarding themes and patterns that emerged. When necessary, the interview schedule was amended to reflect newfound understandings. These interviews included pre- and post-focus-group discussion questionnaires by which I collected data on individuals' demographic characteristics; impressions of the films in regard to social or historical accuracy, pacing, genre, alternative climactic scenes, and overall structure; and several questions about their racial identity and their attitudes on various aspects of modern race relations. Some variables (see Table 4.1) were self-reported, and some were constructed by me (e.g., for socioeconomic status, I created a variable drawn from participants' education, their parents' education, yearly income, whether they rent or own, car ownership, outstanding loans [aside from home mortgage], and attained or expected inherited wealth).

Making Sense of It All

Data were collected through pre- and post-focus-group interviews, audio recordings of focus group discussions, notes from participants, and field notes from my own observation in focus group meetings, allowing a methodological triangulation of findings (Denzin 1978). My attention was focused on how audiences made sense of these films and how the dynamics of group discussion affected the variability of cinematic interpretations.

The data was coded akin to how I approached films (Appendix A) and reviews (Appendix B). First, a paragraph of transcribed interview data, participants' notes, my notes, and transcribed focus group discussion served as the unit of analysis (n = 3,122). This data was read in its entirety, after which I made note of patterns, themes, and categories to develop "sensitizing concepts" (Blumer 1954: 7) that, in turn, provided an important starting point for deeper analysis. Second, with these emergent themes in mind, I turned to the extant literature on white savior films (e.g., race, racism, inequality, power, education, authority, and bureaucracy [see Bernardi 2007; Chennault 1996; Giroux 1997; Moore and Pierce 2007; C. Rodríguez 1997; Stoddard and Marcus 2006; Vera and Gordon 2003]). This deductive approach helped refine the secondary and inductive coding process. As before, the search for first-level frames and second-level themes (Altheide 1996: 31) guided this step. And third, I did the formal coding process to determine the presence and frequency of frames and themes. As many of these categories overlapped, I scored a 1 for each time they were observed (0 = not present, 1 = presents). This third stage of coding took place from July to December 2012. In the end, the data resulted in the following (see Table 4.3): four frames and eleven themes based on 2,139 of 3,122 units of analysis (69 percent).

References

Alliance for Audited Media. 2012. "Research and Data: Top 25 U.S. Newspapers for September 2012." Available at http://www.auditedmedia.com/news/research-and -data/top-25-us-newspapers-for-september-2012.aspx.

Altheide, David L. 1996. *Qualitative Media Analysis*. Thousand Oaks, CA: Sage.

———. 2000. "Identity and the Definition of the Situation in a Mass-Mediated Context." *Symbolic Interaction* 23 (1): 1–27.

Anderson, John. 1999. "'Music of the Heart' a Long, Hard Pull on the Heartstrings." *Los Angeles Times*, October 29. Available at http://articles.latimes.com/1999/oct/29/enter tainment/ca-27356.

Appelbaum, Nancy P., Anne S. Macpherson, and Karin Alejandra Rosemblatt. 2003. *Race and Nation in Modern Latin America*. Chapel Hill: University of North Carolina Press.

Apple, R. W., Jr. 1986. "A New Deal; Tax Changes May Take the Economy on a Bumpy Road." *New York Times*, August 24. Available at http://www.nytimes.com/1986/08/24 /weekinreview/a-new-deal-tax-changes-may-take-the-economy-on-a-bumpy-road .html.

Aridor, Yariv, David Carmel, Ronny Lempel, Aya Soffer, and Yoelle S. Maarek. 2000. "Knowledge Agents on the Web." *Lecture Notes in Computer Science*, no. 1860: 15–26.

Austin, Bruce. 1983. "A Longitudinal Test of the Taste Culture and Elitist Hypotheses." *Journal of Popular Film and Television* 11:157–167.

Axtell, James. 1975. "The White Indians of Colonial America." *William and Mary Quarterly* 32 (1): 55–88.

Bagdikian, Ben H. 2004. *The New Media Monopoly*. Boston: Beacon Press.

Baker, Andy, and Jennifer Fitzgerald. 2012. "Racial Paternalism and Mass Support for Foreign Aid." Institute of Behavior Science, University of Colorado at Boulder, Working Paper Series INST2012-04.

Baker, Eric J. 2012. "'Django Unchained': Race Is On." *Pure Film Creative*, December 30. Available at http://purefilmcreative.com/baker-street/django-unchained-race-is-on .html.

Barthes, Roland. 1977. "The Death of the Author." In *Image, Music, and Text*, translated by Stephen Heath, 142–149. New York: Hill and Wang.

———. 1980. "Barthes on Theatre." Translated by Peter W. Mathers. *Theatre Quarterly* 9:25–30.

Barton, P. E., and R. J. Coley. 2010. *The Black-White Achievement Gap: When Progress Stopped.* Princeton, NJ: Educational Testing Service.

Basuroy, Suman, Subimal Chatterjee, and S. Abraham Ravid. 2003. "How Critical Are Critical Reviews? The Box Office Effects of Film Critics, Star Power, and Budgets." *Journal of Marketing* 67 (October): 103–117.

Baumann, Shyonn. 2002. "Marketing, Cultural Hierarchy, and the Relevance of Critics: Film in the United States, 1935–1980." *Poetics* 30:243–262.

Becker, Howard. 1982. *Art Worlds.* Berkeley: University of California Press.

Bell, Joyce M., and Douglas Hartmann. 2007. "Diversity in Everyday Discourse: The Cultural Ambiguities and Consequences of 'Happy Talk.'" *American Sociological Review* 72 (8): 875–914.

Benjamin, Walter. (1936) 1968. "The Work of Art in the Age of Mechanical Reproduction." In *Illuminations*, edited by H. Arendt, 214–218. London: Fontana.

Bennett, Susan. 1997. *Theatre Audience: A Theory of Production and Reception.* London: Routledge.

Berger, Peter L., and Thomas Luckmann. 1966. *Social Construction of Reality: A Treatise in the Sociology of Knowledge.* Garden City, NY: Anchor Books.

Bernardi, Daniel. 1996. *The Birth of Whiteness: Race and the Emergence of U.S. Cinema.* New Brunswick, NJ: Rutgers University Press.

———. 2007. *The Persistence of Whiteness: Race and Contemporary Hollywood Cinema.* New York: Routledge.

Bertrand, M., and S. Mullainathan. 2004. "Are Emily and Greg More Employable than Lakisha and Jamal? A Field Experiment on Labor Market Discrimination." *American Economic Review* 94 (4): 991–1013.

"Bigger Abroad: Hollywood Goes Global." 2011. *The Economist*, February 17. Available at http://www.economist.com/node/18178291.

Bird, S. Elizabeth. 2003. *The Audience in Everyday Life: Living in the Media World.* New York: Routledge.

Blake, John. 2011. "Are Whites Racially Oppressed?" *CNN*, March 4. Available at http://www.cnn.com/2010/US/12/21/white.persecution/index.html?hpt=T2.

Bliss, Catherine. 2012. *Race Decoded: The Genomic Fight for Social Justice.* Stanford, CA: Stanford University Press.

Blumer, Herbert. 1954. "What Is Wrong with Social Theory." *American Sociological Review* 18:3–10.

Boatwright, Peter, Suman Basuroy, and Wagner Kamakura. 2006. "Reviewing the Reviewers: The Impact of Individual Film Critics on Box Office Performance." *Quantitative Marketing and Economics* 5 (4): 401–425.

Bobo, Lawrence. 1989. "Keeping the Linchpin in Place: Testing the Multiple Sources of Opposition to Residential Integration." *Revue Internationale de Psychologie Sociale* 2 (3): 307–325.

———. 2011. "Somewhere between Jim Crow and Post-racialism: Reflections on the Racial Divide in America Today." *Daedalus* 140:11–36.

Bobo, Lawrence, Camille Zubrinsky, James Johnson Jr., and Oliver Melvin. 1995. "Work Orientation, Job Discrimination, and Ethnicity: A Focus Group Perspective." *Research in the Sociology of Work* 5:45–58.

Bodnar, John. 2001. "Saving Private Ryan and Postwar Memory in America." *American Historical Review* 106 (3): 805–817.

Bonilla-Silva, Eduardo. 1997. "Rethinking Racism: Toward a Structural Interpretation." *American Sociological Review* 62 (3): 465–480.

———. 2001. *White Supremacy and Racism in the Post-Civil Rights Era*. Boulder, CO: Lynne Rienner.

———. 2010. *Racism without Racist: Color-Blind Racism and the Persistence of Racial Inequality in America*. 3rd ed. Lanham, MD: Rowman and Littlefield.

Bonnett, Alastair. 2000. "Whiteness in Crisis." *History Today* 50 (12): 38–40.

Bourdieu, Pierre. 1984. *Distinction: A Social Critique of the Judgment of Taste*. Cambridge, MA: Harvard University Press.

———. 2005. *The Social Structures of the Economy*. Cambridge, MA: Polity Press.

"Box Office/Business for Django Unchained." 2013. *IMDb*. Available at http://www.imdb .com/title/tt1853728/business?ref_=tt_dt_bus.

"Box Office/Business for Lincoln." 2013. *IMDb*. Available at http://www.imdb.com/title /tt0443272/business?ref_=tt_dt_bus.

Brodkin, Karen. 1998. "How Jews Became White Folks and What That Says about Race in America." Brunswick, NJ: Rutgers University Press.

Brooks, David. 2010. "The Messiah Complex." *New York Times*, January 7. Available at http://www.nytimes.com/2010/01/08/opinion/08brooks.html.

Bryson, Bethany. 1996. "'Anything but Heavy Metal': Symbolic Exclusion and Musical Dislikes." *American Sociological Review* 61 (5): 884–899.

Burr, Ty. 2008. "Gran Torino." *Boston Globe*, December 25. Available at http://www.boston .com/ae/movies/articles/2008/12/25/dirty_harrys_neighborhood/.

Cameron, Samuel. 1995. "On the Role of Critics in the Culture Industry." *Journal of Cultural Economics* 19 (4): 321–331.

Canby, Vincent. 1990. "Dances with Wolves (1990)." *New York Times*, November 9. Available at http://movies.nytimes.com/movie/review?res=9C0CE6DB1338F93AA35752 C1A966958260.

———. 1992. "City of Joy (1992)." *New York Times*, April 15. Available at http://movies .nytimes.com/movie/review?res=9E0CEEDC1F3DF936A25757C0A964958260.

Cantril, Hadley, and Gordon W. Allport. 1935. *The Psychology of Radio*. New York: Harper.

Cassell, Catherine, and Gillian Symon, eds. 1994. *Qualitative Methods in Organizational Research*. Thousand Oaks, CA: Sage.

Chan, Vera. 2012. "Race Controversy over 'The Hunger Games.'" *Yahoo! Movies*, March 27. Available at http://movies.yahoo.com/blogs/movie-talk/race-controversy-over-hunger -games-182705585.html.

Charity, Tom. 2007. "Review: 'Freedom Writers' Barely Passes." *CNN*, January 5. Available at http://www.cnn.com/2007/SHOWBIZ/Movies/01/05/review.freedom/.

Charles, Jeff, Larry Shore, and Rusty Todd. 1979. "The *New York Times* Coverage of Equatorial and Lower Africa." *Journal of Communication* 29 (2): 148–155.

Charmaz, Kathy. 2003. "Grounded Theory: Objectivist and Constructivist Methods." In *Strategies of Qualitative Inquiry*, 2nd ed., edited by N. K. Denzin and Y. S. Lincoln, 249–291. London: Sage.

Chennault, Ronald E. 1996. "The Minds behind a Dangerous Film." *Review of Education, Pedagogy and Cultural Studies* 18 (4): 385–396.

Childress, C. Clayton, and Noah E. Friedkin. 2012. "Cultural Reception and Production: The Social Construction of Meaning in Book Clubs." *American Sociological Review* 77 (1): 45–68.

"Cinema: Boxers Triumph." 1940. *Time*, July 15. Available at http://www.time.com/time /magazine/article/0,9171,777399,00.html.

Cloud, Dana L. 1992. "The Limits of Interpretation: Ambivalence and the Stereotype in *Spenser: For Hire.*" *Critical Studies in Mass Communication* 9:311–324.

Cole, Teju. 2012. "The White-Savior Industrial Complex." *The Atlantic*, March 21. Available at http://www.theatlantic.com/international/archive/2012/03/the-white -savior-industrial-complex/254843/2/?single_page=true.

Collins, Andrew. n.d. "The Great Pyramid Was Not Built by Aliens: It's Official." *AndrewCollins.com*. Available at http://www.andrewcollins.com/page/articles/shaheen .htm (accessed July 24, 2013).

Collins, Suzanne. 2008. *The Hunger Games*. New York: Scholastic.

Cooney, Terry. 1995. *Balancing Acts: American Thought and Culture in the 1930s*. New York: Twayne.

Cooper, B. 2000. "'Chick Flicks' as Feminist Texts: The Appropriation of the Male Gaze in *Thelma and Louise.*" *Women's Studies in Communication* 23:277–306.

Corliss, Richard. 2012. "*Compliance*: Sundance Torture Porn." *Time*, August 17. Available at http://entertainment.time.com/2012/08/17/compliance-sundance-torture-porn/.

Crust, Kevin. 2007. "To Her with Love." *Los Angeles Times*, January 5. Available at http:// articles.latimes.com/2007/jan/05/entertainment/et-freedom5.

D'Angelo, Paul. 2002. "News Framing as a Multi-paradigmatic Research Program: A Response to Entman." *Journal of Communication* 52 (4): 870–888.

Daniels, Roger. 2002. *Coming to America: A History of Immigration and Ethnicity in American Life*. 2nd ed. New York: HarperCollins.

"Danny Glover's Slavery Film Lacked 'White Heroes,' Producers Said." 2008. Agence France-Presse, July 24. Available at http://www.google.com/hostednews/afp/article /ALeqM5i_e3UYOiNEhW03rcVTpcB2e15IMg.

Dargis, Manohla, and A. O. Scott. 2011a. "Big Questions, Smart Women, Mann's Movies." New York Times, April 22. Available at http://www.nytimes.com/2011/04/24/movies /ao-scott-and-manhola-dargis-qa-on-film.html.

———. 2011b. "More 'Ask the Film Critics.'" *New York Times*, April 22. Available at http:// artsbeat.blogs.nytimes.com/2011/04/22/more-ask-the-film-critics-2/.

Davis, Peter. 1996. *In Darkest Hollywood: Exploring the Jungles of Cinema's South Africa*. Johannesburg, South Africa: Ravan Press.

Dawes, Amy. 1990. "Review: 'Dances with Wolves.'" *Variety*, November 11. Available at http://variety.com/1990/film/reviews/dances-with-wolves-2-1200428612/.

Deane, Donald. 2010. "Vanessa Williams Bashes 'The Blind Side' on 'The View.'" *Huffpost TV*, March 8. Available at http://www.aoltv.com/2010/03/08/vanessa-williams-bashes -the-blind-side-on-the-view-video/.

Deloria, Philip Joseph. 1999. *Playing Indian*. New Haven, CT: Yale University Press.

Denzin, Norman K. 1978. *The Research Act: A Theoretical Introduction to Sociological Methods*. New York: McGraw-Hill.

———. 1992. *Symbolic Interactionism and Cultural Studies: The Politics of Interpretation*. Cambridge, MA: Blackwell.

———. 2001. "Symbolic Interactionism, Poststructuralism, and the Racial Subject." *Symbolic Interaction* 24 (20): 243–249.

———. 2002. "The Cinematic Racial Order." In *Reading Race: Hollywood and the Cinema of Racial Violence*, 17–46. London: Sage.

De Silva, Indra. 1998. "Consumer Selection of Motion Pictures." In *The Motion Picture Mega-industry*, edited by Barry R. Litman, 144–171. Needham Heights, MA: Allyn and Bacon.

"Detained Americans Say They Had Good Intentions in Haiti." 2010. *CNN*, January 31. Available at http://www.cnn.com/2010/WORLD/americas/01/31/haiti.border.arrests /index.html.

Dirks, Tim. n.d.a. "The History of Film: The 1940s." *Filmsite*. Available at http://www .filmsite.org/40sintro.html (accessed July 11, 2011).

———. n.d.b. "The History of Film: The 1950s." *Filmsite*. Available at http://www.filmsite .org/50sintro.html.

———. n.d.c. "The History of Film: The 1960s." *Filmsite*. Available at http://www.filmsite .org/60sintro.html.

———. n.d.d. "The History of Film: The 1970s." *Filmsite*. Available at http://www.filmsite .org/70sintro4.html.

Doane, Ashley W. 1997a "Dominant Group Ethnic Identity in the United States: The Role of 'Hidden' Ethnicity in Intergroup Relations." *Critical Sociology* 38 (3): 375–397.

———. 1997b. "White Identity and Race Relations in the 1990s." In *Perspectives on Current Social Problems*, edited by G. L. Carter, 151–159. Boston: Allyn and Bacon.

Doyle, Michael J. 1996. "Sunset Park." *Mike's Midnight Movie Reviews*, April 22. Available at http://mdoyle.com/m3review/1996/sunset.htm.

Dryden, John. 1990. "The Conquest of Granada." In *The Works of John Dryden*, vol. 20, edited by George R. Guffey, Alan Roper, Vinton A. Dearing, and A. E. Wallace Maurer, 260–269. Berkeley: University of California Press.

Duan, Wenjing, Bin Gu, and Andrew Whinston. 2008. "Do Online Reviews Matter? An Empirical Investigation of Panel Data." *Decision Support Systems* 45 (4): 1007–1016.

Du Bois, W.E.B. (1935) 1999. *Black Reconstruction in America, 1860–1880*. New York: Simon and Schuster.

Duster, Troy. 2001. "The 'Morphing' Properties of Whiteness." In *The Making and Unmaking of Whiteness*, edited by E. B. Rasmussen, E. Klinenberg, I. J. Nexica, and M. Wray, 113–133. Durham, NC: Duke University Press.

Dyer, Richard. 2011. "White." In *Critical Visions in Film Theory*, edited by T. Corrigan, P. White, and M. Mazaj, 822–839. Boston: Bedford/St. Martin's.

Ebert, Roger. 1987. "Cry Freedom." *Chicago Sun-Times*, November 6. Available at http:// www.rogerebert.com/reviews/cry-freedom-1987.

———. 1990a. "Dances with Wolves." *Chicago Sun-Times*, November 9. Available at http:// www.rogerebert.com/reviews/dances-with-wolves-1990.

———. 1990b. "Glory." *Chicago Sun-Times*, January 12. Available at http://www.rogerebert .com/reviews/glory-1989.

———. 1991. "The Long Walk Home." *Chicago Sun-Times*, March 22. Available at http:// www.rogerebert.com/reviews/the-long-walk-home-1991.

———. 1992. "Thunderheart." *Chicago Sun-Times*, April 3. Available at http://www.roger ebert.com/reviews/thunderheart-1992.

———. 1999. "Music of the Heart." *Chicago Sun-Times*, October 29. Available at http:// www.rogerebert.com/reviews/music-of-the-heart-1999.

———. 2003. "The Last Samurai." *Chicago Sun-Times*, December 5. Available at http:// www.rogerebert.com/reviews/the-last-samurai-2003.

———. 2008. "Gran Torino." *Chicago Sun-Times*, December 17. Available at http://www .rogerebert.com/reviews/gran-torino-2008.

Edelstein, David. 2003. "Shafted in Africa." *Slate*, March 7. Available at http://www.slate .com/articles/arts/movies/2003/03/shafted_in_africa.html.

Eliashberg, Jehoshua, and Steven M. Shugan. 1997. "Film Critics: Influencers or Predictors?" *Journal of Marketing* 61 (April): 68–78.

Eliasoph, Nina, and Paul Lichterman. 2003. "Culture in Interaction." *American Journal of Sociology* 108 (4): 735–794.

Emerson, James. 1988. "Mississippi Burning." *Cinepad*, January.

Emirbayer, Mustafa, and Ann Mische. 1998. "What Is Agency?" *American Journal of Sociology* 103 (4): 962–1023.

Entman, Robert. 1993. "Framing: Toward Clarification of a Fractured Paradigm." *Journal of Communication* 43 (4): 51–58.

Entman, Robert M., and Andrew Rojecki. 1993. "Freezing Out the Public: Elite and Media Framing of the U.S. Anti-nuclear Movement." *Political Communication* 10:155–173.

———. 2001. *The Black Image in the White Mind: Media and Race in America*. Chicago: University of Chicago Press.

Faires, Robert. 1995. "Losing Isaiah" *Austin Chronicle*, March 24. Available at http://www.austinchronicle.com/calendar/film/1995-03-24/142806/.

Faludi, Susan. 1991. *Backlash: The Undeclared War against American Women*. New York: Vintage.

Fanon, Frantz. (1952) 1967. *Black Skin, White Masks*. New York: Grove Press.

Farber, Stephen. 1990. "Dances with Wolves." *Movieline*. Previously available at http://movieline.com/reviews/dances_w_wolves.shtml.

Feagin, Joe. R. 2006. *Systemic Racism: A Theory of Oppression*. New York: Routledge.

Fear, David. 2012. "Sundance: Compliance Riles Everyone Up." *Time Out New York*, January 22. Available at http://www.timeout.com/newyork/film/sundance-compliance-riles-everyone-up.

Ferber, Abby. 1999. *White Man Falling: Race, Gender, and White Supremacy*. Lanham, MD: Rowman and Littlefield.

Feuer, Lewis S. 1991. "From Pluralism to Multiculturalism." *Society* 29 (1): 19–22.

Fineman, Howard. 1995. "Race and Rage." *Newsweek* 125 (13): 22.

Finn, Aidan, and Nicholas Kushmerick. 2006. "Learning to Classify Documents According to Genre." *Journal of the American Society for Information Science and Technology* 57 (11): 1506–1518.

Fish, Stanley. 1976. "Interpreting the *Variorum*." *Critical Inquiry* 2:463–468.

Foner, Eric. 1998. "The Amistad Case in Fact and Film." *History Matters*, March. Available at http://historymatters.gmu.edu/d/74/.

Foucault, Michel. (1975) 1995. *Discipline and Punishment: The Birth of the Prison*. New York: Vintage.

Frankenberg, Ruth. 1993. *White Women, Race Matters: The Social Construction of Whiteness*. Minneapolis: University of Minnesota Press.

Fu, W. Wayne, and Achikannoo Govindaraju. 2010. "Explaining Global Box-Office Tastes in Hollywood Films: Homogenization of National Audiences' Movie Selections." *Communication Research* 37 (2): 215–238.

Fuller, Jennifer. 2006. "Debating the Present through the Past: Representations of the Civil Rights Movement in the 1990s." In *The Civil Rights Movement in American Memory*, 167–196. Athens: University of Georgia Press.

Gallagher, Charles A. 1995. "White Reconstruction in the University." *Socialist Review* 24 (1–2): 165–187.

———. 2003. *On the Fault Line: Race, Class and the American Patriot Movement*. Lanham, MD: Rowman and Littlefield.

———. 2004. *Rethinking the Color Line: Readings in Race and Ethnicity*. New York: McGraw-Hill.

Gamson, William A. 1992. *Talking Politics*. Cambridge: Cambridge University Press.

Gandy, Oscar H., Jr. 1998. *Communication and Race: A Structural Perspective*. London: Arnold.

Gates, Henry Louis, Jr. 2012. "Tarantino 'Unchained,' Part 3: White Saviors." *The Root*, December 25. Available at http://www.theroot.com/views/tarantino-unchained-part-3-white-saviors.

Geller, Adam. 2008. "Obama's Moment Also a Major Juncture in US History." *USA Today*, June 3. Available at http://usatoday30.usatoday.com/news/politics/2008-06-03-2497141011_x.htm.

Gemser, Gerda, Martine Van Oostrum, and Mark A.A.M. Leenders. 2007. "The Impact of Film Reviews on the Box Office Performance of Art House versus Mainstream Motion Pictures." *Journal of Cultural Economics* 31 (1): 43–63.

Gilson, Dave. 2011. "The Machine Gun Preacher: Saint or Scoundrel?" *Mother Jones*, September 23. Available at http://www.motherjones.com/mixed-media/2011/09/sam-childers-machine-gun-preacher.

Giroux, Henry A. 1993. "Reclaiming the Social: Pedagogy, Resistance, and Politics in Celluloid Culture." In *Film Theory Goes to the Movies*, edited by J. Collins, A. Collins, and H. Radner, 37–55. New York: Routledge and American Film Institute.

———. 1997. "Race, Pedagogy, and Whiteness in Dangerous Minds." *Cineaste* 22 (4): 46–49.

Gitlin, Todd. 1980. *The Whole World Is Watching: Mass Media in the Making and Unmaking of the New Left*. Berkeley: University of California Press.

Gleiberman, Owen. 1990. "Dances with Wolves." *Entertainment Weekly*, November 16. Available at http://www.ew.com/ew/article/0,,318636,00.html.

———. 1991. "The Long Walk Home." *Entertainment Weekly*, January 18. Available at http://www.ew.com/ew/article/0,,312999,00.html.

———. 1995. "Dangerous Minds." *Entertainment Weekly*, August 11. Available at http://www.ew.com/ew/article/0,,298327,00.html.

Goffman, Erving. 1963. *Stigma: Notes on the Management of Spoiled Identity*. New York: Simon and Schuster.

Goldberg, David Theo. 1993. *Racist Culture: Philosophy and Politics of Meaning*. Hoboken, NJ: Wiley-Blackwell.

Gordon, Milton M. 1964. *Assimilation in American Life: The Role of Race, Religion and National Origin*. Oxford: Oxford University Press.

Gorringe, Carrie. 1995. "Dangerous Minds." *Nitrate Online*. Available at http://www.nitrateonline.com/rdminds.html.

Grainge, Paul, ed. 2003. *Memory and Popular Film*. Manchester, UK: Manchester University Press.

Gramsci, Antonio. 1971. *Selections from the Prison Notebooks*. New York: International Publishers.

Graves, Joseph. 2005. *The Race Myth: Why We Pretend Race Exists in America*. New York: Penguin.

Gray, Herman. 1995. *Watching Race: Television and the Struggle for "Blackness."* Minneapolis: University of Minnesota Press.

Grazian, David. 2005. *Blue Chicago: The Search for Authenticity in Urban Blues Clubs*. Chicago: University of Chicago Press.

Griffin, Larry J., and Peggy G. Hargis. 2008. "Surveying Memory: The Past in Black and White." *Southern Literary Journal* 40 (2): 42–69.

Griswold, Wendy. 1987. "The Fabrication of Meaning: Literary Interpretation in the United States, Great Britain, and the West Indies." *American Journal of Sociology* 92:1077–1117.

———. 1993. "Recent Moves in the Sociology of Literature." *Annual Review of Sociology* 19:455–467.

———. 2002. "American Character and the American Novel: An Expansion of Reflection Theory in the Sociology of Literature." In *Cultural Sociology*, edited by L. Spillman, 189–198. Oxford: Blackwell.

Grossman, Sandra J. 1990. "Dances with Wolves (1990)." *IMDb*. Available at http://www.imdb.com/reviews/08/0852.html.

Guglielmo, Thoma. 2003. *White on Arrival: Italians, Race, Color, and Power in Chicago, 1890–1945*. Oxford: Oxford University Press.

Guthmann, Edward. 1995. "Teacher Role Hokey, but It Works for Pfeiffer." *San Francisco Chronicle*, August 11. Available at http://www.sfgate.com/entertainment/article/Teacher-Role-Hokey-But-It-Works-for-Pfeiffer-3026732.php.

Gutmann, Amy, ed. 1994. *Multiculturalism: Examining the Politics of Recognition*. Princeton, NJ: Princeton University Press.

Halbwachs, Maurice. (1925) 1992. *On Collective Memory*. Chicago: University of Chicago Press.

Hall, Alice. 2001. "Film Reviews and the Public's Perceptions of Stereotypes: Movie Critics' Discourse about the Siege." *Communication Quarterly* 49 (4): 399–423.

Hall, Stuart. 1997. *Representation: Cultural Representations and Signifying Practices*. Thousand Oaks, CA: Sage.

Hallahan, Kirk. 1999. "Seven Models of Framing: Implications of Public Relations." *Journal of Public Relations Research* 11 (3): 204–242.

Handler, Richard. 1986. "Authenticity." *Anthropology Today* 2 (1): 2–4.

Hannity, Sean. 2010. *Conservative Victory: Defeating Obama's Radical Agenda*. New York: HarperCollins.

Harvey, Fred. 1997. "Movie Review: Amistad." *History Place*, December 20. Available at http://www.historyplace.com/specials/reviews/amistad.htm.

Hays, Sharon. 1994. "Structure and Agency and the Sticky Problem of Culture." *Sociological Theory* 12 (1): 57–72.

Herman, Edward S., and Robert W. McChesney. 1997. *The Global Media: The New Missionaries of Corporate Capitalism*. London: Cassell.

Hicks, Chris. 1992. "Film Review: Thunderheart." *Deseret News*, April 8. Available at http://www.deseretnews.com/article/700001845/Thunderheart.html?pg=all.

———. 1998. "Film Review: Dances with Wolves." *Deseret News*, October 14. Available at http://www.deseretnews.com/article/700000406/Dances-With-Wolves.html?pg=all.

———. 2000. "Film Review: Long Walk Home, The." *Deseret News*, May 19. Available at http://www.deseretnews.com/article/700001076/Long-Walk-Home-The.html?pg=all.

Higham, John. 1975. *Send These to Me: Jews and Other Immigrants in Urban America*. New York: Atheneum.

Hinson, Hal. 1988. "Rambo III." *Washington Post*, May 25. Available at http://www.washingtonpost.com/wp-srv/style/longterm/movies/videos/ramboiiirhinson_a0c8ef.htm.

———. 1991. "The Long Walk Home." *Washington Post*, March 22. Available at http://www.washingtonpost.com/wp-srv/style/longterm/movies/videos/thelongwalkhomepghinson_a0a9e5.htm.

Hirschkorn, Phil. 2009. "The Obama-Lincoln Parallel: A Closer Look." *CBS*, February 11. Available at http://www.cbsnews.com/2100-250_162-4731552.html.

Hoberman, James. 2012. "A New Obama Cinema?" *New York Review of Books*, February 11. Available at http://www.nybooks.com/blogs/nyrblog/2012/feb/11/new-obama-cinema-clint-eastwood-halftime/.

Holbrook, Morris B. 1999. "Popular Appeal versus Expert Judgments of Motion Pictures." *Journal of Consumer Research* 26:144–155.

Hollander, Jocelyn A. 2004. "Social Contexts of Focus Groups." *Journal of Contemporary Ethnography* 33 (5): 602–637.

hooks, bell. 1992. *Black Looks: Race and Representation*. Boston: South End Press.

Horn, John. 2001. "The Reviewer Who Wasn't There." *Newsweek*, June 2. Available at http://web.archive.org/web/20010609225327/www.msnbc.com/news/581770.asp?cp1=1.

Hovland, C. I., A. A. Lumsdaine, and F. D. Sheffield. 1949. *Experiments on Mass Communication*. Vol. 3 of *Studies in Social Psychology in World War II*. Princeton, NJ: Princeton University Press.

Howe, Desson. 1987. "Cry Freedom" *Washington Post*, November 6. Available at http://www.washingtonpost.com/wp-srv/style/longterm/movies/videos/cryfreedompg howe_a0b116.htm.

———. 1991. "The Long Walk Home." *Washington Post*, March 22. Available at http://www.washingtonpost.com/wp-srv/style/longterm/movies/videos/thelongwalkhomepg howe_a0b2e3.htm.

Hsu, Greta, and Joel M. Podolny. 2005. "Critiquing the Critics: An Approach for the Comparative Evaluation of Critical Schemas." *Social Science Research* 34:187–214.

Hughey, Matthew W. 2009. "Cinethetic Racism: White Redemption and Black Stereotypes in 'Magical Negro' Films." *Social Problems* 56 (3): 543–577.

———. 2010. "The White Savior Film and Reviewers' Reception." *Symbolic Interaction* 33 (3): 475–496.

———. 2011. "Measuring Racial Progress in America: The Tangled Path." In *The Obamas and a (Post) Racial America?*, edited by G. S. Parks and M. W. Hughey, 1–26. New York: Oxford University Press.

———. 2012. "Racializing Redemption, Reproducing Racism: The Odyssey of Magical Negroes and White Saviors." *Sociology Compass* 6 (9): 751–767.

Hunt, Darnell M. 1997. *Screening the Los Angeles "Riots": Race, Seeing, and Resistance.* Cambridge: Cambridge University Press.

———. 1999. *O.J. Simpson Facts and Fictions: News Rituals in the Construction of Reality.* Cambridge: Cambridge University Press.

Hunter, Joanna, and Matthew W. Hughey. 2013. "'It's Not Written on Their Skin Like It Is Ours': Greek Letter Organizations in the Age of the Multicultural Imperative." *Ethnicities* 13 (5): 519–543.

Hunter, Stephen. 2005. "'Crash': The Collision of Human Contradictions." *Washington Post*, May 6. Available at http://www.washingtonpost.com/wp-dyn/content/article/2005/05/05/AR2005050501878.html.

Ignatiev, Noel. 1995. *How the Irish Became White*. London: Routledge.

Irwin-Zarecka, Iwona. 1994. *Frames of Remembrance: The Dynamics of Collective Memory.* New Brunswick, NJ: Transaction.

Iyengar, Shanto. 1991. *Is Anyone Responsible? How Television Frames Political Issues.* Chicago: University of Chicago Press.

Izadi, Foad, and Hakimeh Saghaye-Biria. 2007. "A Discourse Analysis of Elite American Newspaper Editorials: The Case of Iran's Nuclear Program." *Journal of Communication Inquiry* 31 (2): 140–165.

Jackman, Mary. 1994. *The Velvet Glove: Paternalism and Conflict in Gender, Class, and Race Relations*. Berkeley: University of California Press.

Jacobson, Matthew F. 1999. *Whiteness of a Different Color: European Immigrants and the Alchemy of Race*. Cambridge, MA: Harvard University Press.

Jahandary, Koshrow. 1977. "Modernization Revisited: An Interview with Daniel Lerner." *Communication and Development Review* 1 (1–3): 4–6.

Jedidi, Kamel, Robert E. Krider, and Charles B. Weinberg. 1998. "Clustering at the Movies." *Marketing Letters* 9 (4): 393–405.

Jhally, Sut, and Justin Lewis. 1992. *Enlightened Racism: The Cosby Show, Audience, and the Myth of the American Dream*. Boulder, CO: Westview.

Johnson, Jason. 2010. "Trans-racial Adoption Should Win Sandra Bullock Another Oscar." *Chicago Defender*, May 4. Available at http://chicagodefender.com/index.php/voices/7027-trans-racial-adoption-should-win-sandra-bullock-another-oscar.

Jones, Chris. 2010. "Roger Ebert: The Essential Man." *Esquire*, February 16. Available at http://www.esquire.com/features/roger-ebert-0310.

Katz, Elihu, and Paul Lazarsfeld. 1955. *Personal Influence*. New York: Free Press.

Kaufman, Jason. 2004. "Endogenous Explanations in the Sociology of Culture." *Annual Review of Sociology* 30:335–357.

Kemply, Rita. 1987. "Cry Freedom." *Washington Post*, November 6. Available at http://www.washingtonpost.com/wp-srv/style/longterm/movies/videos/cryfreedompgkempley_a0ca3d.htm.

King, Martin Luther, Jr. 1963. "Letter from Birmingham Jail." April 16. Martin Luther King, Jr. Research and Education Institute, Stanford University. Available at http://mlk-kpp01.stanford.edu/index.php/resources/article/annotated_letter_from_birmingham/.

Kitzinger, Jenny. 1994a. "Focus Groups: Method or Madness?" In *Challenge and Innovation: Methodological Advances in Social Research on HIV/AIDS*, edited by M. Boulton, 159–175. London: Taylor and Francis.

———. 1994b. "The Methodology of Focus Groups: The Importance of Interactions between Research Participants." *Sociology of Health and Illness* 16 (1): 103–121.

Klady, Leonard. 1996a. "Review: 'Sunset Park.'" *Variety*, April 23. Available at http://variety.com/1996/film/reviews/sunset-park-1200445575/.

———. 1996b. "Review: 'The Substitute.'" *Variety*, April 17. Available at http://variety.com/1996/film/reviews/the-substitute-2-1200445607/.

Kochhar, Rakesh, Richard Fry, and Paul Taylor. 2011. "Wealth Gaps Rise to Record Highs between Whites, Blacks, Hispanics: Twenty-to-One." Pew Research Center, July 26. Available at http://www.pewsocialtrends.org/2011/07/26/wealth-gaps-rise-to-record-highs-between-whites-blacks-hispanics/.

Kosicki, Gerald M., and Jack M. McLeod. 1990. "Learning from Political News: Effects of Media Images and Information Processing Strategies." In *Mass Communication and Political Information Processing*, edited by S. Kraus, 69–83. Hillsdale, NJ: Erlbaum.

Kristof, Nicholas. 2010. "Westerners on White Horses . . ." *New York Times*, July 14. Available at http://kristof.blogs.nytimes.com/2010/07/14/westerners-on-white-horses/.

Lamont, Michèle. 1992. *Money, Morals, and Manners: The Culture of the French and American Upper-Middle Class*. Chicago: University of Chicago Press.

Lamont, Michèle, and Marcel Fournier. 1992. *Cultivating Difference: Symbolic Boundaries and the Making of Inequality*. Chicago: University of Chicago Press.

Lange, Willem. 2013. "Column: America Is Still in Love with Its Mythology." *Valley News*, May 29. Available at http://www.vnews.com/home/6633702-95/column-america-is-still-in-love-with-its-mythology.

LaSalle, Mick. 1996. "Film Review: 'Substitute' Teacher Is a Real Gangbuster." *San Francisco Chronicle*, April 19. Available at http://www.sfgate.com/movies/article/FILM-REVIEW-Substitute-Teacher-Is-a-Real-2985519.php.

Laskowski, Mary S. 2004. "Stop the Technology, I Want to Get Off." *Acquisitions Librarian* 16 (31–32): 217–225.

Leab, Daniel J. 1975. *From Sambo to Superspade: The Black Experience in Motion Pictures.* Boston: Houghton Mifflin.

Leddy, Bruce. 2007. "Nice White Lady," *MADtv.* Season 12, episode 15. February 24.

Leeper, Mark. 1990. "Dances with Wolves (1990)." *IMDb.* Available at http://www.imdb .com/reviews/08/0853.html.

———. 1991. "The Long Walk Home (1990)." *IMDb.* Available at http://www.imdb.com /reviews/09/0982.html.

———. 1992. "Thunderheart (1992)." *IMDb.* Available at http://www.imdb.com /reviews/13/1322.html.

Lemesurier, Peter. 1999. *Gods of Dawn: The Message of the Pyramids and the True Stargate Mystery.* London: Thorsons.

Lerner, Daniel. 1958. *The Passing of Traditional Society.* New York: Free Press.

Levy, Emanuel, and Elizabeth Guider. 1997. "Review: 'Amistad.'" *Variety,* November 30. Available at http://variety.com/1997/film/reviews/amistad-111711764/.

Lewis, Amanda E. 2004. "What Group? Studying Whites and Whiteness in the Era of Colorblindness." *Sociological Theory* 22 (4): 623–646.

Lewis, Oscar. 1961. *The Children of Sanchez: Autobiography of a Mexican Family.* New York: Vintage Press.

———. 1965. *La Vida: A Puerto Rican Family in the Culture of Poverty—San Juan and New York.* New York: Random House.

Lieberson, Stanley. 1980. *A Piece of the Pie—Black and White Immigrants since 1880.* Berkeley: University of California Press.

Lipsitz, George. 1998. *The Possessive Investment in Whiteness: How White People Profit from Identity Politics.* Philadelphia: Temple University Press.

Litman, Barry R., and Hoekyun Ahn. 1998. "Predicting Financial Success of Motion Pictures." In *The Motion Picture Mega-Industry,* edited by B. R. Litman, 172–197. Needham Heights, MA: Allyn and Bacon.

Livingstone, Sonia M. 1990. *Making Sense of Television: The Psychology of Audience Interpretation.* Elmsford, NY: Pergamon.

Long, Elizabeth. 2003. *Book Clubs: Women and the Uses of Reading in Everyday Life.* Chicago: University of Chicago Press.

Lunt, Peter, and Sonia Livingstone. 1996. "Rethinking the Focus Group in Media and Communications Research." *Journal of Communication* 46 (2): 79–98.

Lyden, John. 2003. *Film as Religion: Myth, Morals, Rituals.* New York: New York University Press.

Maher, T. Michael. 2001. "Framing: An Emerging Paradigm or a Phase of Agenda Setting." In *Framing Public Life: Perspectives on Media and our Understanding of the Social World,* edited by Stephen D Reese, Oscar H Gandy, and August E Grant, 83–94. Mahwah, NJ: Erlbaum.

Makinen, Gail. 2002. "The Economic Effects of 9/11: A Retrospective Assessment," September 27. Report for Congress. Congressional Research Service, Library of Congress. Available at http://www.fas.org/irp/crs/RL31617.pdf.

Maloney, Frank. 1992. "City of Joy (1992)." *IMDb.* Available at http://www.imdb.com /reviews/13/1347.html.

Malott, Curry Stephenson. 2011. *Critical Pedagogy and Cognition: An Introduction to a Postformal Educational Psychology.* Vol. 15 of *Explorations of Educational Purpose.* New York: Springer.

Manchel, Frank. 1990. *Film Study: An Analytical Bibliography.* Madison, NJ: Fairleigh Dickinson University Press.

Marine, Craig. 1996. "Actors Bail Out Coach in 'Sunset Park.'" *Los Angeles Examiner,* April 26. Available at http://www.sfgate.com/news/article/Actors-bail-out-coach-in -Sunset-Park-3154648.php.

"Market Share for Each Distributor in 2011." n.d. *The Numbers.* Available at http://www .the-numbers.com/market/Distributors2011.php (accessed August 16, 2012).

Martin, John Levi. 2002. "Power, Authority, and the Constraint of Belief Systems." *American Journal of Sociology* 107:861–904.

Maslin, Janet. 1987. "Film: Attenborough's 'Cry Freedom.'" *New York Times,* November 6. Available at http://movies.nytimes.com/movie/review?res=9B0DE6D61239F935A3575 2C1A961948260&pagewanted=print.

———. 1988. "Reviews/Film; Stallone's 'Rambo III,' Globe-Trotting Cowboy for the 80's Audience." *New York Times,* May 25. Available at http://www.nytimes.com/1988/05/25 /movies/reviews-film-stallone-s-rambo-iii-globe-trotting-cowboy-for-the-80-s -audience.html.

———. 1990. "Review/Film; A Personalized View of the Civil Rights Struggle." *New York Times,* December 21. Available at http://www.nytimes.com/1990/12/21/movies /review-film-a-personalized-view-of-the-civil-rights-struggle.html?src=pm.

———. 1992a. "Review/Film; Connery as a Doctor in the Jungle." *New York Times,* February 7. Available at http://www.nytimes.com/1992/02/07/movies/review-film -connery-as-a-doctor-in-the-jungle.html.

———. 1992b. "Review/Film; Val Kilmer as an F.B.I. Agent among the Sioux." *New York Times,* April 3. Available at http://www.nytimes.com/1992/04/03/movies/review-film -val-kilmer-as-an-fbi-agent-among-the-sioux.html.

———. 1993. "Review/Film; "Schindler's List": Imagining the Holocaust to Remember It." *New York Times,* December 15. Available at http://www.nytimes.com/books/97/06/15 /reviews/spielberg-schindler.html.

Massey, Douglas, and Nancy A. Denton. 1993. *The American Apartheid: Segregation and the Making of the Underclass.* Cambridge, MA: Harvard University Press.

Mauer, Marc, and Ryan S. King. 2007. *Uneven Justice: State Rates of Incarceration by Race and Ethnicity.* Washington, DC: Sentencing Project.

McAdam, Douglas. 1982. *Political Process and the Development of Black Insurgency, 1930– 1970.* Chicago: University of Chicago Press.

McCarthy, Todd. 1993. "Review: 'Schindler's List.'" *Variety,* November 19. Available at http://variety.com/1993/film/reviews/schindler-s-list-2-1200434300/.

McChesney, Robert W. 2003. "Theses on Media Deregulation." *Media, Culture and Society* 25 (1): 125–133.

McGurk, Margaret A. 1998. "No Apologies for 'Bulworth.'" *Cincinnati Inquirer,* May 22. Available at http://cincinnati.com/freetime/movies/mcgurk/bulworth.html.

McIntosh, Peggy, 1988. "Unpacking the Knapsack of White Privilege." Working Paper 189, Wellesley College Center for Research on Women, Wellesley, MA.

Mead, George Herbert. 1934. *Mind, Self, and Society.* Edited by Charles W. Morris. Chicago: University of Chicago Press.

Means Coleman, Robin. 2000. *African American Viewers and the Black Situation Comedy: Situating Racial Humor.* New York: Garland.

Media Matters. 2008. "Gender and Ethnic Diversity in Prime-Time Cable News." Available at http://mediamatters.org/research/diversity_report/.

Meek, Tom. 1998. "Bulworth." *Boston Phoenix,* May 21. Available at http://www.boston phoenix.com/archives/1998/documents/00525163.htm.

Merton, Robert K., Marjorie Fiske, and Patricia L. Kendall. (1956) 1990. *The Focused Interview: A Manual of Problems and Procedures.* New York: Free Press.

Meyer, Jeff. 1989. "Mississippi Burning (1988)." *IMDb.* Available at http://www.imdb.com /reviews/04/0484.html.

Miller, Daniel. 2012. "Sundance 2012: Screaming, Anger at Tension-Filled 'Compliance' Premiere." *Hollywood Reporter*, January 21. Available at http://www.hollywoodreporter.com/risky-business/sundance-2012-compliance-premiere-283782.

"Minorities Expected to Be Majority in 2050." 2008. *CNN*, August 13. Available at http://articles.cnn.com/2008-08-13/us/census.minorities_1_hispanic-population-census-bureau-white-population?_s=PM:US.

Montagu, Ashley. 1942. *Man's Most Dangerous Myth: The Fallacy of Race*. New York: Columbia University Press.

Monteith, Sharon. 2003. "The Movie-Made Movement: Civil Rites of Passage." In *Memory and Popular Film: Inside Popular Film*, edited by P. Grainge, 120–143. Manchester, UK: Manchester University Press.

Moore, Wendy L., and Jennifer Pierce. 2007. "Still Killing Mockingbirds: Narratives of Race and Innocence in Hollywood's Depiction of the White Messiah Lawyer." *Qualitative Sociology Review* 3 (2): 171–187.

Moran, Michelle Therese. 2007. *Colonizing Leprosy: Imperialism and the Politics of Public Health in the United States*. Chapel Hill: University of North Carolina Press.

Morgan, David L. 1988. *Focus Groups as Qualitative Research*. Thousand Oaks, CA: Sage.

Morgan, E. P. 2006. "The Good, the Bad, and the Forgotten: Media Culture and Public Memory of the Civil Rights Movement." In *The Civil Rights Movement in American Memory*, edited by R. C. Romano and L. Raiford, 137–166. Athens: University of Georgia Press.

Morreale, Joanne. 1991. "The Political Campaign Film: Epideictic Rhetoric in a Documentary Frame." In *Television and Political Advertising*, vol. 2, edited by Frank Biocca, 181–201. New York: Erlbaum.

Morse, Janice M., and Peggy A. Field. 1995. *Qualitative Research Methods for Health Professionals*. 2nd ed. Thousand Oaks, CA: Sage.

Mortenson, Greg, and David Oliver Relin. 2007. *Three Cups of Tea*. New York: Penguin Books.

Motion Picture Association of America. 2012. "Theatrical Market Statistics, 2012." Available at http://www.mpaa.org//Resources/3037b7a4-58a2-4109-8012-58fca3abdf1b.pdf.

Münsterberg, Hugo. 1916. *The Photoplay: A Psychological Study*. New York: Appleton.

Murray, Steve. 2001. "Finding Forrester." *Dayton Daily News*. Available at http://mo.daytondailynews.com/movies/content/shared/movies/reviews/F/findingforrester.html.

Nama, Adilifu. 2003. "More Symbol than Substance: African American Representation in Network Television Dramas." *Race and Society* 6:21–38.

"National Film Registry 2007." 2011. National Film Preservation Board, July 19. Available at http://www.loc.gov/film/nfr2007.html.

Norton, Michael I., and Samuel R. Sommers. 2011. "Whites See Racism as a Zero-Sum Game That They Are Now Losing." *Perspectives on Psychological Science* 6 (3): 215–218.

Oher, Michael. 2011. *I Beat the Odds: From Homelessness, to "The Blind Side," and Beyond*. London: Penguin.

Olick, Jeffrey K., and Joyce Robbins. 1998. "Social Memory Studies: From 'Collective Memory' to the Historical Sociology of Mnemonic Practices." *Annual Sociological Review* 24:105–140.

Oliver, Melvin, and Thomas Shapiro. 1997. *Black Wealth, White Wealth: A New Perspective on Racial Inequality*. New York: Routledge.

Olson, Scott R. 1989. "Mass Media: A Bricolage of Paradigms." In *Human Communication as a Field of Study: Selected Contemporary Views*, edited by S. S. King, 57–85. Albany: State University of New York Press.

————. 1999. *Hollywood Planet*. Mahwah, NJ: Erlbaum.

Olzak, Susan. 1992. *The Dynamics of Ethnic Competition and Conflict*. Stanford, CA: Stanford University Press.

Omi, Michael. 2001. "The Changing Meaning of Race." In *America Becoming: Racial Trends and Their Consequences*, edited by Neil Smelser, William Julius Wilson, and Faith Mitchell, 243–263. Washington, DC: National Academy Press.

O'Regan, Tom. 1990. "Too Popular by Far: On Hollywood's International Popularity." *Continuum: The Australian Journal of Media and Culture* 5 (2): 302–351.

"Oscars 2010: Sandra Bullock's Acceptance Speech." 2010. *Metro*, March 8. Available at http://metro.co.uk/2010/03/08/oscars-2010-sandra-bullocks-acceptance-speech-152818/.

Padgett, Deborah. 2008. *Qualitative Methods in Social Work Research*. Los Angeles: Sage.

Pager, Devah. 2003. "The Mark of a Criminal Record." *American Journal of Sociology* 108 (5): 937–975.

Pager, Devah, and Hana Shepherd. 2008. "The Sociology of Discrimination: Racial Discrimination in Employment, Housing, Credit, and Consumer Markets." *Annual Review of Sociology* 34:181–209.

Pascarella, John. 2003. "Notes from the Field." *Taboo: The Journal of Culture and Education* 7 (2): 3–6.

Patton, Michael Q. 2002. *Qualitative Research and Evaluation Methods*. Thousand Oaks, CA: Sage.

Perry, Michelle. 1990. "Black Civil War Soldiers Receive Fitting Tribute in *Glory*." *The Tech*, January 24. Available at http://tech.mit.edu/V109/N60/glory.60a.html.

Pescosolido, Bernice, Elizabeth Grauerholz, and Melissa Milkie. 1997. "Culture and Conflict: The Portrayal of Blacks in U.S. Children's Pictures Books through the Mid- and Late-Twentieth Century." *American Sociological Review* 62:443–464.

Phillips, Michael. 2009. "'The Blind Side'—2 Stars." *Chicago Tribune*, November 19. Available at http://featuresblogs.chicagotribune.com/talking_pictures/2009/11/the-blind-side-2-stars.html.

Potok, Mark. 2011. "The Year in Hate and Extremism, 2010." *Intelligence Report* 141. Available at http://www.splcenter.org/get-informed/intelligence-report/browse-all-issues/2011/spring/the-year-in-hate-extremism-2010.

Pratt, Julius. 1927. "The Origin of 'Manifest Destiny.'" *American Historical Review*, July, 795–798.

Pratt, Richard H. (1892) 1973. "Official Report of the Nineteenth Annual Conference of Charities and Correction." Reprinted in "The Advantages of Mingling Indians with Whites." In *Americanizing the American Indians: Writings by the "Friends of the Indian," 1880–1900*, 260–271. Cambridge, MA: Harvard University Press.

Prince, Stephen. 1997. *Movies and Meaning: An Introduction to Film*. Boston: Allyn and Bacon.

"Questions over Greg Mortenson's Stories." 2011. *60 Minutes*, April 15. Available at http://www.cbsnews.com/stories/2011/04/15/60minutes/main20054397.shtml.

"Race Literacy Quiz: What Differences Make a Difference?" n.d. *California Newsreel*. Available at http://www.newsreel.org/guides/race/quiz.htm.

Ravid, Abraham S. 1999. "Information, Blockbusters, and Stars: A Study of the Film Industry." *Journal of Business* 72 (October): 463–492.

Reed, Ismael. 1989. "The Black Pathology Biz." *The Nation*, November 20. Available at http://www.thenation.com/article/black-pathology-biz.

Reese, Stephen D. 2001. "Framing Public Life: A Bridging Model for Media Research." In *Framing Public Life: Perspectives on Media and Our Understanding of the Social World*, edited by Stephen D. Reese, Oscar H. Gandy, and August E. Grant, 7–31. Mahwah, NJ: Erlbaum.

Reskin, Barbara. 2012. "The Race Discrimination System." *Annual Review of Sociology* 38:17–35.

Rhodes, Steve. 1996. "Sunset Park (1996)." *IMDb*, April 29. Available at http://www.imdb.com/reviews/51/5167.html.

Rich, Katey. 2012. "Compliance Director Craig Zobel: Why the Controversial Film Was More Than He Knew Was Walking Into." *Cinema Blend*, September 5. Available at http://www.cinemablend.com/new/Compliance-Director-Craig-Zobel-Why-Controversial-Film-Was-More-Than-He-Knew-Was-Walking-32792.html.

Riley, Naomi Schaefer. 2005. *God on the Quad: How Religious Colleges and the Missionary Generation Are Changing America*. New York: Macmillan.

Ritsert, J. 1972. *Inhaltsanalyse und Ideologiekritik: Ein Versuch über kritische Sozialforschung*. Frankfurt, Germany: Athenäum.

Robertson, Campbell. 2011. "A Victory in Court for the Author of 'The Help.'" *New York Times*, August 16. Available at http://artsbeat.blogs.nytimes.com/2011/08/16/a-victory-in-court-for-the-author-of-the-help/.

Rocchio, Vincent F. 2000. *Reel Racism*. Boulder, CO: Westview.

Rodríguez, Clara E. 1997. *Latin Looks: Images of Latinas and Latinos in the U.S. Media*. Boulder, CO: Westview.

Rodriguez, Gregory. 2010. "The White Anxiety Crisis." *Time*, March 11. Available at http://www.time.com/time/specials/packages/article/0,28804,1971133_1971110_1971119-2,00.html.

Rodriguez, Nelson M., and Leila E. Villaverde. 2000. *Dismantling White Privilege: Pedagogy, Politics, and Whiteness*. New York: Peter Lang.

Roediger, David. 2005. *Working toward Whiteness: How America's Immigrants Became White; The Strange Journey from Ellis Island to the Suburbs*. New York: Basic Books.

Routt, William D. 2006. "The Film of Memory." *Screening the Past*, no. 19. Available at http://tlweb.latrobe.edu.au/humanities/screeningthepast/19/film-of-memory.html.

Rust, Holger. 1980. *Struktur und Bedurtang* [Structure and meaning]. Berlin: Verlag Volker Spiess.

Rux, Bruce. 1996. *Architects of the Underworld: Unriddling Atlantis, Anomalies of Mars, and the Mystery of the Sphinx*. Berkeley, CA: Frog Books.

Sanneh, Kelefa. 2010. "Beyond the Pale: Is White the New Black?" *New Yorker*, April 12. Available at http://www.newyorker.com/arts/critics/books/2010/04/12/100412crbo_books_sanneh.

Schatz, Thomas. 2009. "Film Industry Studies and Hollywood History." In *Media Industries: History, Theory, and Method*, edited by Jennifer Holt and Alisa Perren, 45–56. Pondicherry, India: SPi Publisher Services.

Schieder, Theodor. 1978. "The Role of Historical Consciousness in Political Action." *History and Theory* 17 (4): 1–18.

"'Schindler's List' Added to Film Registry." 2004. *Los Angeles Times*, September 29. Available at http://articles.latimes.com/2004/dec/29/entertainment/et-quick29.2.

Schlesinger, Arthur. 1991. *The Disuniting of America: A Reflection of a Multicultural Society*. New York: Norton.

Schudson, Michael. 2002. "How Culture Works: Perspectives from Media Studies on the Efficacy of Symbols." In *Cultural Sociology*, edited by L. Spillman, 141–148. Malden, MA: Blackwell.

Schultz, Jennifer, and Ronald L. Breiger. 2010. "The Strength of Weak Culture." *Poetics* 38 (6): 610–624.

Schwartz, Barry. 2000. *Abraham Lincoln and the Forge of the National Memory*. Chicago: University of Chicago Press.

Schwarzbaum, Lisa. 1995. "Losing Isaiah." *Entertainment Weekly*, March 24. Available at http://www.ew.com/ew/article/0,,296502,00.html.

———. 1996. "A Time to Kill." *Entertainment Weekly*, August 2. Available at http://www.ew.com/ew/article/0,,293613,00.html.

———. 2003. "The Last Samurai." *Entertainment Weekly*, November 27. Available at http://www.ew.com/ew/article/0,,550781,00.html.

Scott, Allen J. 2002. "Hollywood in the Era of Globalization." *Yale Global Online*, November 29. Available at http://yaleglobal.yale.edu/content/hollywood-era-globalization.

Scott, Damian. 2012. "The 25 Most Racist Tweets about 'The Hunger Games.'" *The Complex*, March 27. Available at http://www.complex.com/tech/2012/03/the-25-most-racist-tweets-about-the-hunger-games.

Scott-Childress, Reynolds J. 1999. *Race and the Production of Modern American Nationalism*. New York: Taylor and Francis.

Seward, Monise. 2010. "When Things Unsaid, Say a Lot." *Race-Talk*, June 24. Available at http://www.race-talk.org/?p=4930.

Sewell, William F. 1992. "A Theory of Structure: Duality, Agency, and Transformation." *American Journal of Sociology* 98 (1): 1–29.

Shaw, Daniel C. 2008. *Film and Philosophy: Taking Movies Seriously*. New York: Columbia University Press.

Shelby, Jim. 1995. "Movie Reviews: Dangerous Minds." *Palo Alto Online*, August 11. Available at http://www.paloaltoonline.com/movies/reviews/Dangerous-Minds?review_id=460.

Shively, JoEllen. 1992. "Cowboys and Indians: Perceptions of Western Films among American Indians and Anglos." *American Sociological Review* 57 (6): 725–734.

Smedley, Audrey. 1993. *Race in North America: Origin and Evolution of a Worldview*. Boulder, CO: Westview.

Snead, James. 1994. *White Screens, Black Images: Hollywood from the Dark Side*. New York: Routledge.

Snowden, Philip. 1983. *Before Color Prejudice*. Cambridge, MA: Harvard University Press.

Sochay, Scott. 1994. "Predicting the Performance of Motion Pictures." *Journal of Media Economics* 7 (4): 1–20.

Son, Jeong-Bae. 2008. "Using Web-based Language Learning Activities in the ESL Classroom." *International Journal of Pedagogies and Learning* 4 (4): 34–43.

Stempel, Tom. 2001. *American Audiences on Movies and Moviegoing*. Lexington: University Press of Kentucky.

Stoddard, Jeremy D., and Alan A. Marcus. 2006. "The Burden of Historical Representation: Race, Freedom, and Educational Hollywood Film." *Film and History* 36 (1): 26–35.

Stoker., Kevin. 1995. "Existential Objectivity: Freeing Journalists to Be Ethical." *Journal of Mass Media Ethics* 10:5–22.

Stone, Alan. 1993. "On Film: Spielberg's Success." *Boston Review*, December, p. 19.

Stratton, David. 1999. "Review: 'Music of the Heart.'" *Variety*, September 8. Available at http://variety.com/1999/film/reviews/music-of-the-heart-2-1117752092/.

"Studio Market Share." n.d. *Box Office Mojo*. Available at http://boxofficemojo.com/studio/?view=company&view2=yearly&yr=2012&p=.htm (accessed May 13, 2012).

Subers, Ray. 2012. "Paramount Wins 2011 Studio Battle." *Box Office Mojo*, January 11. Available at http://boxofficemojo.com/news/?id=3345.

"The Substitute." 1996. *Screen It*, September 20. Available at http://www.screenit.com/movies/1996/the_substitute.html.

Sullivan, John L. 2013. *Media Audiences: Effects, Users, Institutions, and Power*. Thousand Oaks, CA: Sage.

Swidler, Ann. 1986. "Culture in Action: Symbols and Strategies." *American Sociological Review* 51:273–306.

Takaki, Ronald T. 1979. *Iron Cages: Race and Culture in 19th-Century America*. New York: Knopf.

Taylor, Charles. 1994. *Multiculturalism: Examining the Politics of Recognition*. Edited by Amy Gutmann. Princeton, NJ: Princeton University Press.

Thakur, Manavendra K. 1987. "Cry Freedom (1987)." *IMDb*. Available at http://www.imdb.com/reviews/01/0181.html.

Thayer, George P. 1968. *The Further Shores of Politics: The American Political Fringe Today*. 2nd ed. New York: Simon and Schuster.

Thomas, W. I., and Dorothy Swaine Thomas. 1928. *The Child in America: Behavior Problems and Programs*. New York: Knopf.

Tikkun. 1999. "Panther: An Interview with Mario Van Peebles." *FrontPageMag.com*, February 17. Available at http://archive.frontpagemag.com/Printable.aspx?ArtId=22287.

Titone, Connie. 1998. "Educating the White Teacher as Ally." In *White Reign: Deploying Whiteness in America*, edited by J. L. Kincheloe, 159–176. New York: St. Martin's.

"'Town & Country' Publicity Proves an Awkward Act." 2001. *Wall Street Journal*, April 27, pp. B1, B6.

Travers, Peter. 1989. "A Dry White Season." *Rolling Stone*. Previously available at http://www.rollingstone.com/movies/reviews/a-dry-white-season-19890920.

———. 1996. "A Time to Kill." *Rolling Stone*, July 24. Available at http://www.rollingstone.com/movies/reviews/a-time-to-kill-19960101.

Trotman, C. James. 2002. *Multiculturalism: Roots and Realities*. Bloomington: Indiana University Press.

Tuch, Steven A., and Jack K. Martin, eds. 1997. *Racial Attitudes in the 1990s: Continuity and Change*. Westport, CT: Praeger.

Tunstall, Jeremy. 1977. *The Media Are American: Anglo-American Media in the World*. London: Constable.

U.S. Census Bureau. 1997. "Current Population Reports." Available at http://www.census.gov/prod/2/pop/p25/p25-1131.pdf.

Utter, Glenn. 2009. *Culture Wars in America: A Documentary and Reference Guide*. Santa Barbara, CA: Greenwood.

Vaisey, Stephen, and Omar Lizardo. 2010. "Can Cultural Worldviews Influence Network Composition?" *Social Forces* 88 (4): 1595–1618.

Van Belle, Douglas A. 2000. "New York Times and Network TV News Coverage of Foreign Disasters: The Significance of the Insignificant Variables." *Journalism and Mass Communication Quarterly* 77 (1): 50–70.

Van Dijk, Teun A. 1992. "Discourse and the Denial of Racism." *Discourse and Society* 3 (1): 87–118.

Vannini, Phillip. 2004. "The Meanings of a Star: Interpreting Music Fans Reviews." *Symbolic Interaction* 27 (1): 47–69.

Van Riper, Tom. 2007. "The Top Pundits in America." *Forbes*, September 24. Available at http://www.forbes.com/2007/09/21/pundit-americas-top-oped-cx_tvr_0924pundits.html.

Vera, Hernán, and Andrew M. Gordon. 2003. *Screen Saviors: Hollywood Fictions of Whiteness*. New York: Rowman and Littlefield.

Vice, Jeff. 2001. "Film Review: Finding Forrester." *Deseret News*, February 22. Available at http://www.deseretnews.com/article/700002642/Finding-Forrester.html?pg=all.

Vickerman, Milton. 2007. "Recent Immigration and Race" *Du Bois Review* 4 (1): 141–165.

Wagner-Pacifici, Robin, and Barry Schwartz. 1991. "The Vietnam Veterans Memorial: Commemorating a Difficult Past." *American Journal of Sociology* 97:376–420.

Ward, Aubrey. 2011. "Movie Review: The Help (2011)." *Firefox News*, August 14. Available at http://firefox.org/news/articles/3587/1/Movie-Review-The-Help-2011/Page1.html.

Ward, V. M., J. T. Bertrand, and L. F. Brown. 1991, "The Comparability of Focus Group and Survey Results: Three Case Studies." *Evaluation Review* 15 (2): 266–283.

Welling, David, and Jack Valenti. 2007. *Cinema Houston: From Nickelodeon to Megaplex.* Houston: University of Texas Press.

White, Hayden. 1988. "Historiography and Historiophoty." *American Historical Review* 93 (5): 1193–1199.

"Who Owns the Media?" 2006. *Democracy on Deadline*, October 9. Available at http://www.pbs.org/independentlens/democracyondeadline/mediaownership.html.

Winston, Thomas Pillsbury. 2010. "A Critique of the Environmental Savior Trope in Wildlife Film." Master's thesis, Science and Natural History Filmmaking, Montana State University.

Winter, James P., and Chaim H. Eyal. 1981. "Agenda Setting for the Civil Rights Issue." *Public Opinion Quarterly* 45 (3): 376–383.

Wise, Tim. 2009. *Between Barack and a Hard Place: Racism and White Denial in the Age of Obama.* San Francisco: City Lights Books.

Wittkowski, J. 1994. *Das Interview in der Psychologie: Interviewtechnik und Codierung von Interviewmaterial.* Opladen, Germany: Westdeutscher Verlag.

Woodruff, Zachary. 1995. "Head of the Class: 'Dangerous Minds' Gets a Gold Star." *Tucson Weekly*, August 17. Available at http://www.tucsonweekly.com/tw/08-17-95/cinema.htm.

Yen, Hope. 2011. "Census Shows Whites Lose US Majority among Babies." *My Way News*, June 23. Available at http://apnews.myway.com/article/20110623/D9O1HG5G0.html.

Index

Page locators in italics refer to figures and tables.

Academy Awards (Oscars), 1, 14, 22, 160
active reinterpretation, 130
Adams, John Quincy, 68, 69, 107
advertisements, 74
affirmative action, 77, 78, 85, 104–105
African-as-savage trope, 10, 60–61
agency, 126, 130–131
alcoholism of white savior, 43–44
Allport, Gordon, 163
Amazing Grace, 33–34, 42, 117, *162*
American Film Institute award, 22
American Nazi Party, 12
Amin, Idi, 44–45
Amistad, 7, 14, *23*, 68, 105, 107
Anglo conformity, 83
anti-Communist films, 13
Apple, R. W., 105
appropriation of token objects, 173, 174
"Are Whites Racially Oppressed?" (CNN), 6
art world, 73–74
Ask the Film Critics (*New York Times*), 79
assimilation, 8, 11, 41, 83–84, 103
attacking white saviors, 95–96
audience, 8, 16–17; and agency, 126, 130–131;
    appeasing white, *86*, 98–100; film critics as
    influencing choices of, 72–74; and filmgoing
    as ritualized social activity, 75; how film is
    seen by, 126–127, *127–129*; and structure,
    agency, and context, 130–131

audience opinions: black points of view, 136;
    cinematic racial stereotypes, *132*, 146–148;
    color-blind interpretations, *132*, 142–146;
    diversity as danger, *132*, 134–137; diversity
    as exotic fetish, *132*, 139–142; diversity as
    inherent good, *132*, 133–134; dominant
    frames, 131–132, *132*; embracing paternal-
    ism, *132*, 152–156; films as propaganda, 135,
    136–137, 158; ideal whiteness, *132*, 156–157,
    170–171; race as everywhere, *132*, 132–142;
    race matters/racism exists, *132*, 146–152;
    racism as normal, *132*, 150–152; white de-
    fensiveness about race, *132*, 144–146; white
    man's burden trope, *132*, 152–155; white
    pandering to people of color, *132*, 137–139;
    white points of view, 135–136; white su-
    premacy in modern film, *132*, 148–152
Austin, Bruce, 74
authenticity, cinematic, *86*, 98, 100–103, 172
author intention, 130–131, 158, 159
Avatar, 3, 14, *24*, 28, 30–31, 51, 117; box office
    receipts for, 162, *162*
awards, 1, 14, 22, *23–24*, 67, 160
Axtell, James, 11

backlash, white (1993–1998), 6–7, 14–15,
    66–67, 103–116, *106*, 117; as discourse of
    racial neoliberalism, 76–78; grateful "others"
    and, 110; and morality personified, 106–108;

backlash, white (1993–1998) (*continued*)
  and nonwhites as dysfunctional, 111–113;
  and paternalistic figure, 105–110; and saving
  white saviors, 113–116
bad white (racist white character), 25, 26, 47–52,
  166–167
Bagdikian, Ben, 19
Baker, Andy, 173
*Balancing Acts: American Thought and Culture
  in the 1930s* (Cooney), 13
Barthes, Roland, 130
"based on a true story." *See* historiography,
  racialized ("based on a true story")
Basuroy, Suman, 74
Baumann, Shyonn, 73, 74
Becker, Howard, 73–74
Bell, Joyce, 86
Belle, 165
Benjamin, Walter, 101
Bernardi, Daniel, 15–16, 174
Berry, Halle, 14
Bertelsmann, 19
big-budget films, 22
Big Six media conglomerates, 19–22, 163
Birth of a Nation, 13–14, 153
The Birth of Whiteness (Bernardi), 174
blackface performances, 173
Black Hawk Down, 60
"The Black Pathology Biz" (Reed), 113
Black Reconstruction (Du Bois), 76
Black Robe, 34–35, 85
black self-esteem, 148
blaxploitation genre, 14, 149
The Blind Side: Evolution of a Game (Lewis), 66
The Blind Side, 1, 7, 14, 66–67, 117; focus group
  discussions on, 131, 133–134, 136, 140, 143,
  147–148, 153, 154, 155; nonwhites as dys-
  functional in, 168
Blood Diamond, 24, 41, 59, 61–62, 69–70, 117
Boatwright, Peter, 74
Bobo, Larry, 165
Bonilla-Silva, Eduardo, 77, 152, 168
Bonnett, Alastair, 7
bon sauvage character, 64
bootstrapping, 54, 58–59, 110, 118
Bourdieu, Pierre, 161
boxing, 10
box office receipts, 161–162
Brokaw, Tom, 104
Brooks, David, 3
Brown v. Board of Education, 14, 116
Buchanan, Pat, 85
Bullock, Sandra, 1, 2, 7, 14, 67
Bulworth, 23, 105, 108–109

Burke, Edmund, 60
Burr, Ty, 122

cable news networks, 77
cable television, 14
Cameron, Samuel, 74
Canby, Vincent, 93, 95
Cantril, Hadley, 163
celebrating difference, 86, 86–88
census projections, 5–6
Chan, Vera, 79
Charity, Tom, 123
Chatterjee, Subimal, 74
Chicago Defender, 2
Children of Men, 24, 32, 46, 117, *162*
Church Arson Prevention Act (1996), 104
"The Cinematic Racial Order" (Denzin), 171
circuit of culture, 16
circuit of meaning, 16–17, 75
citizenship as white, 83–84
City of Joy, 36, 42, 85, 93
civil rights era, 7, 22, 77–78, 84, 94–95, 97, 102
The Clansman (Dixon), 14
Clinton, Bill, 105
Cold War, 14, 85
Cole, Teju, 7
Coleman, Robin Means, 14
collective memory, 70–71, 98
colonialism, 9
colonialist fantasies, 59–64
colonialist logic, 41
color-blind rhetoric, 2, 76–78, 84, 116
color capital, 90
Columbia Pictures, 19, 74
Comcast, 19
commentary. *See* critics/reviewers
Committee on Public Information, 163
common sense, 4n1, 8; dominant racial dis-
  course as, 78–81
comparative messages, 57
Compliance, 125
Congress, 10
The Conquest of Granada (Dryden), 9
The Constant Gardener, 14, *23*, 28, 59, 61, 65,
  117, *162*
consumption, 16
content analysis, 16, 19
context, 130–131
Contract with America, 105
Cooney, Gerry, 10
Cooney, Terry, 13
Cooper, Abilene, 65–66n6
Crash, 14, *23*, 117, 123, *162*
crisis of legitimation, 7

critics/reviewers, 16; content review and, 75; discourse of racial neoliberalism and, 76–78; dominant racial discourse and, 79–81; fictitious, 72; film advertisements and, 74; film industry and, 73–75; as gatekeepers, 81; as interpretive community, 75–76, 124; perception and racial conflict and, 81–82; during unsettled times, 80–81. *See also* backlash, white (1993–1998); (multi)cultural wars (1987–1992); postracial era and the redemption of whiteness (1999–2011)
critique of Hollywood racism, *86*, 92–93
critique of white savior trope, 61–62, 65
crossing the color and culture line, *25*, *26*, 28–31
crucifixion allusions, 41, 44
Cruise, Tom, 7
Crust, Kevin, 121
Cry Freedom, 14, 19, 22, *23*, 59, 85; as appeasing white audience, 99–100; interracial friendships in, 87; white point of view in, 94
cultural pluralism, 83–84
culture industry, 18
culture of poverty as trope, 154–155, 156
culture war, 24, 85

Dances with Wolves, 14, *23*, 28, 31, 71, 85; defense of white characters and, 96–97; diversity overpowering prejudice in, *86*, 88–89; exotic other in, 91; interracial friendship in, 87; white man's burden trope and, 95
Dangerous Minds, 14, 31, 53–55, 105, 141; morality of white character in, 107–108, 109; nonwhites as dysfunctional in, 111–112, 145
Dargis, Manohla, 79
Davis, Peter, 60
Dawes, Amy, 97
"The Death of the Author" (Barthes), 130
decline of civilization, 103
Deep South, 28
Denzin, Norman, 171
depression of white savior, 42–43
development climate, 163
dialogue, sentimental, 29–30, 34, 67
diamonds, 69–70
Dickens, Charles, 64
difference: celebrating, *86*, 86–88; essentializing, *86*, 90–93
disaster films, 31–41
Disney, 19
distribution, 16
The Disuniting of America: Reflections on a Multicultural Society (Schlesinger), 85

diversity: celebrating, *86*, 86–88; as danger, *132*, 134–137; as exotic fetish, *132*, 139–142; as inherent good, *132*, 133–134
Dixon, Thomas, Jr., 14
Django Unchained, 160–161, 166
dominant racial discourse, 113; as common sense, 78–81
Doyle, Michael J., 114
Dreamworks SKG, 22
Dryden, John, 9
A Dry White Season, 14, 22, *23*, 51, 59, 85; as appeasing white audiences, 100
Du Bois, W.E.B., 4–5n2, 76
Durkheim, Emile, 70
Duster, Troy, 78
dynamic duos, 35–36, 42

Ebert, Roger, 72–73, 89, 94; on *Dances with Wolves*, 89; on *Gran Torino*, 122; on interracial friendship, 87; on *The Last Samurai*, 122; on *The Long Walk Home*, 88, 100; on *Music of the Heart*, 118
Edelstein, David, 120–121
educational pedagogy, 11
egalitarianism, hope for, 165–166
The Elementary Forms of the Religious Life (Durkheim), 70
Eliashberg, Jehoshua, 74
Emerson, Jim, 94, 97
Entman, Robert M., 80
environmental conservation and protection advocates, 11
Esquire, 72–73
essentializing difference, 90–93
ethnic and racial pride movements, 84, 85
exotic others, 28, *86*, 90–91, 93; and diversity as fetish, *132*, 139–142

Faires, Robert, 112
Faludi, Susan, 103
Fanon, Frantz, 142
Farber, Stephen, 91, 96
Farrakhan, Louis, 104
feedback loop, 16, 124
Ferber, Abby, 103
film, eras of, 12–16
film industry, 73–75
The Film of Memory (Routt), 71
Finding Forrester, 58–59, 117, 119–120
Fineman, Howard, 104
Fitzgerald, Jennifer, 173
Focus Features, 19
focus groups, 126–158, *127–129*, *132*; religion-affiliated, 142–143, 158; social influence

focus groups (*continued*)
in, 158–159; socioeconomic status of, 130, 158–159; and use of statistics, 134
Foner, Eric, 68–69
forgetting, 70
Foucault, Michel, 70
Fox Searchlight, 19, 22
Frankenberg, Ruth, 5
Freedom Writers, 31, 49–50, 55–57, 117, 121, 123; focus group discussions on, 131, 133, 140–141, 143, 144–145, 147, 153, 155; non-whites as dysfunctional in, 168; in U.S. and global market, *162*
Fuller, Jennifer, 104

Gallagher, Charles, 105
Gandy, Oscar, Jr., 170
Geller, Adam, 117
Gemser, Gerda, 74
geopolitical realm, 12
Ghosts of Mississippi, 14, *23*, 105
Gingrich, Newt, 105
Gleiberman, Owen, 87–88, 92, 99, 107
globalization of Hollywood film, 17, 161; from color-blind ideology to ideal white identity, 170–171; and dearth of films without white savior, 172–173; neoliberal deregulation and, 163; postracial discourse and, 165–170; seduction of white savior and, 161–164; U.S. and global markets, 161–163, *162*; and white savior beyond the silver screen, 171–174
Glory, 14, *23*, 24, 41, 68, 85, 94, 105
Glover, Danny, 172–173
Golden Globe Awards, 1, 22
Gordon, Andrew, 8
Gordon, Milton, 83
Gorringe, Carrie, 111–112
Grainge, David, 70
Gramsci, Antonio, 79
Gran Torino, 24, 28, 37–38, 41, 117, 168; focus group discussions on, 131, 134, 137–138, 137–140, 139–140, 143, 147, 149–150; sacrifice of white savior in, 46–47
gratitude for white benefactor, 110
Great Depression, 13
great migration, 76–77
great white hope, 10, 15, 39, 123
Griffith, D. W., 13–14
Griswold, Wendy, 131
Grossman, Sandra J., 92
group awareness, perception of, 82, 186–187, *187*
group relations, perception of, 82, 186–187, *187*
group threat, perception of, 82, 186–187, *187*

Gruwell, Erin, 157
Guaspari, Roberta, 119
Guider, Elizabeth, 107
guilt, white: alleviating, *118*, 120–121; "everyone's racist, not just whites," 122–124
Guthmann, Edward, 114
Gutmann, Amy, 84

Haiti, 12, 172–173
Halbwachs, Maurice, 70
Half Nelson, *24*, 31, 53, 117
Hall, Alice, 80
Hall, Stuart, 16
Handler, Richard, 101
Hansberry, Lorraine, 13
Hardball, 30, 32, 39, 42, 117; bad white in, 50–51
"harmless entertainment" argument, 12
Hartmann, Douglas, 86
Hawaii, 12
hegemonic whiteness, 112, 157–158, 161, 167, 171
The Help, 7, *24*, 40, 63–64, 65, 117, 123, 167
Hicks, Chris, 88–89
Hinson, Hal, 95–96
his saving grace, *25, 26*, 31–41
historiography, racialized ("based on a true story"), 1, 8, 15, 33–34, 64–71, 96–103; critics/reviewers and, *86*, 98–103; and fiction and lies, 66–67; history as linear, 169
historiophoty, 98
History Place (history website), 69
Hitler, Adolf, 10, 12
Hoberman, James, 165
Hollywood: and Academy Awards (Oscars), 1, 14, 22, 160; and critique of racism, *86*, 92–93; global dominance of, 161; top billing for white actors in, 94, 95, 100. *See also* globalization of Hollywood film
Homes, Larry, 10
hooks, bell, 142
hope and change, 165–166
Horn, John, 72
Hotel Rwanda, 60
House Un-American Activities Committee, 13
Howe, Desson, 97, 99
Hsu, Greta, 75
human rights movement, 10
The Hunger Games, 79
Hunter, Stephen, 123
hyper-segregation, 103–104
hypodescent (one-drop rule), 9

I Beat the Odds: From Homelessness, to "The Blind Side," and Beyond (Oher), 66

idealism, 5
identity politics, 84
immigration, 4, 6, 82–83, 155; audience opinions of, in films, 137–139, 155
Immigration Act of 1924, 83
In Darkest Hollywood (Davis), 60
Independence Day, 80
Independent (magazine), 173
independent ("indie") films, 22
Indiana Jones and the Last Crusade, 23, 34, 85
Indiana Jones trilogy, 14
individualism, 166–167, 168
interpretive community, film reviewers as, 75–76, 124
interracial interactions: film reviewers' mediation of, 74–75; interracial friendship, 86, 86–88, 115–116; in neocolonialist framework, 70–71, 170, 173; and paternalism disguised as cooperation, 169–170
Invasion, U.S.A., 13

Jackman, Mary, 169
James, Jesse, 2
Jaws, 22
Jerry Maguire, 80
Johnson, Jack, 10
Jones, Chris, 72
journalism, 2–3

Kamakura, Wagner, 74
Katz, Elihu, 74
The Keeping Room, 165
Kemply, Rita, 99–100
King, Martin Luther, Jr., 34, 117
Kipling, Rudyard, 10
A Knight's Tale, 72
K-Pax, 117
Kristof, Nicholas, 3
Ku Klux Klan, 76

Lakoff, George, 166
The Last King of Scotland, 24, 44–45, 51, 59, 117
The Last Samurai, 7, 23, 28, 29–30, 64, 117, *162*; white guilt alleviated in reviews of, 121–122
Lazarsfeld, Paul, 74
Lee, Harper, 13
Leenders, Mark, 74
Leeper, Mark R., 87, 92, 96–97
left-leaning saviorism, 2–3
Lerner, Daniel, 163
Levy, Emanuel, 107
Lewis, Amanda, 157
Lewis, Michael, 66

Lewis, Oscar, 154
Lincoln, 160–161
Lincoln, Abraham, 12, 166
Lipsitz, George, 15, 173–174
Long, Elizabeth, 131
The Long Walk Home, 65, 85, 87–88, 98; authenticity of, 102; defense of white characters in, 97
Losing Isaiah, 105, 106–107, 112–113
Louis, Joe, 10
Lucas, George, 22

Machine Gun Preacher, 172
MADtv, 3
magical powers, 63–64, 92
Maloney, Frank, 95
manifest destiny, 9, 15, 96
Manning, David, 72, 74
Marine, Craig, 115
Marvel Studios, 19
Maslin, Janet, 91, 96, 99, 115
master status identity, 158–159
materialist influence of films, 163
The Matrix, 23, 31, 117
The Matrix Reloaded, 117, *162*
The Matrix Revolutions, 117, *162*
McCarthy, Todd, 106
McCarthyism, 14
McConaughey, Matthew, 7
McGee, Michelle, 2
media: as American, 161; as ignoring voices of nonwhite people, 77; white savior stories in, 7
media conglomerates, 19–22, 163
Medicine Man, 85, 92
melting-pot ideology, 83–84, 122
memory, 70–71, 98
meritocracy, 25, 26, 52–59
Meyer, Jeff, 99
Million Man March, 104
Miramax, 19
Mississippi Burning, 14, 23, 24, 85, 99; and critique of white point of view, 94–95; defense of white characters in, 97
Monster's Ball, 14, 23, 41, 117
Montagu, Ashley, 4
morality personified, 106–108
Mortenson, Greg, 172
Moss, Kate, 173
Motion Picture Association of America, 162
Movieline, 91
multiculturalism, 84; essentialism and, 90–91; film critics' support of, 102–103
Multiculturalism: Examining the Politics of Recognition (Gutmann), 84

(multi)cultural wars (1987–1992), 82–103, 117;
    and celebrating difference, *86*, 86–88; and
    essentializing difference, *86*, 90–93; and
    watching whiteness, *86*, 93–96; and white
    historiography, *86*, 96–103
multiplex theaters, 13
Münsterberg, Hugo, 73
Music of the Heart, 14, *23*, 65, 117, 118–119
myth: of race, 4, 7, 66; of white superiority, 10,
    11–12, 15
mythological tales, 18

narrative arc, 29, 95
National Film Registry, 71
National Opinion Research Center survey, 105
Native Americans, 4n1, 9, 11, 89, 92, 96–97,
    101, 103
"native" as dysfunctional, 47–52
nativist laws and policies, 6
Neeson, Liam, 115
neocolonialist framework, 70–71, 170, 173
neoliberalism, 17, 24, 124, 163, 167; racial, 76–
    80; and scapegoating of nonwhites, 79–80
"Neo-Minstrel Era," 14
News Corporation, 19
Newton, John, 33–34
New York Times, 3, 79, 85, 102, 105
New York Times Index, 16, 81–82, *83*, 185–187,
    186, *187*
"Nice White Lady" (skit), 3
noble savage, 9–10, 64
nonwhites: as dysfunctional, 9–10, 47–52, 105,
    107, 111–113, 165, 167–168; "exceptional," 59;
    light-skinned political leaders, 12; mind-sets
    of, transformed by white savior, 37, 39, 41;
    as in need of redemption, 2; scapegoated as
    source of racial inequality, 79–80; stereo-
    types of sexuality of, 57–58; struggles of, as
    foil for white savior, 47; white civility, black
    savagery, *25*, *26*, 59–64
normativity as white, 5, 7, 8, 83, 117, 141, 151–
    152
The North Star, 165

Obama, Barack, 6, 15, 24, 78, 117, 165, 166
objectification, racial, 141–142
Obregón, Álvaro, 12
Oher, Michael, 66–67
On Deadly Ground, 105
organizational interaction (group style), 126,
    130

Panther, 172
Paramount Pictures, 19, 22

*Parents Involved in Community Schools v.
    Seattle School District No. 1*, 116
Parker, Alan, 94–95
Parks, Gordon, 14
paternalism, 18–19; bad whites as foil for, 47,
    49–50; disguised as cooperation, 169–170;
    embracing, *132*, 152–156; right-wing, 2;
    violence and, 41
paternalistic figure, 105–106; blatantly racist,
    108–109; grateful "others" and, 110; as mo-
    rality personified, 106–108; vengeance and,
    108–110
Pathfinder, 117
Pavilion of Women, 117
Pelosi, Nancy, 6
perception of racial conflict, 81–82, *82*
Perry, Michelle, 102
Personal Responsibility and Work Opportu-
    nity Reconciliation Act of 1996, 105
Pfeiffer, Michelle, 53, 107, 114
Phillips, Michael, 1
Pixar, 19
Podolny, Joel, 75
point of view, white, *86*, 93–95
The Political Mind (Lakoff), 166
politics, 11–12, 104–105
The Possessive Investment in Whiteness
    (Lipsitz), 173–174
postracial discourse, 15, 81; distinguishing
    characteristics of, 165–170; individualism
    in, 166–167, 168; minimization of racial
    inequality in, 169–170; nonwhite people as
    dysfunctional in, 167–168; racial fatigue in,
    165, 168–169; seduction of white savior and,
    161–164
postracial era and the redemption of whiteness
    (1999–2011), 24, 82, 116–124; alleviating
    white guilt, *118*, 120–122; everyone's racist,
    not just whites, *118*, 122–124; salvaging su-
    periority, *118*, 118–120
postracial state, 14–15
The Principal, 24, 31, 53, 85
production of white savior films, 19–24; com-
    panies controlling, 19–22
propaganda, films as, 163–164; audience opin-
    ions on, 135, 136–137, 158
Proposition 209, 104–105
Protestant ethic, 9

race: as everywhere, *132*, 132–142; modern
    meanings of whiteness and, 4–8; race mat-
    ters/racism exists, *132*, 146–152; as relational
    concept, 8–9, 29; as social construction, 4;
    white defensiveness, *132*, 144–146

race-based literature, 13
race films, 14, 168
race relations in 1990s, 24
"race themes," 118
racial fatigue, 165, 168–169
racial inequality: color-blind rhetoric and, 76–78; and educational inequality, 66; minimization of, 169–170
racial media spectacles, 85
racial narratives, 28
racial schizophrenia, 14
racism: cinematic stereotypes, *132*, 146–148; critique of Hollywood racism, *86*, 92–93; denial of, 146; as normal, *132*, 150–152; refusal to acknowledge, 122–124
racist white characters, 67–68; bad whites, 47–52, 166–167
Raiders of the Lost Ark, 22
A Raisin in the Sun, 13
Rambo III, 22, 41, 85, 95–96
Ravid, S. Abraham, 74
reactionary stasis, 81
Reagan, Ronald, 84
rebirth allusions, 44
Reconstruction, 6, 76
Reddick, Lawrence, 13
redeemers (whites), 2, 18, 47
redemption: hagiographies of, 117–124; interracial relations and, 15; nonwhites as in need of, 2, 41; sacrifice of white savior and, 42, 45–47; of whites, 7, 32–33, 82. *See also* postracial era and the redemption of whiteness (1999–2011)
redemption stories, 15, 18, 45, 71
Red Planet Mars, 13
Reed, Ishmael, 113
relational concept of race, 8–9, 29
religious metaphors and imagery, 32–34, 41; Christian, 32–35; Egyptian, 35–36
Relin, David Oliver, 172
resegregation, 14
resurrection imagery, 36
reverse racism, 15, 103, 138–139
revisionism, 98
Ridgefield Press, 72
Roberts, John, 116
Rocchio, Vincent, 15
Rockwell, George Lincoln, 12
Rodriguez, Gregory, 6
Rodriguez, Nelson, 5
Rojecki, Andrew, 80
romanticism, 3, 9, 64
Roosevelt, Franklin, 13
Routt, William D., 71

sacrifice of white savior, 12, 24, 41, 42, 45–46, 61, 68
saintliness of white savior, 47
Sanneh, Kelefa, 68
savagery as nonwhite, *25*, *26*, 59–64; noble savage, 9–10, 64; in science fiction films, 62–63
Savannah, 166
savior, the bad white, and the natives, *25*, *26*, 47–52
saviorism, 2; religious foundation of, 11
Schatz, Thomas, 19, 22
Schindler's List, 23, 71, 115; paternalism in, 105, 106, 110
Schlesinger, Arthur, 85
Schmeling, Max, 10
Schwarzbaum, Lisa, 106–107, 115
science fiction–based savior films, 62. *See also Avatar*; *Stargate*
Scott, A. O., 79
Scott-Childress, Reynolds, 11–12
Screen Actors Guild Awards, 1, 22
Screen Saviors: Hollywood Fictions of Whiteness (Vera and Gordon), 8
segregation in postracial state, 14–15
sentimentalism, 29–30, 34, 67
sequels, 22
setting, unfamiliar, 28
sexuality, myths about, 57–58
Shaft, 14
Shake Hands with the Devil, 60
Shaw, Robert Gould, 68, 102
Shelby, Jim, 114
Shugan, Steven, 74
The Siege, 80
Sierra Leone civil war, 61–62, 68
Simpson, O. J., 104
Sisk, Tim, 11
slavery: in film, 160–161, 165–166; in United States, 68–69
Snead, James, 168
Snow Falling on Cedars, 23, 117
social facts, 4
Social Frameworks of Memory (Halbwachs), 70
social systems, racialized, 151–152
socioeconomic status, *127–129*, 130, 158–159
sociology of culture, 125–126
The Soloist, 117
Something Whispered, 165–166
Sony, 19, 22, 72, 74
Sotomayor, Sonia, 6
soundtracks, 39, 160
Spielberg, Steven, 22

spiritual journey, common, *132*, 142–144
sports films, 57–58
standpoint, *86*, 93–95
Stargate, 35–36, 42–43, 105
Star Wars, 22
stereotypes, 3–4, 14, 97; as apolitical, 60, 65; cinematic racial, *132*, 146–148
stock caricatures, 14
Stockett, Kathryn, 65–66n6
Stone, Alan, 110, 115
Stone, Emma, 7
"stranger in a strange land" motif, 28–29
Stratton, David, 118
structure, 130–131
The Substitute, 53, 105, 108
suffering of white savior, *25*, *26*, 41–47
Sundance Film Festival, 125
Sunset Park, 48, 57–58, 105, 110, 112; as predictable, 114–115
superiority, salvaging, 118–120
Supreme Court, 68–69, 116
Sweet Sweetback's Baadasssss Song, 14

Takaki, Ronald, 9
teacher and tough kids trope, 3, 11, 24, 48, 111, 114. *See also Dangerous Minds*; *Freedom Writers*; *Sunset Park*
Teach for America, 11
Tea Party, 6
Tears of the Sun, 59, 60, 117, 120–121, *162*
testing and screening, 22
Thakur, Manavendra K., 99
Three Cups of Tea, 172
Thunderheart, 85, 89–90, 91, 92; Ebert on, 101–102
A Time to Kill, 7, *23*, 80, 105, 115–116
Time Warner, 19
Titone, Connie, 11
To Kill a Mockingbird, 13
TriStar, 22
tropes, 8
Tula, 166
Tunstall, Jeremy, 161
12 Years a Slave, 165
Twentieth Century Fox, 19, 22

United States: manifest destiny ideology of, 9; and national memory, 70; slavery in, 68–69; white supremacy and foundations of, 66, 83–84
United States Magazine and Democratic Review, 9
Universal Pictures, 19, 22
urban classroom films, 24, 31, 49–50, 52–53

van Dijk, Teun A., 146
Vannini, Philip, 76
Van Oostrum, Martine, 74
Van Peebles, Mario, 172
Van Peebles, Melvin, 14, 172
The Velvet Glove (Jackman), 169
Vera, Hernán, 8
Viacom, 19
Vickerman, Milton, 84
Victoria, Queen, 10
The View, 1–2
Villaverde, Leila, 5
violence: paternalist, 51; of white savior, 35–38, 41, 111; white threats of, 68
virtuous republicanism, 9

Walk East on Beacon!, 13
Walters, Barbara, 2
Ward, Aubrey, III, 123
Warner Bros, 19, 22
Washington Post, 102
watching whiteness, *86*, 93–95
web-based film reviews, 16
Weisz, Rachel, 14
White, Hayden, 98
"The White Anxiety Crisis" (Rodriguez), 6
white civility, black savagery, *25*, *26*, 59–64
white man's burden, 10, 15, 47, 95, *132*, 152–155, 171
"The White Man's Burden" (Kipling), 10
whiteness: bifurcated, 160–161; erosion of power and, 138–139; ideal, *132*, 156–157, 170–171; and identity as crisis, 7; modern meanings of, 3–8; myth of, 12; as normative, 7, 8, 83, 141, 151–152, 174; unnamed, 93
white-nonwhite binary, 8–9
white savior: bad white compared with, 47–52, 166–167; blatant racism of, 37–38; color of meritocracy and, *25*, *26*, 52–59; common denominators of, 24, *25–27*; critique of, 61–62, 65, 95–96; as crossing the color and culture line, *25*, *26*, 28–31; defense of, 96–98; dynamic duos, 35–36, 42; as dysfunctional, 29, 42; environmental, 11; genealogy of, 8–10; global seduction of, 161–164; as only reason for black life and agency, 40–41; as only source of stability, 37, 39–40; political, 11–12; sacrifice of, 12, 24, 41, 42, 45–46, 68; saving, 113–116; saving grace of, *25*, *26*, 31–41; beyond the silver screen, 171–174; sinister aspects of, 10; sports and, 10; suffering of, *25*, *26*, 41–47; transformation of white protagonist into, 31–34, 36–37, 42, 61; as transforming nonwhite mind-sets, 37, 39, 41;

triumph after testing of, 117–118; violence of, 35–38, 41, 111; as widespread, 11–12
white savior films, 1, *20–21*; in 1980s, 14; as cultural devices and artifacts, 15–16; as progressive, 153–154. *See also specific films*
White Savior Industrial Complex, 7
white supremacist groups, 78
white supremacy, 2, 6, 8–9, *132*; in foundations of U.S. culture, 66, 83–84; and ideal stock character, 171; in modern film, *132*, 148–150; threats to, 5–7
white-victimization narrative, 78
Wilberforce, William, 33–34

Williams, Vanessa, 1–2
Wilson, Woodrow, 163
Woods, Donald, 94, 99
work ethic as white, 5, 53, 58, 137, 151, 154, 155, 161
World War II, 13
Writers Guild of America award, 22

xenophobic narratives, 28

Yahoo! Movies, 79

Zobel, Craig, 125

Matthew W. Hughey is an Associate Professor of Sociology at the University of Connecticut. He is the author or coauthor of seven books, including *White Bound: Nationalists, Antiracists, and the Shared Meanings of Race.*